T0158543

The Gwilliam Seasons

Also by David Parry-Jones

Prince Gwyn

The Gwilliam Seasons

John Gwilliam
and the Second Golden Era
of Welsh Rugby

David Parry-Jones

seren

Seren is the book imprint of
Poetry Wales Press Ltd
Nolton Street, Bridgend, Wales
www.seren-books.com

ISBN 1-85411-327-5

A CIP record for this title is available from the British Library

*The publisher works with the financial assistance of the Arts Council of
Wales*

Printed in Plantin by CPD (Wales), Ebbw Vale

The Gwilliam Seasons

FOREWORD

One of the most enjoyable aspects of writing this book was the series of rail journeys I made from Cardiff to North Wales to speak with John Gwilliam. The train departed at seven a.m. and dashed through some of Britain's best scenery: along the Marches, in and out of Chester, up the Dee estuary and finally along the north Wales riviera to Llandudno Junction. Here John, still upright, lean and fit, would whisk me by car to Llanfairfechan and, perched above the village, 'Araulfan', where we talked until it was time for me to catch the return train southwards.

So this is a word of thanks to Pegi, who always gave me delicious home cooking for lunch, and to John for his patience. Despite the scrap-books which he keeps, bulging with Press cuttings from more than half a century ago, being ceaselessly prodded for accurate recall and analysis of long-gone days is taxing, and I acknowledge gratefully what he delivered.

A number of his contemporaries have also talked willingly and enthusiastically about what I choose to call the Second Golden Era of Welsh Rugby, containing as it did two Grand Slams and – at the time of writing – the last Welsh defeat of New Zealand. Thanks are also due to Bleddyn Williams, Jack Matthews, Billy Cleaver, Cliff Morgan, 'Stoker' Williams and John Robins who all stretched their memories almost to breaking point. I spoke only briefly with Lewis Jones, but his book *King of Rugger* (1958) contains much useful data.

This volume is not exactly a biography of John Gwilliam. It is, rather, about a period in the Welsh game when his influence on it was paramount. In my narrative he makes his appearances and is then absent for a number of pages.

It was the same during the actual Gwilliam Seasons. He would parachute in, take command, and lead his team before, job done, departing across Offa's Dyke or Hadrian's Wall.

DP-J, Radyr, 2002

PREFACE

In nearly a century and a quarter, attacks by politicians upon the Welsh Rugby Union and its adherents have been rare. Generally, the principle that sport and politics do not mix has been accepted and was only seriously tested during the third quarter of the twentieth century. At that time, although the apartheid system in South Africa was at its most repressive, Wales and, it should be added, the British Lions fell out of step with large sectors of the free world by seeking to maintain contact with the Republic on the Rugby field. They cited tradition, sporting bonds and 'mind your own business' as justification for their stance, while opponents accused them of 'giving comfort' to an odious regime. Tempers flared, hostile demonstrations were commonplace, stadia at which the 1969 Springboks were due to play in Britain were festooned with barbed wire against protesters. The period was unforgettably grievous as political activists mixed it with the hearties.

Three decades on, it is now the summer of 2002, and the finishing touches are being put to this book. The date is 26 April, and I am hearing on the radio that the Welsh Rugby Union has been ordered to put its house in order by Rhodri Morgan AM, First Minister of the National Assembly. Not by a former player with fifty caps. Not by a past-President of the WRU. Not by some Professor of Physical Education. Not even by a media critic. Instead, by Wales's leading politician, who is telling the nation and the Union's top dogs that they are "drinking in the last chance saloon." His extraordinary and unprecedented intervention highlights the gravity of the perceived situation: "The national game," he adds, "is in tatters at the top."

There is no doubt that the early years of the professional game here have been the saddest period for our Rugby since 1897 when the Welsh Rugby Union left the International Board over the 'Monkey' Gould affair (he was given the deeds to a house to mark his retirement after a glittering career, a gift which other Unions deemed an act of professionalism). The word 'Union' still describes the formal nature of the ruling body, but at this point in time it is cruelly inappropriate. All sectors of the game at senior level are at each others' throats like ferrets in a sack.

Big money being tossed into the arenas has bred division, throwing into relief conflicts of interest. Millionaires generously funding the top echelon of clubs seek rewards in the shape of cups, trophies and prestige. Top players pursue fast cash pay-packets for the years when they are in their prime and, unless they get their way, put themselves on the market. Demoralised coaches whose teams fail to deliver results leave the game, taking experience and dedication with them. The way Rugby is played here, with its emphasis on confrontation and collision, diminishes its appeal for fans. Television's desire to control kick-off times has altered spectator habits which date back over a century, leaving stands and terraces bare of paying customers whose Saturday afternoon habits and loyalties are disrupted. The big Welsh competitions can no longer attract the scale of sponsor-type backing which they have traditionally enjoyed.

Given such a scenario, it is not surprising that the WRU appears bewildered and aimless despite commissioning an in-depth investigation by a Working Party under the President, Sir Tasker Watkins VC. The WRU's Rugby aristocrats are vastly out-numbered by second and tertiary strata which resent the fame and fortune enjoyed by the favoured few and are inclined to frustrate creative change.

All this amounts to a sporting maelstrom, a crisis from which the Welsh game will find it hard to extract itself. Thus the author inviting readers to ponder achievements of a bygone era – albeit a 'golden' one – has to query whether there are lessons to be learned from the past which are relevant and useful to the health of our 'national game' today. The effort is worth making.

My belief is that the Welsh of the Third Millennium should first accept that in terms of the world game we are a Rugby nation whose man-power resources are minuscule, and always have been, compared with those of the dominant powers in the Game. Our Rugby-playing population is relatively small. Hence for a start we are entitled to feel gloom at today's mediocre standards, but that should not degenerate into despair. Instead the starting-point should be pride that, during a twentieth century which brought regular confrontation with giant-sized opponents, this small nation enjoyed three distinct periods when our National XVs were unsurpassed, as measured by successes and style. There were the early years a hundred years ago when Gwyn Nicholls's sides were pre-eminent; the nineteen seventies under men like Dawes and Mervyn Davies; and the Gwilliam seasons.

There are two common factors in the Golden eras which warrant contemplation, and which are well illustrated in the period with which this book is concerned. First, the packs who played under John Gwilliam reached a boiling-point of expertise and aggression which gave them parity with and sometimes dominance over the seven other Rugby nations with whom they locked horns from time to time. There was huge skill at lines out, where the skipper himself and the sky-climbing Roy John could contain and out-do the great opponents of their day; and there was concerted action at loose and set scrummages which meant that good possession without rubbish ball was consistently deliv-ered to the half backs. My reading of Welsh sides' uneven displays of the nineteen twenties and thirties suggests that the brilliant backs of those decades never enjoyed such luxury.

So point one is that domination up-front has to be secured, and has to be achieved consistently. Though Wales has produced some fine forwards in recent years, and the early eights fash-ioned by Graham Henry were within sight of this excellence, it is a long time since the National XV radiated the menace of yester-year. The modern spectator often sighs for a merciless presence like that of Geoffrey Wheel or Denzil Williams or Graham Price who bear-hugged opponents into submission throughout a full eighty minutes of conflict.

The other factor common to Golden Eras of the twentieth century is that the history-making Welsh sides always had two, three or even four match winners in the back division. That is, not just the cultured, mistake-free play-makers but the devastat-ing movers and shakers who could shatter a defence with a waggle of the hips or an unbelievably extravagant change of pace. In the Gwilliam seasons men like Lewis Jones, Bleddyn Williams, Cliff Morgan, Ken Jones and Gareth Griffiths were able to change the course of a game so as to win it. They were physically equipped to achieve these ends, with powerful limbs and electric heels; a joy to watch and a nightmare to mark.

It is fairly certain that, after going through a kind of Rugby kindergarten where they learned to walk, run, and then attack, such men did not suffer the regimentation experienced today when all too often foresight is limited to the next defender and 'taking the tackle'. Gwilliam's backs had wide-angle vision which showed them where there was space to exploit, and where was a team-mate who needed to off-load. The captain sometimes wound them up by suggesting that they should use a training session to improve their passing; but otherwise he left them to weave their devastating mischief without having to pause and attempt the recall of pre-match orders. As will emerge, to his back divisions he shouted encouragement rather than moves.

The Welsh game of recent years has possessed these two vital ingredients, but not consistently and all too rarely at the same time in the same team. Sporadically the coaches have managed to create some well-drilled packs capable of fury and *hwyl*. But free spirits behind the scrum have been few and far between, backs being tutored to play by rote and all too often ignoring open space in order to trigger pre-ordained 'moves' (in which forwards are encouraged to join at a tortoise pace always likely to mess up the best intentions). Robert Howley has often been outstanding, and Ieuan Evans ranks among the finest-ever wings. Now, Iestyn Harris may blossom into a great 15-a-side midfield player; but the recently-imported New Zealand coaches do not see number ten as the vital cog in a Welsh back division. And do they recognise match-winners when they see them, unless they are wearing number five or seven?

So what if anything, I ask myself, does an account of a glittering period of Welsh Rugby half a century ago have to offer to the present and to today's practitioners and administrators in the game? Well: it may show what has been lost from the traditional Welsh approach and highlight its eternal verities. In the Gwilliam seasons selectors took decisions that made jaws drop; and there were no coaches passing orders down from the grandstand by mobile phone. But for a few short years control was exerted by a captain who was always at the heart of the battle setting an example which could not but inspire his men to play a little bit better than they believed they could. They trusted him.

ONE

In 1941 my father accepted a call to become pastor of the Presbyterian Church at Hoylake, a pleasant resort in Cheshire. After his Sabbath-day exertions in the pulpit he liked to play a round of golf next morning on the municipal course where I was sometimes allowed to watch. However, my little school pals and I much preferred to roam the Royal Liverpool links, the championship venue at the north west extremity of the Wirral peninsula. It borders the 'Red Rocks', from which the Welsh in exile can look over the River Dee to Clwyd and the Land of their Fathers.

To eight-year-olds in short pants this area was a boundless prairie of rolling hillocks and beckoning fairways. And here, on its remote thirteenth green, my friends and I committed an ultimate sporting outrage, by pitching wickets and playing limited over cricket. This cultured patch of turf, we thought, afforded a truer surface than the adjacent sea-shore and yielded a good bounce.

My team was set 48 to win, but scarcely had we begun to bat than a grey-haired old retainer in a shiny blue serge uniform and cap appeared over a nearby sand dune waving his arms and bellowing at the small marauders. Had he been young and sprightly he could certainly have collared one or two of us as we fled, but elderly limbs and lungs slowed his pursuit and soon he had perforce to stop for breath without managing to exact retribution. As a deterrent he was effective, for I do not recall us returning, ever, to smack stumps into one of those greens again. But he would never have caught us, being well into his sixties.

You see, this was war-time. The young green-keepers who would easily have apprehended us were otherwise occupied fighting Hitler's armies. I would not go so far as to say that children like us were regarded as a kind of Fifth Column; but certainly to elderly, traditionalist ground staff looking after gorgeously manicured turf in the absence of their rightful guardians our presence was an abomination.

You have to be in your seventh decade, at the very least, to recall the huge disruptions to normal life caused by Total War. If he was below the age of forty, your father would have been 'called up' for military service as a soldier, sailor or airman in remote locations from Benghazi to Burma. Maybe your mother would be filling a vacuum by teaching at a junior school, or even making bombs and bullets for the armed forces. Now and again you heard that so-and-so's father or husband or brother had died in action, or that a friend's house had been blitzed and its occupants killed. Death, destruction, depravation, man's inhumanity to man: these were the serious, grievous aspects of World War II. There were other considerations, as will become clear, which kept morale afloat.

All professions, trades and occupations suffered, certainly including the sector that had moved up decisively to big-time status in the thirties – sport. Not so much the playground kick-arounds of schoolboys, or the golf enjoyed by vicars on a Monday morning, or gentile tennis played by middle-aged ladies at leafy clubs, but palpably the professional or top-level amateur fixtures that had become huge crowd-pulling events. Because the Armed Forces' need for manpower was paramount there could be no favouritism. Top centre forwards, Wimbledon finalists and Test batsmen went obediently into uniform. Some never came back from theatres of war: leading England bowlers Kenneth Farnes and Hedley Verity lost their lives, as did Wales' Maurice Turnbull who had played International cricket and Rugby football. Others like Wilfred Wooller returned after VJ-Day ('Victory over Japan' Day) weak and emaciated from internment in Japanese prison camps.

There was concern in official circles about staging Association or Rugby football on the grand scale: not necessarily because it might be deemed frivolous, but since large crowds of spectators on a popular bank in broad daylight would be sitting ducks for a malevolent Luftwaffe bomb-aimer. However the argument that the staging of occasional International matches and club games would smack of normality and thus be good for civilian morale won the day, and such encounters took place sporadically, often depending on whether there was a quorum of first-class players based at a nearby Army or RAF camp. In South Wales a good deal of soccer and Rugby was played involving miners, who were excused call-up. So were medical students – like Jack Matthews (destined to be an International centre in peace-time), whose College 'meds' XV beat a Cardiff side 28-26 in a match to raise money for charity. Towards the end of the War a Europe-based Australian services XI, which included the incomparable Keith Miller, played swashbuckling Tests against England, while the Second New Zealand Expeditionary Force's Rugby squad, nick-named the Kiwis, went on a whirlwind tour of Britain before their return home.

On Merseyside, too, there was a fair amount of soccer being played at a senior level which was an on-going topic of conversation for my little circle at junior school. A recent arrival from Cardiff, I could hold my own in class, but lack of local knowledge meant that I had to bit my lip in the heated debates and argument about sport which engaged my small friends. One had an elder brother who played for the local Deeside Rovers and – ah, bliss – owned a pair of shin-pads. Others had seen the Birkenhead-based Tranmere Rovers and could speak of a gifted inside forward called Danny Glidden, a name that I thought worthy of a film star. Boys who had been to Goodison Park or Anfield, and actually seen Lawton, Mercer or T.G. 'Tommy' Jones were the most authoritative.

The chat was endless, and after a while I began taking part in it. I never actually saw top-flight soccer on Merseyside, for those stadia were twenty miles away and petrol rationing precluded the use of the family car for such outings. But I soon appreciated that this did not prevent small boys from passing strong opinions on the players or their clubs – does it ever? My sole claim to spectatorial fame was to have seen a certain Matt Busby take part in a services fixture on the Hoylake AFC pitch; but given my age and height he was no more than a fleeting figure in a large landscape and I cannot claim to remember his involvement in the action. I do remember, though, that he was not a goal-scorer.

We all loved to play football. Soccer is, of course, a simple game – some would say a case of arrested development when only two of four limbs may be used by ten of the eleven participants. Mostly we used a much-punished, threadbare tennis ball, pursued from end to end of the school yard. I was certainly ten years of age before I took part in a game which featured a full-size football with the huge, stitched-together panels of the day. The leather was held in place by a slimy shoe-lace, pulled tight to close the gap through which the bladder was inflated. Early on I headed this ball, seeing stars and nearly passing out under the impact. My first pair of football boots were borrowed and too big. They were also iron-like and unbending.

In years of austerity this was, roughly, the norm. The horns of sporting plenty which later generations of children have come to take for granted were simply undreamed-of. Further, with no enthusiastic young men and women free to coach the young, or even referee their games, war-time children enjoyed no more than a modicum of on-field activity, just as at senior levels properly-structured competitive soccer, Rugby, cricket and other games scarcely existed. From 1939 to 1945 sport at all levels was phoney – *ersatz*, as the Germans would have put it.

But there was something to cheer, boo and get excited, even hysterical, about: the War itself. In terms of sheer heroics, foul play, expenditure of energy, desperation, ruthlessness and will to win, sport has never held anything as compelling as the circumstance of great, ostensibly civilised, nations giving their all for six years to wipe each other out. If you were a child, despite the little local sadnesses experienced earlier you did not, could not, comprehend the enormous, macro-issues at stake. Thus the War was perceived by my age-group as an all-embracing, on-going Match between two factions – involving the whole of the world, and destined to continue until one of the 'teams' gave in. This, I guess, was an impression deliberately created in the media of the day so that the population's primary emotion would not be fear but optimism – confidence that everything would be all right in the end.

'Our side' were the Goodies. The boys' stories in the books and comics of the period portrayed Rockfist Rogan and Gimlet (yes, and Worralls for the girls) as super-stars, death-defying and able to emerge from crises bloody (maybe) but unbowed. On 'their side' we knew from *The Beano* of Nazis and Fascists like Hitler, Goering and Mussolini. But in that fortnightly comic and other publications like *The Dandy, Knock Out, Wizard* and *Hotspur* such ogres, who in due course included the Japs, were portrayed as buffoons or bullies who presented no real threat to Our Side. Should one of their ships manage to sink the *Hood* or *Prince of Wales* – well, that was a blip, a misadventure.

Such a win-some, lose-some theme was sustained in the morning Press, which I would glance at while carrying out a delivery round for pocket money. The newspapers featured maps which antedated those computer graphics which accompany Test Rugby on television and show the territorial dominance of Wales over Italy or England versus France. In similar fashion, with big black superimposed arrows, those charts of 1941 showed you the advances and retreats of the warring armies. Vividly, they configured Rommel's forces pushing the Eighth Army back through the Western Desert towards Cairo (groan) or the Russians bravely repelling the Germans from Stalingrad and pursuing them westwards (hooray).

Looking back, it seems likely that the sporting illusion was sparked by the introduction of competitive slants into the 'War Effort' mounted by the Ministry of Information acting for the coalition Government of the day. There were prizes for school pupils who could make the best model Spitfire or Hurricane fighters. One challenge involved the recognition of aeroplane silhouettes: was that 'one of ours' or 'one of theirs'? – the practical implication of which was that children would know when to take cover and when there was no need to. There were shrapnel drives in which boys and girls were encouraged to collect, like beachcombers, fragments of bombs which had exploded. Some fell locally, and we examined their jagged remains with curiosity.

Such sporadic 'finds' were insufficient to allow the schoolchildren of a relatively unscathed Hoylake to compete with rivals living in Liverpool or Birkenhead. The banks of the Mersey and its docks became prime targets for the Luftwaffe once the Panzer divisions had overrun France, Holland and Belgium and could use their air-strips for long-haul bombing raids deep into Britain's hinterland. Sometimes my parents would take us up Caldy Hill, from which we could see the sky above Liverpool turn crimson as the incendiary bombs straddled whole suburbs. I have heard Carmarthenshire folk speak in similar vein about vantage points from which they watched Swansea roasting in the blitz.

Through the first few war-time years there was, in truth, little to cheer. London was in agony from nightly raids by the enemy. Other great cities in Britain also counted the cost. In Cardiff Llandaff Cathedral was wrecked in January 1941. And on the same night the state-of-the-art north grandstand at Cardiff Arms Park, only eight years old, took a hit which blasted its facilities. Though the Royal Air Force was at full stretch to shoot down as many German bombers as it could and minimise the blitz, many raiders were getting through. In the Far East and North Africa British troops were in disarray. At sea merchant ships carrying raw materials and food from the Empire and the Americas were savaged by German U-boats, and food rationing was introduced. All this was brought home to youngsters when they contemplated their weekly sweets ration: two ounces – a small bar of chocolate or a packet of pastilles.

Alamein and Stalingrad marked the turn of the tides, plus the United States' entry into the conflict goaded by Japan's outrageous attack on Pearl Harbour. My generation will well remember how the mood now began to change, to a feeling that the worst was over. The convoy system made the North Atlantic a safer place for our shipping; Montgomery put Rommel's Afrika Korps to flight and forced Italy to surrender. In 1944 and 1945 along came D-Day and the invasion of Europe, V-E Day, and finally V-J Day.

Now, triumphant but exhausted, Britain's demobilised fighting men desired only normality and the fruits of peace. Since the vast majority of them were still youthful it is natural that the resumption of sporting pursuits and competitions ranked high on lists of priorities. Their wish to run around in the sunlight without fear of being machine-gunned or bombed, and engage in mimic warfare rather than the real thing, drew a response from administrators who swiftly worked out schedules that included football league programmes and cup competitions, Wimbledon, Open Golf and big cricket – with India as the first tourists to play a peacetime season in the UK of Test and County matches.

The appetite of players and performers for such involvement and competition was only matched, and probably outstripped, by the craving of fans for entertainment, spectacle and victory. Everything meaningful and laudable in their sporting experience was six years out of date and often secondhand, culled from books and yellowing newspapers. There had been only titivation, not satisfaction. Now, suddenly, the real thing was within reach, and in their millions men and women of all ages and persuasions wanted to stand on terraces or sit in grandstands to watch goals being scored and cricket balls hit for six. One of the teams they cheered would finish up exultant and triumphant – but their opponents would not have been shot to bits.

Alive to the opportunities, Rugby football was not slow to re-open for business. The Welsh Rugby Union, which had spent the War years in suspended animation, was quick to accept a game against the Kiwis (which Wales lost), and then embraced the idea of 'Victory Internationals' scheduled for the first months of 1946. No caps were awarded for these matches, and some distinguished players lamented that oversight. But they were useful for highlighting the available talent, often miners and medics who had been excused from call-up, but by now also including returning servicemen. Some of these were veterans who had played at a high level before the War, while others were new to the first-class scene and bursting to make an impact.

Among the clubs, Cardiff were swiftly back into action, playing forty games in 1945-46 which included a home-and-away double over Llanelly (as they were then spelt) but defeat at the hands of the Kiwis. That was a fate also suffered by Swansea, who had suspended themselves for the duration. However, run by an unofficial volunteer group in which Rowe Harding, a great wing of the twenties, wielded influence, some wartime Rugby did take place at St Helens. Thus the ground, which hosted Welsh International games until the fifties, managed to stage Services international matches featuring sides like the Army, RAF, AA Command, Combined Dominions and Civil Defence. Rugby League men (paid) played alongside (unpaid) amateurs during hostilities, and one of these occasions featured the great Gus Risman's final appearance on Welsh soil.

Newport came flying out of the blocks in 1945-46. As at Cardiff, Rugby activity on Uskside had been kept ticking over during the War years through the efforts of dedicated club servants like Alf Panting and Bill Everson. Opponents on a regular basis were Newbridge, where 2,000 men were employed in the several local pits, and Abertillery whose teams also included miners. Other opponents from time to time were St Mary's Hospital, RAF St Athan, Filton and Cheltenham.

Now, therefore, in peace-time the Black and Ambers were strong enough to secure a draw against the Kiwis, before supplying half the Monmouthshire side which sensationally beat the New Zealanders 15-0 with never-to-be-capped Hedley Rowland scoring three tries. They lost only one game in the season's second half, to Cross Keys, but beat Cardiff home and away. Besides Rowland, the Rodney Parade roll-call included 'Bunner' Travers, Roy Burnett, R.T. 'Bob' Evans and Ken Jones, names that were to lighten post-War seasons with dash and Rugby bravado.

A young man – indeed, a teenager – of promise was among the raw recruits that Newport threw into action while the grown-ups were away at the Front. This was a certain John Albert Gwilliam, educated at Monmouth School, who first pulled on the club jersey at the age of eighteen in the 1941-42 season and whose name reappears inaccurately as 'J.L. Gwilliam' in the club's 1945-6 appearance list compiled by its historian Jack Davis.

The interim three missing years were those in which the young Gwilliam went, first, to Cambridge University and then into the Army. There is no doubt that the second of these experiences had a sizeable, positive influence upon the strapping back-five forward who was soon to lead his country on the Rugby field. In an essay published after his retirement, he wrote:

> Rugby Football, like Chess, has much in common with warfare. The difference is that the law, and in Rugby the referee, prevent the use of total warfare. But anyone leading a national Rugby team would do well to apply some of the principles which famous generals have adopted. Napoleon always looked for energy in his generals... all through the game you will be stirring up the brilliant player who is inclined to be idle.

It was natural for those who had been in the Forces to think and write in these terms, for such men and women took huge experience out into civvy street. The way in which the Services trained their officer class was characterised by great clarity in the identification of aims and objectives. John Gwilliam brought this capability to a fine art as he moved through Rugby's ranks and, ultimately perchance, attained command status.

In 1947 he was only one of a group of highly-gifted players who came together in Welsh teams of the immediate post-War years. Under him these men were to touch heights and assert themselves on the world scene. Not immediately: the fans, who had last cheered a Triple Crown season by the National XV in 1911 had to be patient for a little longer. But glory lay in store.

TWO

Early in 1946 the Parry-Jones family was on the move again, back to Cardiff whence it had gone to Hoylake. My parents secured a transfer for me from Birkenhead School, where my secondary education had commenced and where I was introduced to the strange game of Rugby football, to Cardiff High School. Here, too, the 15-a-side game held sway in the winter terms.

The school was one whose pupils were, in the main, those who had fared best in the scholarship, or 'eleven-plus', examinations. Although there was a tier of excellent suburban grammar schools, the best-placed scholars came to CHS from all corners of the city. The result of this was that if you wished to visit a friend out of school hours you might have to travel some distance, from Rumney to Ely for example or from the Docklands – picturesquely known as Tiger Bay – to Llandaff. Such trips could be aboard one of the clattering tramcars which serviced principal routes, but we boys preferred to go by bicycle. The machines of the day, manufactured by Raleigh or Humber or Rudge were beyond dispute status symbols. The most sought-after were low-slung and painted in sexy colours, sporting narrow racing saddles and bottles with straws from which, the idea was, long-distance cyclists could satisfy thirst without having to stop for a drink and suffering a delay.

The Second World War was now no more than a memory, albeit one from the very recent past. However, because my friends were far-flung, I could not possibly avoid noting the blitz damage as I cycled to call on them. My guess is that its extent could not compare with the havoc wreaked upon Merseyside; yet as you pedalled around the city you were left in no doubt of the German bombers' intentions, which were to cause as much mayhem and demoralisation, with loss of life, as possible. Some streets in the Roath area, where I now lived, had been razed to the ground and among the ruined buildings was Marlborough Road junior school. Allensbank Road lost a terrace near its junction with Whitchurch Road. Neville Street's tall villas were disfigured, while the big city-centre hit was upon the fashionable cafe-ballroom of R.E. Jones in Queen Street which the incendiary bombs reduced to a heap of smouldering rubble. A sad loss was the Howard Gardens High School, which stood just off Newport Road near the Royal Infirmary. Eyewitnesses who saw it burning under the incendiary bombs said it was like a giant yellow, red and orange torch of flames. When I arrived at Cardiff High School, a mere half a mile distant, Howard Gardens pupils attended classes held on our premises, for all the world like other 'displaced persons' in Europe. Canton High School was hit too.

There is a tale that things would have been much, much worse for Cardiff had the Luftwaffe pilots been given correctly-drawn maps; their targets were wrongly marked between the Rivers Taff and Ely, in the west, instead of delineating areas to the east between Taff and Rumney which featured docks and steelworks. If this is true, it explains why a lot of bombs fell on open ground and fields adjoining Grangetown and Canton, with few landing on the strategically vital installations to the east. Maybe that is true, maybe not; what is baffling is how the raiders missed the gleaming white buildings of Cathays Park or the picturesque ramparts and battlements of the Castle.

It was not always easy, as a 12-year-old, to comprehend what had happened in the houses, offices and factories that had been hit. Their remains seemed to generate a kind of anodyne effect, as if you were looking at an ancient monument that might have been knocked about a bit by Owain Glyndwr or Cromwell. It was a long time before I discovered, or was told, that in that house over there, for instance, a whole family perished when a bomb struck it; or here once stood a bakery where workers took cover from the bombs, only to die when it caught a direct hit.

There were two Cardiff buildings which enjoyed a higher profile than others and suffered grievously in the raids of 2 January 1941. One was the cathedral church of St Michael, located in the village-city of Llandaff. The roof of its nave took the full force of a land-mine, a parachute-borne device which drifted earthwards aimlessly before exploding some feet above ground. This ensured that the blast was effective over a far greater area than would have been the case had the explosion occurred on impact. Thus although the nave's sturdy pillars stood firm, the roof's beams and tiles which it supported were shattered beyond repair. The cathedral was a piteous sight, especially when it was realised that the spire had been de-stabilised and needed to be cut to a stump in the interests of safety.

So there were tears on the cheeks of parishioners who came to inspect the damage in the morning. Some groaned that if only the wind had blown the land-mine a hundred yards to the east its force would merely have caused a few ripples on the surface of the Taff. Others said that had it fallen a similar distance to the west it would have wiped out other old-established buildings in Llandaff with a substantial attendant death-toll. For the cathedral itself to be struck was, indeed, a mixed blessing.

The second spectacular, if equally irrelevant, strike achieved by the German bomb-aimers laid waste to a large sector of Cardiff Arms Park's Rugby stadium, including grandstand seating and terracing at its western end, which bordered the Taff in days when the Rugby pitch ran at right angles to the river. A giant crater dented the in-goal area; and one of the most inspired Welsh cartoons of the twentieth century (by the *South Wales Echo's* J.C. Walker) portrays a diminutive member of Cardiff's Home Guard showing the wreckage to a cigar-smoking Yankee visitor. "The last International match played here," the American is being told, "was between Wales and England."

"Gee!" comes the reply. "That sure must have been a helluva game."

Now it was the Welsh sporting fraternity's turn to grieve. The great centre Bleddyn Williams, himself a wartime flier, thinks that the German bomb-aimer may have imagined that he had a steelworks in his sights, or an arms depot or a giant hangar: "Whatever the case, the hit amounted to nothing short of catastrophe." Not until 1949 was the stadium completely re-furbished, completion being celebrated with a club match between Cardiff and Newport which the home side won 5-0. A few graphic photographs of the damage survive, notably one from Wales' game against Scotland in 1948, showing that while the north terrace had been repaired the 'shelf' above it remained in ruins: empty.

It so happened that Cardiff High School's junior sides played their Rugby on Saturday mornings. Thus my contemporaries and I could, if we chose, get to Cardiff Arms Park in time to watch a match that featured our local heroes against a succession of charismatic opponents, ranging from Penarth (no pushovers in those days) to English clubs like Coventry and Wasps. Our attendance was both encouraged and facilitated by the issue of small yellow entrance passes which you had to hand back to the Rugby master on Monday mornings. A number 2a or 2b tram took us joyfully into the city centre for seventy minutes (not eighty as it would soon become) high-octane sporting entertainment. Graham Hale, a Cardiff High School Old Boy who played on the wing for Wales in the 'Victory Internationals', ascribes this privilege to the good relations built between Cardiff RFC and Eric Evans who, besides teaching us English and organising our Rugby, was honorary secretary of the Welsh Secondary Schools Rugby Union and knew about up-and-coming youngsters.

The passes allowed us access to the terraced South Enclosure. This standpoint meant that the wrecked North Stand was for long a back-drop to the matches that we watched. Some of us once sneaked across the field after a final whistle and emerged after a tortuous climb at the level which had suffered the bomb damage. I remember that the seating had been reduced to matchwood; and that the damaged area was no more than casually roped-off. Any careless schoolboy who lost his footing could easily have plunged to his death on the concrete terracing below.

Later we will dwell on the talents that were being paraded before the big crowds of the day. Let us stay with the atmospheres and enthusiasms of those post-War years for a little longer, and the voracious appetites of players and spectators for action and spectacle. As a result, there was the manifestation of a glorious exuberance on the pitch, greeted and acknowledged by applause from the side-lines that was constant, generous and sometimes tumultuous. The post-War crowds were huge; 25,000 was a regular gate for Cardiff's matches; and an encounter between the home team and Newport in 1951 drew the astonishing figure for a club game of 48,500 spectators. They gorged themselves on huge feasts of points and tries.

It is fair to say that as a result the youngsters who stood on tip-toe to see over the railings onto the pitch became hooked on Rugby football at this time. I can remember only one contemporary who changed codes in later life. That was the late Graham Vearncombe, who before leaving school broke our long-jump record, kept wicket for the First XI and performed superbly in the First XV's three quarter line. He opted for professional Soccer, however, at which he was a superb goalkeeper for Cardiff City and won a number of caps for Wales.

From Cardiff RFC's point of view there was every reason for feeding the stars of the future on a diet of rich action. The dreams of small hero-worshippers were focussed on the distant demigods and their heroic deeds. We wanted to emulate Bleddyn, or Jack, or Haydn, or Les (Manfield) or Cliff (Davies). Blue and Black was beautiful. The free pass privilege, by the way, was not confined to Cardiff High School boys. Derek Williams – 'C.D'. – remembers the introduction of a a similar system at Canton High School, and it appears that in the west Swansea RFC ran a similar concessionary system in their town (as it then was).

There was a second vital motive in those amateur Middle Ages for capturing the imagination and loyalty of the young, at the earliest possible age. Welsh stars often hailed from relatively indigent backgrounds compared with those of England, a large proportion of whose top players had grammar and public school backgrounds and did not need or want recompense for playing. The immediate pre-War days had seen men like W.T.H. and Idwal Davies cash in their talent and take money to 'go North', as the terse saying had it, and the amateur game's administrators in Wales were now bent on keeping the rising generation in the homeland. One way of doing this was to secure their allegiances with calculated blandishments like free passes.

Another method, which won collusion by the media of the day, was to banish for eternity any 'defector' from the amateur ranks. Merely speaking to an agent from the Yorkshire and Lancashire badlands could spell doom for an ingenuous boy from the Valleys who simply listened to a sales pitch. But still they went. With hindsight it is perhaps surprising that Rugby League and the big financial rewards held out, never took root in Wales. Part of the answer is that the clubs had become controlled down the years by powerful, self-perpetuating oligarchies who owned facilities like stadia and pitches and had their own ways of rewarding men who stayed loyal.

These circumstances, however, overshadow a more constructive approach by Welsh Rugby's Establishment to the nurturing of its teenage prospects. It stemmed from a realisation that while the educationally-elect – grammar school products and a public school minority – had a well-signposted route up to top-quality club Rugby and thence to International level, boys who left school at fourteen, or even seventeen, too often encountered no beckoning avenue of progress. Not big or mature enough to be required by the clubs, they all too often turned their backs on the game forever or came back fortuitously in their late twenties. The formation of the Welsh Youth Rugby Union early in 1949 acknowledged these factors and tapped a huge new reservoir of raw talent from which players of great talent would soon come on stream.

Although John Gwilliam's upward progress in Rugby Football differed in many respects from that of other South Wales valleys boys, it began in a manner that was common enough in the mid-twentieth century. Edward Evans had been a face-worker at one of the Rhondda collieries; his daughter, John's mother, spoke vividly to her son of the 1911 Tonypandy riots when troops joined forces with the local constabulary to quell industrial action taken by the miners against the coal-owners.

During a week when shop windows were smashed and scuffles broke out in the main street she recalled being escorted to school by her mother so that she would come to no harm.

Her husband Bert was also familiar with subterranean Wales, though not one who earned a living with pick and shovel. Rather, he was a surveyor who plotted underground routes for shafts and levels by which colliers could access rich seams. He would calculate how a tunnel, begun from two different ends, would meet precisely at its projected half-way point. Off duty he was a good cricketer, but seems to have been more of a spectator than a player of Rugby football. He evidently travelled out of Pontypridd if there was an attractive fixture down on the coast and often spoke of George Nepia, the great All Black full back who toured Wales in the year that John was born, 1924. He would have seen him at Newport or Cardiff, for Wales met the tourists at Swansea.

Gwilliam junior proved to be a bright pupil and an equally good performer on the sports field, his favourite game at that juncture being cricket. Tall and sturdy for his tender years, while still only ten he was chosen for the school's under-12 Rugby XV which was coached for a few weeks by the charismatic Ronnie Boon, the first 'star' he saw in the flesh. This hero in 1933 of Wales' first-ever win at Twickenham came up a year later to Pontypridd to undertake the practical stints of teacher training.

Outside classroom and playground, occasions Gwilliam quickly learned to look forward to were Ponty's mid-week fixtures against top Welsh sides such as Llanelli or Neath. When they were the visitors Llanwood, like other schools in town, would finish early (in days before floodlights became common), so that pupils could go to see the action. On such evenings Gwilliam's father would come to meet his son for the short walk to Ynysangharad Park where they would watch the giants from the west, who often included household names like the brilliant, bald-headed Llanelli stand off half Dai John. Often, a Pontypridd 'regular' would disappoint the local fans by suddenly going missing; and, in those days of depression, Bert would have to explain to his son that so-and-so had been lured away in search of employment. Young John was particularly upset by the departure of a promising player called Loosemore, attracted to Torquay RFC by the promise of a job as a town council dustbin man. Now in his late seventies Gwilliam laments, "It's the on-going tale of Pontypridd. Their talent is always being burgled."

On another occasion he remembers climbing the fence around Ynysangharad Park with some pals to watch Cliff Jones train. The boys wondered: was this the nearest bit of flat land to his home town of Porth? Gwilliam regrets that he never watched the little man play, though he did catch a wartime game at Gloucester in which Jones's rival W.T.H. Davies was in action.

John Gwilliam's all-round abilities seemed set to be refined and polished at Pontypridd Grammar School when he passed the eleven-plus scholarship examination. At this crucial point in the boy's education and up-bringing, however, Gwilliam senior decided that he would perforce quit underground working because of the adverse effect it was having upon his health. The decision appears to have been taken suddenly, so that John found himself withdrawn after only three weeks from his new, exciting educational establishment and travelling eastwards to Monmouth with his parents.

So abrupt a departure from Pontypridd, a bustling, pleasant town at the confluence of the rivers Taff and Rhondda, can be explained in terms of the prevailing economic climate. The years between the wars were catastrophic for South Wales: a period of severe economic depression when, as the demand for coal fell, the mining industry contracted. Jobs were scarce during a decline in general prosperity. Rather, therefore, than kicking his heels and enduring frustrations in the quest for new work locally Bert Gwilliam sensibly turned to his mother, who ran an off-licence establishment in the Forest of Dean and was evidently not short of capital assets. She responded by helping her son to acquire a retail business at Monmouth. A transfer was arranged for John from Pontypridd GS to the town's Direct Grant semi-public school.

Monmouth School's sports fields lie just east of the River Wye, on which John Gwilliam learned to scull beneath picturesque hills. Enough space is available for several Rugby pitches while, in summer, cricket is the resident game on decent wickets. Here the gifted Pontypridd newcomer enjoyed himself to the utmost. A batsman who put a large, growing frame behind huge drives and hooks, he brought off a highly unusual, if not unique, feat in scoring two centuries on the same Saturday: one for a House XI and the other for the Town team the same evening against a local Services side. His father, whom John does not recall as a wildly enthusiastic parent, passed on congratulations in his capacity as captain of Monmouth CC.

To pursue the Cricket theme briefly, a year or two after the War ended Gwilliam was deemed good enough for a trial by Glamorgan CCC on whose behalf the skipper, Wilfred Wooller, invited him to report at the County office in Cardiff at ten am one spring morning. Gwilliam's appetite was hugely sharpened by the prospect of rubbing shoulders with Gilbert Parkhouse, Phil Clift, Allan Watkins and other members of a successful Glamorgan side which won a first Championship title in 1948. Alas, a blunder of gigantic proportions resulted in his arrival at 6 High Street (Glamorgan's HQ in those days) at a quarter past twelve to find the office closed. The would-be recruit had blown his chance of a big career with bat and ball, and was mortified.

There was, however, Rugby football. At the School his skills steadily grew and his technique at set scrum and, particularly, the line out was being polished. Gwilliam enjoyed a scary debut in chocolate and white hoops for the First XV away from home against a Llandovery College side coached by T.P. Williams (revered by Carwyn James). It included Rees Stephens, a year older than him and destined before long to start winning his 32 caps for Wales. At this time both boys were props who packed down against each other. Gwilliam admits that it was hard coping with an opponent twelve months his senior. "Llandovery were a bit too good for us," is his sober recall.

Another early Rugby acquaintance who would become an

International team-mate in due course was the wing Ken Jones. When Monmouth's XV visited West Mon school, by whom they had never been beaten, Jones was on a wing for the pride of Pontypool. His team chose that day to make history, winning 13-12 in a match that the two men often talked of in later years.

The headmaster at Monmouth, a Mr Lewin, believed firmly that prowess at Rugby Football was an influence on the academic intake by Oxbridge colleges and would help boys to win scholarships (in those days he was not far from the mark). That in turn would reflect well on his School and keep its registers full. Thus he recruited Peter Hordern, who held four England caps, to coach Rugby. Another recruit, who seems to have had more influence upon the young Gwilliam, was one Mike Marshall. This Yorkshireman arrived at Monmouth following a stint in the Isle of Man and began preaching the Rugby principles of the great Wavell Wakefield. Between the Wars England were the most successful of the Home Countries; the Sedbergh-educated 'Wakers' had made thirty-one appearances for his country, captaining it on thirteen occasions and his thoughts on the game would repay study. Gwilliam did as he was told; a few short years later he grieved to hear of Marshall's wartime death when his ship was sunk by a U-boat in the Mediterranean.

The boy's frame stretched as he practised jumping to catch throw-ins; it broadened to carry muscle; he spent time dissecting and analysing the game. Eric Evans ran an 'Anglo-Welsh' schools XV for which the young Monmothian turned out in vacations, and it was probably he who advised the Cambridge Rugby establishment that a major new talent was in the pipeline. It was about this time too – probably in the 1941-42 winter – that Newport took an interest in the up-and-coming second or back row youngster and gave him a few outings whenever he happened to be available.

Sport apart, Gwilliam confesses to experiencing a scholastic culture shock. It is hard enough to cross the gap dividing secondary from primary education; but here, as boys dropped anchor at Monmouth, there were forces at work already scheming their path up to and beyond the 'matric' examinations of the day and the 'Higher Cert' sat by sixth formers. To ensure that boys gave a respectable account of themselves they were required to start the working day study schedule at 08:30 hours, snatching meal-breaks at 13:00 and 16:30 before pressing on to a mid-evening finish.

Despite this fierce discipline the next step, to further education, caused some furrowed brows. The problem was not that the young Gwilliam was short of brain power; rather, it was indecision which caused a minor crisis. Yes, he wanted to go to University; yes, Cambridge would be a good idea. But, to read what? That was the question.

Now Mr Lewin saved the day, unearthing an award offered at Trinity College for undergraduates considering the teaching of history as a career. To his faint surprise Gwilliam was given an Exhibition which he could take up straightaway – worth all of £30 a year. Though this was not a fortune, the recipient remembers a sure feeling that Lady Luck had smiled upon him: he had been lucky to move to Monmouth School, it was lucky that his paternal grandmother had enough money to set the family on its feet; it was sheer luck that his Headmaster's keen research identified a scholarship which lay within his grasp: "I didn't like maths, or physics, or chemistry," he admits. "I quite fancied history. That was lucky too."

The much-heralded boy from Pontypridd, via Monmouth school, scarcely set University Rugby on fire when he took up residence at Cambridge in 1941 aged 18. Teenage sportsmen who go up to Oxbridge step suddenly into a man's world, and Gwilliam was still a boy. He played once for the University team before being demoted to the Sixty Club, Cambridge's second fifteen. It became one of thirteen distinct teams for which he claims to have played during war-time.

Another of these was Cilfynydd RFC which he represented on a return trip to Pontypridd. It was a tough game against tough opponents: a Welch Regiment XV which included two strong-running backs who had been capped by Wales during the thirties in F.J.V. Ford and Barney McCall. The invitation to play in this match had been procured by a local contact from earlier days called Will Dixon. This family friend appears to have had an important influence on the youngster and had taken him regularly to chapel on behalf of parents who were lukewarm about religion. Gwilliam says that it was about the time of this second meeting with Dixon that he decided to live a good, clean life and "not to be inebriated, ever."

The point should be made that this decision was a brave and unusual one to make at the time in the context of Rugby football, its ethics, and the behaviour which was once expected of all its aspiring adherents. It may be that in his first year at Cambridge he had witnessed post-match alcohol effecting a devastating influence on the personalities of otherwise sensibly behaved companions. So he took up a stance from which he has never retreated. It may be partly for this reason that former team-mates and opponents are willing to use terms like 'austere' and 'aloof' of him. As we shall see, a certain distance between him and the men he led was, in the end, literally the case because of the direction his career took. For his part an element of mystique and unpredictability cannot have greatly harmed his command status.

The War Office permitted successful entrants twelve months at the University to which they had gained entry before 'call-up' to the colours. By 1943 therefore, having finished basic training and been identified as 'officer material' John Gwilliam had moved to Sandhurst where his six month posting included appearances in the Rugby XV. His team-mates included C.B. Holmes, a leading British sprinter of the inter-War years, and W.E.N. 'Wendy' Davis who had propped for Wales, plus the double International Maurice Turnbull. In charge of PE was none other than Matt Busby, destined to become one of the great managers of Manchester United.

This agreeable interlude came to an end when he was commissioned into the Royal Tank Regiment. By now the new subaltern was a very large young man who, half a century on, still recalls the struggle it took to get his frame down through the turret to the innards of his war-chariot. Once there he learned the meaning of claustrophobia. Such considerations, however, were not deemed uncomfortable enough to delay his posting across the Channel in August 1944, a little way behind the full-blooded Allied landings on the Normandy beaches. He and his squadron landed on a 'Mulberry', or floating harbour before driving inland to join the Fifth 'Desert Rats' in the push towards Caen under Field Marshal Montgomery. At this time the British and American invaders had devised an elaborate 'pocket' where they had trapped two German field armies, the Fifth and Seventh Panzers, and because of which the war in north west France was about to be concluded. This was the nightmare scenario behind the German lines into which Lt Gwilliam and a column of British tanks strayed and got lost for an hour and a half. The young commander mopped his brow with relief when radio contact helped him to bring his squadron to safety.

The Germans resisted until the following spring without ever being able to halt the Allies' progress towards Berlin and 'Victory in Europe' day. Gwilliam and his tanks moved steadily eastwards with the flow, helping to overcome tough German resistance at locations like the Ardennes, Arnhem and the Rhine crossing. He and his men were sad that all too often the combatants whom they encountered were aged veterans and boy members of the Hitler Youth.

After the War ended with the Nazi surrender on 8 May the Forces were critical of the lack of urgency on the part of officialdom and the delay in their longed-for repatriation. While difficult logistics were worked out, sport was one way of fending off impatience and keeping the troops busy. Thus 1945 saw the first Army Cup tournament in which the Royal Tank Regiment got to the Final at Wuppertal, only to go down decisively to the Fourth Battalion, the Welch Regiment. As if native talent were not enough, Gwilliam remembers that their opponents' 21-3 success owed much to one of the best English Rugby league players of his day, Peter Stott.

Demobilisation, however, came eventually and back on Welsh

soil Gwilliam, at 23, was knuckling down in Black and Amber colours to Rugby at its highest level as one of the Rodney Parade squad. Very much in his sights, however, was a return to Cambridge to resume progress towards his Tripos and, with luck, a Blue. Not in his sights at this stage, perhaps, was International Rugby. Yet it lay only a couple of years in the future.

THREE

And so, eagerly and energetically, normal service was resumed. Instead of being directed at Nazi Germany, hostile energies could be worked off healthily once more upon the posh Rugby club from down on the coast or local rivals from further up the valley. I cannot resist quoting the Risca RFC historian Jack Strickland on a famous defeat of near neighbours Cross Keys and the fervour which it generated after years on a starvation diet of spectator sport. This is how a small boy experienced it:

> Hundreds came down from Cross Keys on bikes and walking... kick-off time arrived and I was on the spot where the players ran onto the field. Cross Keys came first, and the very sight of them frightened the wits out of me! Faces covered in grease and smelling of wintergreen. Forwards wearing scrum caps, huge legs, sleeves tucked up and faces like gargoyles... Then out came Risca. Heavens above, they looked just as tough. This game will never be finished, I thought. They will kill each other.

With only seconds left at the end and two points adrift, Risca won a free kick on the half way line. Scorning a line-kick 'Tosh' Evans dropped for goal.

> The silence was so profound that I swear if somebody had struck a match it would have sounded like a clap of thunder. A thousand eyes were staring at that lump of leather travelling, oh so slowly, on its way to the posts. Would it reach, or wouldn't it? I am sure all breathing stopped for what seemed to be an hour yet was but a matter of seconds. The ball then started to drop earthwards – Everything that goes up must eventually come down – and that ball did come down. Just over the bar! The referee's whistle blew for the end of the match... Suddenly all hell was let loose. Home supporters jumped over the fence by the hundred, and grabbed every man in a Risca jersey to hold him up high.

More than half a century on such partisanship, such total commitment, at such a village level of the game is difficult to credit. But since 1945 there have been powerful influences at work which have eroded such passions.

The latter part of the twentieth century brought, first of all, the closure of a myriad collieries which had bestowed unity, identity and a vibrant self-respect upon the communities living close to pitheads no more than three or four miles apart. The young working men of today's Valleys are more likely to be employed in distant factories up towards the Brecon Beacons or down on the coast, so that beating the boys who live two miles away is not the be-all and end-all of their sporting ambitions. The allegiances which survive are no longer blind or one-eyed.

The second factor that has diluted much of the frenzy that once accompanied club Rugby in the Welsh hotbed is the construction of the dual-carriageways and motorways which now criss-cross Gwent, Glamorgan and the western outposts. In the immediate post-War years a simple journey by road between Cardiff and Swansea might take four hours. A Llanelli player considering a transfer to, say, Newport's ranks would need to address serious domestic issues such as moving house and changing jobs. Such moves were therefore rarer and men stayed loyal to the local clubs which had nurtured them. Thus Haydn Tanner's decision to leave Swansea RFC and join Cardiff in 1946 caused a minor sensation. Nowadays the two-way traffic between east and west is non-stop. The first objective of top professional players in the twenty-first century is not to bring glory to their locality but to negotiate a good wage package anywhere.

Thirdly, and perhaps most important, today's ardent supporters of the Rugby game across South Wales have new choices. Where their fathers would have crowded ever closer to the ropes to savour the old-fashioned, robust exchanges with their flying fists, careless studs and bloodied noses, the fans of the new millennium can choose to stay before the fire on a wet winter's night to watch televised 'super' Rugby from the southern hemisphere or so-and-so's selection of *A Hundred Best Tries* on video, with scoring passes to be viewed from every conceivable angle and match-saving tackles played over and over again.

Of course, the stars of the future often shine first at Pandy Park or the Welfare Ground or Broadacre, and the smaller clubs will always be important to the future of the game in Wales. But when television's Rugby hypermarket is crammed with quality goods it is inevitable that the corner-shop's appeal is diminished.

Half a century ago, just as cinema was the great evening entertainment, so Rugby, both at top level and parochially, continued to hold sway during daylight hours and at weekends, as it had done for nearly a hundred years. The clubs were prosperous, partly because players – the principal human resource – were not paid professionals. Their boots may have been regularly and furtively filled with cash rewards but plenty of money was left over for administrators and committees to use. If little of it found its way into improvements of stadia, pitches and other facilities, then too bad; the people who might have been able to explain where the bulk of it went are no longer alive to render account.

But some clubs remained scrupulously amateur, either through exigence or on principle. And it so happened that one of those in the latter category was enjoying a golden era of its own. Players with Cardiff RFC at that time took no secret cash; but the total experience was like living at a luxury hotel. You probably used your own boots for matches (even International players owned no more than one pair); but every other piece of kit was supplied by the club. Transport was laid on, in first class carriages if a rail journey was necessary (and this was quite frequent in days before the first Severn Bridge was constructed). When the Blue and Blacks visited London, five-star accommodation was the norm and a pre-match night at the theatre commonplace. In return for such star treatment Cardiff's teams gave displays that dazzled big crowds at home and at top clubs around Britain. Danny Davies's 1976 book names the 1947-48 season as the greatest in the club's history, narrowly ahead of 1905-06 and the heyday of Gwyn Nicholls.

Part of the reason for this pre-eminence was the quality of the available players. Though not yet the nation's Capital, Cardiff was by 1946 a big, important city holding out employment opportunities which were prestigious and lucrative enough to over-ride the local loyalties alluded to earlier. Employers were only too happy to be influenced by an application from a big-name Rugby player, who having secured a post naturally proceeded to offer his services to the Arms Park club.

Critics and committees based elsewhere thought that head-hunting went on and that top players were brought to the club by inducements. There is no evidence for this and Cardiff stoutly deny the use of blandishments. Sometimes, it has to be said, the newcomers' arrival caused sadness and some acrimony, as when Haydn Tanner came on strength; his move dislodged the popular Billy Darch, who had perforce to accept second string status until his emigration to Canada in 1949.

But no club would have closed its doors against a world-class player like the Swansea-bred scrum half. Before the War, aged just seventeen and still at Gowerton Grammar School, Tanner had figured in the two defeats of the 1935 All Blacks, by Swansea and Wales, picked up another twelve International caps and gone on the 1938 Lions tour of South Africa. In 1947-48 he became captain of Cardiff, turning his side into a scoring machine which won 39 of its 41 matches averaging close on twenty points per game.

Though I do not recall ever seeing moving pictures of Tanner in action, I was at Cardiff Arms Park just before he first donned Cardiff colours. It was Eastertime; he was in the touring Barbarians' side; and like the vast majority of folk on the field or in the crowd I completely lost sight of the ball and the scrum half as he ghosted past the opposing back row for a try that swung the game his side's way. He made these breaks judiciously, no more than twice or three times during a half. But when he went it was into space, with opponents momentarily off-guard. If a defender did manage to get an arm or a shoulder into him, at six feet and thirteen stone the scrum half was big enough to brush off the challenge and in this respect probably compares with Terry Holmes rather than Gareth Edwards. To the rest of the world the last-named is supreme, partly because he is better-known; but the older Welsh generation who saw both men in their prime find it hard to separate them.

It is interesting that the late Hermas Evans, a contemporary at Gowerton and latterly an elder statesman in Welsh Rugby, said that Tanner was arrogant; but his judgement may stem partly from disappointment at the perceived defection of a major figure away from west Wales. Maybe, too, the supreme self-confidence needed to dominate a match can be mistaken for arrogance and conceit. Here, finally, is how Wilfred Wooller summed up his skills in an article written after his retirement in 1950:

> ...The outside half never had to take a bad pass. Indeed the force and direction demanded that his partner must be running straight and fast if he was to get the best advantage from it. He thereby fulfilled the primary duty of an inside half to a degree which I have never seen before or since.

Outside Tanner Cardiff's stand off half for the six post-War seasons was Billy Cleaver, a mine manager who grew up in the Rhondda valley. A well-muscled man with wavy fair hair, he crouched ever so slightly as he ran with the ball, and thus seemed able to bounce tacklers off a sturdy-frame. His hands were reliable, and he was quick to pass on useable possession. But his great talent was with the boot, and under the Laws of the day he could employ it to close a game down to rest his pack (at that time this was easier since players were allowed to kick straight out from anywhere on the field); or just as easily make huge gains of territory with raking screw kicks which bobbed and rolled into touch just beyond a full back's grasp.

The Cardiff midfielders were as great a centre pairing as club Rugby has ever seen – Bridgend-born Jack Matthews who had earned a Welsh Trial just before the War and led the club in its first post-War season and Bleddyn Williams, a native of Taff's Well just north of Cardiff whose Rugby finishing school was Rydal, (which Wilfred Wooller had also attended). The full-blown club careers of both men were interrupted by six years of hostilities and by September 1945 they were clearly fired up for the fray with energy to burn.

In days before 'inside' and 'outside' centres the pairing of the two men was a felicitous accident. Jack, short of stature with legs which pounded like pistons, is best remembered for defence in which he was what today is known as a big 'hitter', seriously dedicated to shocking his opposite number out of the game. He had also been a sprint champion in his teens, so that in attack he could use vivid acceleration to achieve an outside break and get into space. Whoever were the visitors, their midfield frequently found itself back-pedalling in disarray.

'Jink' was the word used to describe a main weapon in Bleddyn Williams's armoury. Not coined, it appears in the Oxford English Dictionary which defines it as "making a quick elusive turn so as to dodge a pursuer". This scarcely does justice to the panache with which Williams executed the manoeuvre. Its crucial ingredient, as I recall it, was an abrupt check of his stride which halted defenders – followed by a tremendous acceleration through the space which had been created. The difference between him and his partner was effortlessness: a limousine compared with a hot-rod.

Also, whenever Williams was photographed he was smiling, and you felt that he probably grinned with pleasure as the markers stumbled in his wake. Immaculately-timed passes could put wings like Les Williams, Terry Cook and Russell Burn in at the flag, but Bleddyn also reached the line on his own account. Still standing is his record 41 tries for Cardiff set in 1948, one of the reasons why Danny Davies named him "one of the greatest centre three quarters of all time".

People who saw him, or played with him, found him unforgettable. This, I surmise, is partly why John Gwilliam's recall of the first time he appeared with Bleddyn remains vital and vivid a full sixty years on. He says they were both in an 'Anglo Welsh Public Schools' XV which met a Rhondda select side.

He adds:

> I have never forgotten what I saw. He dominated the game, mesmerising the poor lads from the Rhondda. At one stage

he must have side-stepped every one of them at least once...
then his acceleration was remarkable too. It was unfair to pit
him against ordinary mortals!

The forward play of this period will be examined in detail
later. For now let us simply recall names like Maldwyn James, a
hooker, lock Les Manfield (later his position would be re-named
'number eight'), flanker Gwyn Evans, prop Cliff Davies and
second row man Bill Tamplin who could kick prodigious goals.
These were men who appreciated the quality of the club's back
division, accepting that their job was to win possession and let
the backs do the scoring. Jack Matthews recalled that back-row
players 'corner flagged' in defence and 'stayed out of the backs'
way in attack'. So intensive support play by packs was not yet the
norm, though Manfield liked an occasional run close behind the
back-line.

These were the stalwarts of a team which drew big crowds
wherever they appeared in Britain (or France: Cardiff went there
for an Armistice Day fixture with Nantes by air, the club's first
flight). Jack Matthews recalls with enormous pleasure the taking
of Coventry's ground record, which had lasted for 63 games, in
1945 by sixteen points to three in front of 15,000 spectators.

For all these reasons it is fair to conclude that Cardiff were
setting the pace in Welsh club Rugby. But other clubs were also
regaining momentum, notably Newport for whom Gwili Jenkins
and the inspirational Hedley Rowland were good captains. Ken
Jones, soon to become an Olympic athlete, came down from
Blaenavon for a first season in 1946-47, R.T. Evans was making
an impact, Malcolm Thomas would soon take centre stage.

Newport's results at this time show how Welsh club Rugby
remained immeasurably stronger than that of England. From
1945-6 to 1948-9 the club lost only five games (out of 58) to
English opposition. Swansea would not pick up momentum for
a few seasons and supplied no more than a prop, Dai Jones, for
the International games of the late forties. Even Llanelli could
only point to Ossie and Stan Williams as consistent cap-winners,
though the romantically-named Christmas Howard Davies

stayed in the game long enough to add four caps at full back to the two he had won in 1939. Handel Greville won a solitary cap as a stand-in when Tanner chipped an elbow, and Peter Rees played two Tests on the wing. But the immediate post-war years were not quite vintage Scarlet.

It was at this time, too, in a socialist political climate when elitism was coming under fire, that the junior clubs of Wales were setting their sights high and jostling for acceptance in the top echelon. Maesteg completed an ambitious new grandstand project just in time for their astonishing 'invincible' season of 1949-50 (though it should be noted that at that time neither Cardiff nor Newport, for example, figured on their fixture list). Newbridge had been runners-up in the championship race of 1947-48. Glamorgan Wanderers lived a Bohemian-style existence with a playing centre out at Ely whose headquarters was in an attic above the Wyndham Arcade – afficionados who drank there tried not to think of their possible fate in the event of fire. Bridgend, too, lived a hand-to-mouth existence in these post-War years, actually using the Island Farm PoW camp which had accommodated Gerd von Runstedt and Rudolf Hess among other Nazi notables.

For sure, club Rugby in Wales was quickly up and running as peace returned.

John Gwilliam, by now 23 years of age, had been de-mobbed and continued to be selected by Newport when available. This was less often than the club would have liked, and between 1946 and 1949 the young man made no more than a handful of appearances in a Black and Amber jersey. He had other things on his mind, notably the return to Cambridge. His secondary education at Monmouth would have prepared him admirably for life beside the Cam in which scholarly habits were cultivated but sport caught the imagination.

The autumn term of 1947, when he became a major force in the light blue pack, had seen a torrent of pent-up, frustrated talent and Rugby creativity pouring into Cambridge, and Oxford too. The shoulders rubbed by Gwilliam belonged to men who are still revered more than half a century later. Team-mates and opponents at Twickenham in the first of his two Varsity matches included Clive van Ryneveld, Vic Perry (his fellow lock forward), Jika Travers, David Swarbrick, John Kendall-Carpenter, Peter Kinninmonth and a fellow countryman educated at Ammanford Grammar School called Lloyd Davies who won the game with two penalties as the Dark Blues' place kickers failed miserably. Gwilliam recalls with a grin how the laid-back full back almost failed to reach Twickenham in time to play after over-sleeping and nearly missing the small fleet of saloon cars hired to take the 'Tabs' to the match. Cambridge celebrated in 1947 while a year later the Welshman was on the losing side and even the presence of Wales stand off half Glyn Davies could not deny Oxford victory by fourteen points to eight.

Top players at the two Universities have been dubbed Rugby Union's 'first professionals'. This is because, certainly in those post-War seasons, their commitment to training was total with three to four sessions per week in term time, in addition to, probably, two major fixtures against opponents who might include Cardiff, Harlequins and London Scottish. The physique of players in their early twenties might not have measured up to that of Welsh miners or brawny Leicestershire farmers, but the undergraduates made up for this by training like demons. An average outing at Grange Road would last for ninety minutes, ending as exhausted squad members dripping with sweat staggered their way to a hot bath.

Such fanaticism was fuelled by two considerations. One had to do with the importance of the 'Blue', which is only awarded for an appearance in the Varsity match and, arguably, is a testament to excellence that lasts a lifetime. Secondly there was the business of beating Oxford each December. The intensity of the inter-Varsity rivalry and its on-field fury is well-nigh impossible to convey to the uninvolved or even to the huge crowds – 38,000 in 1947 and 45,000 a year later – who pack the stadium. The testimony of the Blues has to be accepted; my good friend the late Andrew Mulligan, who was at scrum half for Cambridge in the fifties, used to draw a comparison from boxing: Ireland v England, he would say, or Wales v France is Rugby's heavy-weight division. The Varsity match is a cruiser-weight contest – faster than an International match and twice as frantic.

John Gwilliam bears this out: "My two Varsity matches were the quickest I ever played in. We had trained to exhaustion level – and after one training stint I blacked out. After the first game against Oxford I woke up in the middle of the night quite unable to move."

The modern idiom for such single-minded dedication is 'focussed'. Concentration was a key aspect of the young team-mates of Gwilliam, and all around him in the training squads were men who not only excelled at their particular skills but had also thought hard about how to win Rugby matches. Two years in such stimulating company were the privilege conferred by Cambridge upon Gwilliam, and must have under-pinned the steering of his International teams to the high successes of the mid-twentieth century.

In contrast the picture he paints of training night in Wales in those days is a stark one:

> After complaining about the coldness of the air, the damp-ness of the shirts and the muddiness of the ground all present assume an expression of deadly seriousness and begin their ritual. This consists of trotting steadily around the perimeter of the field until exhaustion is imminent... about twenty five players are soon to be observed waiting hopefully for someone to kick the ball in their direction or continuing the ritual lapping. After three quarters of an hour of this, enlivened only by a few sporadic bursts of passing, the session ends for all except the full back. He comman-deers the only available ball to take a few pot-shots at goal.

This is not the sneer of a Rugby patrician. The evocation is borne out by other University men who were astonished on their return to club Rugby to discover how rudimentary was the big-match preparation of many top Welsh clubs.

A first-hand account of Cardiff RFC's training schedules was given to me by Graham Hale, a three quarter in the so-called 'Victory Internationals' of 1945-6 (which, sadly, never qualified participants for full cap status) who is adamant that the Blue and Blacks trained only once a week. Recalling the greyhound track which ran around the Rugby pitch until the 1980s, he said that its lights were just adequate enough for simple jogging and passing to be undertaken, but complex moves involving combined play by backs and forwards could never be rehearsed after September and before April. Similarly tactics for match day were 'spur of the moment' rather than pre-planned. Nor, Hale told me, was there any figure generally acknowledged to be in charge. Even Haydn Tanner did not run training.

These were days before track suits became commonplace. Flannel shorts were worn, plus a jersey no longer spruce enough to be worn in a match. Scrum caps were a rarity, mainly because they were expensive, though they were worn by the great Neath locks Roy John and Rees Stephens. Even a club like Cardiff would boast no more than two or three well-used balls for training nights which, like match balls, quickly became leaden in wet or muddy conditions. This is possibly the reason why the place kickers of the day remembered by Graham Hale were strong, burly men like his clubmate Bill Tamplin and the Newport lock Ben Edwards.

Kicking at goal in this era was done with the toe, so that although leading players like Bleddyn Williams and Ken Jones quickly took to light boots such as those being turned out by Law and Elmer Cotton, most footwear was clumsy. Heavy swathes of leather were the fashion, with hard toe-caps to absorb the impact. My recall is that rubber, and then aluminium, studs did not become generally available until the start of the fifties. Up until then leather studs were the norm, attached to the boot by three small nails. When the leather wore away, the nails were exposed and could deeply gash an opponent's flesh. Luckily feet were mainly used for dribbling at that time and the ruck had yet to be imported from New Zealand. All in all, no wonder Graham Hale habitually left the Rugby stadium on training nights and went to the cricket enclosure which then lay next to it. Here he would don spikes and practise sprints on short grass and springy turf.

If training was less than intensive it is tempting to conclude that the players of this post-War era were less fit than those of the new professional era. However, it is worth bearing in mind that more matches were played than is the case today. Newport's side of 1947-48 for instance, in which Gwilliam figured a few times, played forty-five games, no fewer than seven of which took place before September was out. Such regular activity, it is his belief, contributed to the attainment and preservation of high fitness levels. He also points out that his generation, charged with going to war in defence of their country, had been obliged to reach a distinct level of fitness during their time in the armed services, a point borne out by Jack Matthews. Dr Jack recalls that a lot of valuable road-work was done in those days – "and despite the surges of speed that were part of my game I never once pulled a muscle!"

However demanding or otherwise training was in those days, Gwilliam was more than ready to praise the organisation which lay behind the on-field successes of Newport. "Fred Cox [the groundsman] was in a class of his own. A new player entering the changing room would find that Fred had every item of kit laid out for him in perfect order. In due course Ray Lewis would arrive with his remarkable powers of physiotherapy and non-stop banter. In the background were committee-men such as Vernon Parfitt, himself an International referree... who were almost paternal in their attitude to the team."

Gwilliam speaks, too, of the sheer friendliness of Newport, from his first outings in 1941-42 up to 1949 and the last games before he left Wales to work in Scotland. Men like R.T. Evans, Haydn Thomas, 'Bunner' Travers (a pre-War cap making a come-back at hooker) and skipper Rowland were kind to nervous newcomers, encouraging them to participate to the full in expansive, crowd-pleasing Rugby – which also happened to be successful, despite a 4-8 defeat by the Wallabies. Wrote the club Historian Jack Davies, "Gates soared beyond Newport's wildest dreams: 22,000 for the Australia game, 19,500 and 24,500 for the two home games with Cardiff, 15,000 for the Watsonians and 14,000 for the Barbarians game. It was clear that this was the sort of Rugby the public wanted to watch".

But John Gwilliam was no longer destined to play a role in the Welsh club game. His priority, in those dear, dead amateur days, was to earn a living. The quest would take him far away from Wales.

FOUR

In the immediate post-War years, then, the clubs of Wales quickly rediscovered winning habits. In contrast, despite the availability of great players and the frenzied support which urged them on, the National XVs of the period were unable to give consistent performances. Perhaps other countries would have been satisfied with the results that came along; but the Welsh were, are and always will be hyper-critics who demand more of their representatives than the putting up of a good show.

The first sign that results in peace-time Rugby might disappoint the Welsh as a nation came when the Second New Zealand Expeditionary Force's 'Kiwis' arrived in Wales. This was an impromptu side made up of players who stayed for some months in Britain after the end of hostilities on the European mainland in 1945. Yet they won twenty nine of their thirty three games, beginning in October with thumping victories over Swansea, Llanelli and Neath. An amazing three-pronged turn-of-the-year programme in Wales began with the seizing of Cardiff's unbeaten record by 3-0 and a 3-3 draw with Newport at Rodney Parade. Nonetheless a 'Welsh XV', whose members were not awarded caps, was confidently expected to win the unofficial Test of 5 January 1946. Informed opinion suggested that the servicemen from Down Under would suffer their country's third defeat at a venue where New Zealand had already lost twice, in 1905 and 1935.

After an hour the prediction looked well-based. Wales were leading through a prodigious penalty goal kicked by that same Hugh Lloyd Davies who would soon come close to missing a Blue through over-sleeping. Alas, he also delivered the possession which the Kiwis turned into a winning score. On his first tour assignment was the commentator Winston McCarthy who described the crucial try in *Haka*.

> Lloyd Davies was forced to kick hurriedly with his left foot for the Welsh left-hand touch, a low hard kick which, nine

times out of ten would have skidded into touch. But Sherratt had his ideas too. He took the ball at top speed when it was shin-high. That was on his ten-yard line and five yards from touch. Then came one of the most thrilling runs of all time. Looking neither to right nor left but with his eyes glued on the goal-line sixty-five yards ahead he set sail with the weight of his fourteen colleagues on his shoulders. Lloyd Davies went after him, so did Graham Hale... the Kiwis just stood where they were and cheered and yelled encouragement to the big wing. As he got to the corner Sherratt swung in towards the posts to touch down for a try that must rank with the greatest ever.

The Kiwis' full back R.W.H. Scott kicked a straightforward conversion to put the tourists ahead and added two penalty goals in the final minutes. Just under thirty thousand expectant fans, who had packed the war-damaged stadium, went home with tails between legs. There was a consolation prize when Monmouthshire not only beat the Kiwis but were the only European side to prevent them from scoring.

During the War years Welshmen serving as fighter pilots or infantrymen, old gentlemen nursing memories of halcyon days, and youngsters dying to emulate the greats whose legendary exploits they had read of – all of these had fondly believed that International Rugby needed only to re-start for Wales to soar back to an imagined pre-War golden era.

These hopes were more than a little overblown. Between 1920 and 1939 Welsh sides won only two Championship titles outright, shared the title four times and could not add to their seven Triple Crown successes up to 1911 when they had been a dominant force in International Rugby. As World War II receded into history the reverse at the hands of the Kiwis was a sign that the presence of individual match-winning players who might be great to watch at club level would not guarantee Championship-winning performances and victories over the 'Dominions'.

Nevertheless the historic stadium named 'Cardiff Arms' Park, after the coaching inn which once stood nearby, was packed for the first post-War Championship game on 18 January 1947. The North Stand's ruined upper deck was still cordoned off, and the attendance was capped at 43,000. In those days players changed in rooms which looked out over the county cricket ground and took the field via a passageway that led between the North Terrace and the West (river end) Terrace, and as the Welsh side stepped over the touchline onto the field of play thirteen of them were winning first caps. Only the captain, Tanner, and full back Howard Davies had played Test Rugby before the Hitler war. England fielded eight new men.

What sort of preparations had the Welsh and English players of the day undertaken? In Rugby's mediaeval days the answer is, next to none. We have seen that training and preparation was minimal in the clubs; so it was at International level. It is the case, if hard to credit, that some selected players who might be packing down together or attempting some intricate 'moves' in the afternoon might have met each other for the first time on the Saturday morning in Cardiff or Swansea, or on the train to an away venue.

This state of affairs accounts for a maxim of those days to the effect that the selection of 'club pairings' made excellent sense. This was true; but only because club half backs, having played together for some time, at least knew each other's names – and even then, sometimes, selectors could ignore the obvious. The Cardiff back division of the post-War years did contain the best Welsh players of the day. But, recalls Bleddyn Williams: "The 'Big Five' selectors never had the gumption to pick me and Jack Matthews together in our club positions at centre." He exaggerates a little: they did play there together five times. But all too often Bleddyn would be selected at stand off half; Billy Cleaver would play at centre; Jack Matthews might be on a wing. The cohesion that was evident when they played for Cardiff was missing when they swapped Blue and Black for Red.

Clearly, in these times when Welsh International sides were picked by the 'Big Five', selectorial shortcomings must bear responsibility for the inability of Welsh XVs to combine and achieve consistency. Bleddyn Williams adds:

> There is no question about it – selectors' knowledge of the game was strictly limited. They did not even know players whom they had just been watching in a Trial. Before an International match they might enter the changing room to wish players good luck, but we would realise that they did not know most of our names. In days before TV they relied heavily on the Press.
>
> It was rare for a selector to be a former International. Arthur Cornish of Cardiff and Vince Griffiths of Newport were exceptions. They were, of course 'District reps'. Thus a major part of the problem was that they felt under pressure to favour clubs in their locality in order that their quest for re-election as a District Rep would be successful.

To take another example, the man who probably suffered most from this vacillation was the fair-haired Billy Cleaver, perceived incontrovertibly by Cardiff RFC, though not the Big Five, as a stand off half. His International career had begun felicitously, it seemed, when, on the morning that the news broke of his selection, he was called from the coal-face to the mine manager's office and given coffee. The conversation went thus:

Boss:	Hello, Cleaver. I hear you've been picked for Wales this weekend.
WBC:	Yes, sir.
Boss:	Congratulations! Take Saturday morning off.
WBC:	That's kind of you, sir. I will.
Boss:	Good, good. Come in on Sunday instead.

Certainly in those days the idea that an International player deserved a certain latitude from employers had not been born. However, if his boss did him no favours, neither can the selectors be said to have treated Cleaver sensibly. His International career began with an appearance in the 1947 game against England at centre. He was chosen there five more times, made seven appearances at stand off half, and played once at full back – no wonder he was to be taken to New Zealand by the British Isles as a 'utility' player. In the 1950 season when the Cardiffian was given four straight caps at stand off half it cannot be coincidence that Wales pulled off a Grand Slam.

The English would not disagree that in those far-off days their club Rugby lacked huge quality. The game, they fiercely argued in those days, was an amateur one. Englishmen played for fun. Their club, whether it was Sleepy Hollow RFC or Wasps or Coventry, was not worth any final sacrifice. For the cause of their country, however, those who donned the white kit with its rose upon the breast like a badge of blood were prepared to give their all. During the inter-war seasons such fortitude had meant that they won the Championship outright seven times and jointly three times. They beat the fast-emerging French nine times in eleven matches, lost narrowly to South Africa in 1932 and obtained a first win over New Zealand in 1936.

As a general rule England's great asset is discipline. In the first years of the Third Millennium Clive Woodward coached free thinking into his selections; but, for a century and a quarter before that, well-drilled packs and a series of stand off half backs who kept cool heads were the factors that counted when pride and the honour of the English nation were at stake. Half a century ago the Celts relied, as always, on inspiration and heaven-sent improvisation. Those were, and mainly remain, essential differences which feature when England visit Cardiff or defend Twickenham.

So it was in 1947, when N.M. 'Nim' Hall's dropped goal (worth four points at the time) clinched a narrow victory for the visitors, all the more remarkable in that the centre E.K. Scott sustained a serious injury after fifteen minutes. He remained on the field to offer nuisance value, but the visitors deemed it necessary to remove Micky Steele-Bodger from the pack to strengthen the three quarter line. Wales were still unable to subdue a pack in which Mycock, Perry and Walker were heroic. Don White, England's outstanding open side flanker of the day, scored a try which Gray converted, while Wales' two unconverted tries by Rees Stephens and Gwyn Evans were not enough to stave off defeat.

The scribes were suitably gloomy, with a *Western Mail* columnist pointing out that the visitors could have won by another ten points if the St Mary's Hospital centre Bennett had given two scoring passes to the sprinter-wing Dickie Guest instead of going for non-existent gaps himself. "The form of some of the Welsh forwards... was too bad to be true," wrote another contributor. Such match reports and analysis were in complete contrast to previews which had appeared during the build-up to the game. For example, an article in the official match programme stated, "The Welsh selectors have chosen a team as near as possible to perfection." Hm.

A fortnight later, after a magnificent afternoon in Edinburgh, the critics were falling over themselves to congratulate the selectors for the five changes deemed to have effected a total turn-around in Welsh fortunes and the defeat of Scotland. Four of the newcomers were forwards, including a beefy policeman at lock who could kick goals, Cardiff's Bill Tamplin. A re-shuffle of the back division, however, had seen the moving of Bleddyn Williams to his natural centre position where he would play not with his club partner Jack Matthews, who was discarded, but with Cleaver.

As it happened the reports say that the Welsh midfield performed well, thanks to the iron control of Tanner at scrum half and a wondrous debut in the International Championship by the Pontypridd stand off half Glyn Davies. Selected in 'Victory Internationals' a year earlier, the nineteen-year-old was thought by many to need another season before being exposed to the ruthless marking of the big game. They need not have worried. The critics wrote that Davies ran straight, checking defenders so that his centres enjoyed space in which Bleddyn Williams revelled and got his first try at this level of Rugby. That in turn benefited the wings: Ken Jones scored twice and Les Williams once, while Tamplin placed seven points with the boot.

Davies's display meant that an ongoing saga of welsh Rugby was being perpetuated, and in fact throughout the twentieth century the stand off half position has agonised our selectors. Is a level-headed, low-risk approach allied to a sturdy physique the best characteristic for a Welsh stand off half? Or should the smaller, elusive genre with speed off the mark be preferred? – or the latter can usually side-step, too, a spectacular part of the Welsh game.

Perversely, the selectors favoured first one, then the other style. So there was Bowcott from 1929 to 1933, a calm general who was sent packing soon after his Lions tour to New Zealand to make room for the sensational little Cliff Jones who buzzed here and there like a wasp behind his forwards. Jones in turn gave way to W.T.H. Davies – "A clean, straight runner," said the *Western Mail* – before the post-War Cleaver-Glyn Davies debate. Cliff Morgan wore the number six jersey (which soon became number ten) through much of the fifties despite the claims of Roy Burnett and Carwyn James. Later David Watkins's vivid bursts of speed were weighed against the spectral running of Barry John, while the final years of the century witnessed the attempts of Arwel Thomas, a will o' the wisp, to assert himself in the shadow of Neil Jenkins' wonderful goal-kicking and sheer dependability.

The debate sways to and fro between the adventurous Welsh and those who cannot tolerate error. It is important in this country because the Welsh concept is that the stand off half is the playmaker. Despite the long reign as captain of Sean Fitzpatrick, New Zealand prefers her scrum halves to exercise control – which is not necessarily the same as captaincy – while England, Scotland, Ireland, South Africa and France as often as not will appoint a forward to call the shots. But in Wales number ten, in the Scot Norman Mair's memorable phrase, "wears the Turin shroud."

High tension characterised the build-up to the next game, against France at Stade Colombes (which I always considered a misnomer for a place where Rugby blitzkrieg was the norm). First Glyn Davies missed the chance to build on his triumphant debut because of a knee injury sustained in a Services clash. Cleaver, at last, was picked at stand off half.

Then, as lock forward George Parsons stood on the platform at Newport, waiting with some team-mates as the Paddington Express steamed in on the first lap of the boat-train trip to Paris he was approached by a WRU delegation under its Secretary Walter Rees. They told him that alleged negotiations [sic] with Rugby League scouts had cost him his amateur status. Parsons denied any such contact, but was disbelieved and, in an age of Draconian amateurism, not allowed onto the train. He walked from Newport station into obscurity, soon bowing to the inevitable and leaving the Union game for League Rugby and its rewards.

The French, who were in no way distracted by the sacro-sanctity of amateurism, had been in the same sort of trouble as Parsons just before the War. Soon after their first-ever victory over Wales (1928: 8-3 in Paris) they were banished from the Five Nations tournament for alleged monies being paid by leading clubs to their players. Relations with member nations of the International Board could not therefore be resumed, said the IB, "until France has put its house in order."

Besides games against the Home Countries this cost the French lucrative, high-profile fixtures against the South African tourists of 1931 and the 1935 All Blacks. But their domestic game thrived in this decade as fans transferred their enthusiasms from basketball to Rugby Football with its intensified physical contact. International ostracism was painful; but there seems little doubt that the thirties were used by France to shape and refine the kind of game they liked and at which they would excel. Right up until the game went 'open' in 1995 there would be claims and counter-claims about France's cavalier attitude to the amateur regulations. In 1946, however, there was forgiveness for a Wartime ally symbolised by a welcome at Richmond Athletic Ground where her Forces team played an Empire Services XV. A year later she took the Rugby public aback by winning the first game of the re-born Championship 8-3 against Scotland at Colombes. Three weeks later there followed a remarkable 12-8 victory at Lansdowne Road against an Irish side which included J.W. Kyle, J.C. Daly and Karl Mullen, soon to be captain of the British Isles. The Welsh knew that France was no longer the pushover she had been in 1931 at Swansea when their last meeting had ended 35-3 to the home team.

Wales' 3-0 win says a lot about a game that was evidently gruelling. Tamplin's boot was again decisive and his winning penalty goal was placed from just inside France's half. Since the visitors' full back Howard Davies spent much of the middle part of the game in the changing room having an injury attended to, a fourteen-man Welsh effort is worth commending. Although defeated France proved that she had arrived as a Rugby power to be respected, a nation that could put onto the field top-flight players like Prat, Basquet, and two lock forwards who in those days were giants – Alban Moga and Robert Soro. This healthy new status was underlined when France held England to 6-3 at Twickenham in the Championship's last match.

The season could have been worse for Wales, who ended this first post-War winter in second place on points difference behind England. But the manner of two of the three victories was far from satisfactory to the purists, owing more to Bill Tamplin's boot than to the twinkle-toes of the three-quarter lines. It was the same in the 29 March finale against Ireland at St Helen's where the lock forward's penalty goal ("almost inevitable", the critics were writing) along with an R.T. Evans try were the crucial scores. But perhaps the most penetrating observation, and one to which the selectors would soon have to pay attention, came from the columnist E.R.K. Glover: "We are no nearer an appreciation of the principles of the loose heel. We must study the new duties that forwards must perform and how they should be carried out."

John Gwilliam was a non-participant in this resumption of peace-time club Rugby activity. As a 1943 conscript into the Army he was later than others being 'demobbed' (slang for 'demobilised' or discharged) from the forces and managed to play only nine games for Newport in the 1946-47 winter. In 1947-48 this total was down to eight as the young man resumed his studies at Cambridge.

Here he was not short of friendly compatriots. While Oxford benefited greatly from the presence of its Rhodes Scholars who included South African and New Zealand Test players, a convey-

or belt stretching eastwards from Offa's Dyke was a balancing factor which moved exceptional Welsh talent to Cambridge. Ken Spray, a centre who played numerous games for Newport, was already in residence, had won one Blue, and would be with Gwilliam in the 1947 Varsity match. Other Welshmen to be at Cambridge in the forties and fifties included Clem Thomas (Blundells), Peter Davies (Llandovery), Harry Morgan (Usk-bred, schooled at Wycliffe), Alan Barter (Cardiff HS), Alun Prosser-Harris (Llanelli GS) and Brian Richards (Neath GS). This momentum was kept up later as Gerald Davies, Brian Thomas and Brian Rees went the same way. The Welsh end of this mechanism featured the aforementioned Eric Evans, who narrowly missed a Blue before being appointed to teach English and coach Rugby at Cardiff High School. At the opposite end from this 'mole' was one Windsor Lewis, educated at Christ College, Brecon, a winner of Blues in 1926 and 1927 who was capped six times by his country at stand off half. There seems no doubt that as a player he possessed genuine pace and was very elusive.

In the post-War years, as Treasurer and then President of the CURFC, this medical don poured much energy into persuading the most promising Welsh talent to apply for admission to Cambridge, a policy which certainly helped the University to stem, perhaps reverse, a tide which had of late been favouring Oxford. He would have known that Gwilliam was to resume his studies at Trinity College in 1947 and made sure his renewed availability was noted by the Rugby club. This time, once he was picked for the University, the Monmothian was not dropped.

The game in which he won his first Blue took place, unusually but happily, in late November rather than mid-December. Hence when the Welsh selectors decided that they might need him for the 20 December Test against the Wallabies, no University commitment prevented him from appearing for the Possibles in a 6 December Final Trial. As it happened Cambridge won the 1947 Varsity match, albeit only by 6-0, thus strengthening their second row forward's claim to International recognition. He was named in Wales XV to meet Australia.

Such a debut was not so forbidding as it would have been fifty years later. In most parts of Australia the Union code was experiencing huge competition, from Rugby League and, in Victoria, a form of the 'hurling' game popular with immigrants from Ireland. Wallaby touring sides in Britain, therefore, for most of the twentieth century depended to a great extent on players from Queensland and New South Wales. The latter State – nick-named Waratahs – beat Wales in 1927, but the only full Test match between the two nations had been won by Wales 9-6 in 1908. The continuity of Australia's Tests in the UK was sadly interrupted in 1939 when the Second Wallabies arrived for a 28-match tour. Before they could leave Plymouth the start of World War II forced a return home without playing a single game.

Nevertheless a Test match is a Test, and the 1947-48 Wallabies beat Scotland, Ireland and England before taking the field at Cardiff shortly before Christmas. The writers John Billot and J.B.G. Thomas note Gwilliam's debut, in the second row, without stating how well he played. Two penalty goals by Tamplin clinched the result for the home side, but Gwilliam missed the next three International matches (a win, a draw and a first-ever defeat in Wales by France, 11-3 at Swansea). His return in Belfast was in a Welsh XV beaten 6-3 by Ireland.

Why, then, was he side-lined? Gwilliam puts an amusing spin on the reason:

> Early in the game I jumped, successfully, three times at line-outs. Three times referee A.S. Bean blew against me for a penalty. I didn't know what I was doing wrong, but I suppose it inhibited my approach in the remainder of the game.
>
> Subsequently I learned from Windsor Lewis – he was my GP! – that he and Bean had spoken together. The former said, 'With his height, Gwilliam doesn't need to barge. He goes for the ball, and usually gets it.'
>
> Mr Bean replied, 'I suppose you're right. Better talk to him, I think.'
>
> And he did, taking me to a nice restaurant where he made generous amends.

Gwilliam and Cambridge licked their wounds after the 1948 Varsity match, won 14-8 by Oxford, but Welsh spirits soared with the three-try victory over England at Cardiff which started the 1949 Championship campaign. In those days the fixtures followed a similar sequence each year; and if the first result against England was a defeat or a draw the Welsh groaned – yet another Triple Crown was instantly out of reach. A win, however, would mean that all things were possible.

This time, though 'Nim' Hall dropped his usual goal (now worth three, not four, points), two tries by Les Williams and another by Alun Meredith saw the Welsh through. Two iron-hard Newbridge forwards, Don Hayward and Ray Cale, made strong debuts ahead of long, excellent careers, but the perceptive R.T. Gabe commented in the *Western Mail*, "The Welsh forwards were grand... in the loose and especially at the line outs where Gwilliam and Meredith towered above everybody they were definitely the fresher."

From that point on, however, there came a series of numbing set-backs. Not huge defeats – in fact the points difference in the remainder of the Championship was only 8-16. But reverses – which began at Murrayfield where Scotland's skipper, the Wallaby Scot Keller, abetted by Peter Kininmonth and Doug Elliott shattered the Welsh back division which could contrive only a Bleddyn Williams try, converted by Trott, against two by Gloag and Doug Smith (later a Lions manager supreme).

Then, at Swansea, it was Ireland's hunger for honours which swung the match her way. Generously acclaimed by 40,000 spectators the victory stemmed from a Kyle break down the blind-side, a lofted cross-kick off which Jim McCarthy scored near the posts, and a final conversion by George Norton. The Irish celebrated their Triple Crown while Wales stumbled home in disarray. Nobody was very surprised when a campaign that had begun so well closed with a 5-3 defeat at Colombes, the first time for Wales to lose back-to-back against France.

So: the season ended almost apologetically. Welsh pride (Carwyn James had yet to call it *hubris*) had been punctured.

Rugby in the Principality, it seemed, was not advancing. It was ordinary. Over-rated. Not the stuff of which dreams were made, rather Wooden Spoons – with one of which the Welsh now had to eat humble pie for the second time in a dozen years.

Because of the success of club sides in the immediate post-War years, and the complete absence of anything resembling a coaching system (which had it existed might have been held to blame) reporters and critics were at a loss to explain away three successive defeats for the enlightenment of their readers. They and the sub-editors sometimes got lines crossed in the confusion: after the Swansea game, for example, the *Western Mail's* match report said "Wales lacked the youthful spirit to gain victory" while a nearby close-up photograph was captioned "DAI JONES (Swansea): best Welsh forward." Dai was thirty four years of age.

At times like this one man could always restore Welsh spirits, whether there had been a one-off reverse or a row of defeats like that of 1949. In true Celtic fashion he warned his readership beforehand that alien spirits capable of mischief and malevolence were bent on undermining visiting excellence. There was a 'Twickenham Bogy', which had haunted England's great stadium since it opened in 1910, denying the Welsh victory in all but one of their fourteen visits to HQ. Another hobgoblin was the 'Murrayfield Bogy' which perched above the great East stand at Murrayfield and, though less successful than its Twickenham relative, also swung the balance against visiting sides, notably Wales.

These spooky figures were the creation of the *Western Mail's* Chief Rugby Writer of the period (later its Sports Editor) J.B.G. Thomas. After a Welsh defeat they encouraged his readership to believe that the better side had lost (compare sundry New Zealanders who have observed, "You never beat Wales – you just score more points than them"). After the frantic dashing-off of literary or broadcast contributions in all directions and to all markets Bryn had been taken on by *Western Mail* Editor D.R. Prosser, and was cutting his teeth in these early peacetime seasons.

The confidence of later years when he reached icon status was not yet in place, for he once asked his deputy John Billot whether he should drop the 'J.B.G.' by-line (which colleagues in the office said meant 'Just Below God') in favour of simply 'Bryn'. Billot remonstrated with him, saying that 'J.B.G.' was what differentiated him from all the other Bryn Thomases in Wales. Maybe his boss needed reassurance that he truly belonged among the well-established Rugby writers of the day who boasted ample supplies of initials – like E.H.D. Sewell, E.W. Swanton O.L. Owen, D.R. Gent, R.C. Robertson-Glasgow and the Welsh-based E.R.K. Glover. As his stature grew with the years it was even suggested that Bryn invented second initials for certain Welsh players who, he thought, could do with greater gravitas.

In print he was not a great stylist. Modestly, he once introduced his son Craig to me with the remark, "This is the real man of letters in our family" – and indeed in due course Craig did become a best-selling author. Often *Western Mail* Rugby previews by their 'Chief Rugby Writer' began with something like, "This promises to be a close game which Wales should win, but might come unstuck" and (allegedly) "to win Wales must score more points". He could also begin a major match-report on a home victory with, "Well Done, Wales! Well done, Glyn Davies!" – ingenuous lines but ones which, in fairness, probably summed up the emotions of most fans (unless they were Cleaver) on the January Monday morning after beating England at Cardiff.

The best journalists find ways of giving their output a cutting edge, plus a reputation for accuracy and sound forecasting. John Billot says that J.B.G. did this by cultivating the company of Cliff Jones, who had dazzled European teams at stand off half just before the War. Although the Llandovery-educated stand off half was out of the limelight at this time, the Welsh selectors of the day were more than ready to take his views on board and reflect them in their chosen teams. Realising this, J.B.G. created an alliance with Jones which effectively enhanced the reputations of the Big Five, their trusty consultant, plus one of the rising stars of British Rugby journalism.

His match reports were accurate. They were also kind, in the sense that often he would rather ignore a man's performance than say that he had had a bad game. This attitude to the controversial may well have been rooted in prudence: a visit to Neath after Bryn had criticised a local hero, the international wing Elgan Rees, for possessing 'dodgy hands' attracted fist-waving spectators to the Press box baying for his blood. Similarly, only rarely did he explicitly indicate preferences. For the reasons touched on earlier, the time came when he needed to express an opinion on candidates for the key stand off half position in one of the the post-War Welsh sides. When he plumped for Cleaver, some close relatives of the rival Glyn Davies invaded the *Western Mail* offices bent on doing Bryn a revengeful mischief.

Above all, his readers will recall, his opinions were his own. After his time, as the twentieth century neared its end, match coverage of Rugby relied heavily on interviews with key players for insight and interpretation. In practice, as both participants and the reporters of the period will acknowledge, no such ingredients found their way on air or into print as a result. Players do not want to upset management lest they are dropped and will not criticise team-mates for fear of undermining team-spirit or a good friendship.

In such a position speakers fall back upon platitudes and bland cliches. 'At the end of the day'; 'We gave it our best shot'; 'We're still on a learning curve' – these have become formulae which many top Rugby players are happy to mouth rather than say anything which a viewer or a listener might find interesting. Readers, listeners and viewers stifle huge yawns – and turn to broadsheets and broadcasters for genuine expressions of opinion. All this, incidentally, is not strictly the players' fault.

As far as I and my contemporaries are concerned J.B.G. also effected one sea-change in Wales. Aided and abetted by large headlines, good supporting reportage, any amount of space plus good photography he made us feel that Cardiff and Wales were the epicentre of the Rugby world. The litmus test which other Rugby nations had to pass was how their quality related to that of the Welsh. This was valid certainly until the middle of the twentieth century, even if it ignited the fury of All Black writers in the mould of T.P. McClean.

All of which did have a down-side. Young, impressionable fans came to believe that Welsh primacy was a fact of Rugby. It followed that in defeat the chagrin quotient was higher and more difficult to swallow.

The other cult figure in mid-century media was a Cardiff centre from pre-War days called G.V. Wynne-Jones, 'Jeevers' to friends and admirers. Broadcasting of 'commentaries' on Rugby Football's fast-moving action had been broached with the Welsh Rugby Union by the infant BBC Wales office as early as 1928. Seen as a competitor, rather than a generator of interest and audiences, its 'live' debut had initially been discussed and dismissed by the ruling body (though Welsh games at Twickenham were described on air by Teddy 'Square One' Wakelam with the blessing of the RFU). In due course the WRU relented and bowed to the inevitable, only for the War to put the idea on the the back-burner.

Broadcasting debuts are often the result of happy accidents, and in 1946 Wynne-Jones, by now a contributor to the *Sunday Express*, found himself travelling on a tube train with the Executive Officer of the BBC's Welsh region, Heber Jenkins. Said the latter, "We are looking for a Rugby commentator. Why don't you give it a crack?" Accordingly Jeevers entered a competition on radio called 'Choose Your Commentator'. Despite being described by more than one listener as 'Too la-de-da' the Christ College Brecon product was voted the winner and swiftly embarked on his radio career with a match commentary on Wales v France at Paris in 1947.

It is true that Wynne-Jones had English overtones in his voice, but when he was in full cry there was no doubt that this was a Celt. My main recall of him is that he had worked out the basic cadences of commentary; that is, the vocal output should play a solo role to the orchestra that is the crowd. If nothing of note is happening on the field of play broadcasting must be matter-of-fact. Once the crowd starts to roar the commentator has to go with the flow and express his own excitement (never hysteria). Jeevers knew how to do that, and did it well.

His broadcasting on Rugby was cruelly ended by the WRU who put pressure on the BBC to drop him after he wrote in his 1951 autobiography *Sports Commentary* that "some clubs make a habit of remunerating their players", adding that he had seen money change hands at the end of games "in such quantities that it far exceeded expenses". He might conceivably have got away with that had he not thrown in some explicit words which implied that the top administrators in Wales knew about such payments and condoned them. Certainly these were Rugby's Dark Ages.

So some barren years rolled by, with journalists, commentators and fans thirsty for champagne only for successive Welsh XVs to deliver small beer. Why? The analysts of the day do us few favours, identifying no trends in the Welsh game and merely chronicling under-performances.

One aspect of Welsh play is apparent, however, and features frequently in the Press coverage of the day. The Welsh had moved ahead of the field in the century's early decades by choosing what came to be known as 'Rhondda forwards' who introduced steel to the National XV's packs. Often miners, these were tough, very strong, men who gave Wales a bludgeoning capacity which other nations initially found hard to match.

By the middle of the twentieth century brute force alone was no longer enough. What was crucial (and always will be) was now the delivery of quality possession by the pack. In training forwards still practised 'dribbling', an ancient skill by Rugby standards which, though still championed by Scotland, harked back to the game's pre-handling era and was fast becoming a waste of time. 'Rucking' had not yet arrived from New Zealand.

'Ripping' and 'mauling' were understood and practised by forwards, but only as individuals – we have noted that little preparatory training took place with International team-mates –

though good work by a pack in the loose requires as much, if not more, combined preparation as a back division puts in. So it seems certain that the possession which reached scrum halves was of unpredictable quality. Wales were lucky to have Tanner just behind the pack; but it is clear that his attacking instincts plus the speed with which the ball reached mid-field were diminished by the uneven performance of the men in front.

E.R.K. Glover's words in his *Western Mail* Notebook after Wales's 1947 win over France at Swansea are relevant:

> As usual there was never a heel from the loose... we are no nearer an appreciation of the principles of the loose heel than we were before... Mauls are still conducted with the players standing nearly upright and worse still forwards join them from the side rather than from the back.

A final reflection on the three post-War International seasons concerns Tanner himself. Apart from the win over Australia, which he missed, the scrum half played twelve Tests, all of them as captain. As a survivor from pre-War Test Rugby he enjoyed a special status as an international scrum half, which he built on between 1947 and 1949 without a serious challenge to his supremacy. Nor did the Big Five look elsewhere for a skipper.

It is not recorded, however, that Tanner was a great captain. He had little to say about leadership in his 1950 book *Rugby Football*, which contains stunning advice like, "The captain must give careful thought to the game to be played every week" or "if the tactics likely to be employed by the opposition have been correctly forecast then the captain can work out his best plan of campaign... If his forecast is inaccurate then a revision of plans might be necessary."

His superb skills, of course, were lauded by Wilfred Wooller in his foreword for the book. Other critics were equally fulsome: "The greatest of all footballers," wrote E.R.K. Glover. In his book *Great Rugger Players* (1955) J.B.G. Thomas calls him "masterly" in attack, technically perfect and one who dominated the scene. However he also describes him as "unobtrusive" and "even his greatest admirers tended to blame him for the Welsh defeat at Murrayfield in 1949." Do those remarks reveal a man who could not crack the whip?

Almost certainly, scrum half is not the best position from which to captain a side. Seldom does a man in this position get the chance to stand back from the fray and think about tactics. There is time to bark briefly at a pack before a line out or while a scrum is settling down, but if possession is won he needs immediately to avoid his opposite number plus two or three back row forwards out to nail him. No wonder that, except when he broke, Tanner's influence upon games was less than profound. Survival had to be his priority, not leadership.

And that last quality may just have been the missing ingredient which Wales needed in order to capitalise on the great skill levels of those post-War sides: Making quietly-spoken demands on key men at key moments. Words of encouragement and warning at the right time. Driving the team on until the eightieth minute. Cutting out minor squabbles within its ranks. Ignoring attempts by the opposition to under-mine confidence and concentration.

Wales had a man who had served his apprenticeship at the eye of the storm and understood these things. He would lead Wales into a second Golden Era. If only by accident.

FIVE

Des O'Brien was a well-loved Irishman who figured in the back row during Ireland's great seasons in the forties, when he won twenty caps. This impressive sequence was not interrupted despite long periods away from the homeland as a brewery representative, when he played for Edinburgh University and London Irish. Shortly before his retirement from Rugby his career brought him to Cardiff in 1950 for a couple of seasons when he played thirty-one games for the Blue and Blacks. The club were especially glad of his services, since in those days of long journeys by sea their British Lions were not due back from New Zealand until mid-autumn.

O'Brien is remembered in clubhouse debates and discussions for highlighting the baffling failure of Wales to transpose innate brilliance into achievement on the International stage. His team-mates of the day were stars like Bleddyn Williams, Jack Matthews, Cliff Morgan and others, and as captain of Ireland in his last playing days Des would agonise about how to bottle them up.

Then his face would brighten. "When they take the field to represent their nation, your players freeze", he would tell his audience. "Maybe it is anxiety and the burden of representing a nation that gets to them, but they are all fingers and thumbs and don't deliver the goods. For which, by the way, the Lord be praised."

Thus perhaps the most important pre-match sentence spoken to a mid-century Welsh team by its captain was delivered on the morning of the 1950 game at Twickenham against England. The players were told, "There is nothing to be nervous about. This will be no more than the kind of hard club game we are all used to."

By 1949 John Gwilliam had played his second Varsity match and was nearing the close of his University career. Despite the wartime interruption, for the youngster from Pontypridd it had been an eye-opening experience – sometimes literally, as academic giants of the day like Wittgenstein, G.M. Trevelyan and Bertrand Russell sauntered and conversed on Trinity's smooth lawns.

By a far-fetched coincidence, too, he had re-encountered a girl who had made a big impression on him years previously at a school holiday camp in Anglesey. One afternoon in 1948, by now an undergraduette studying maths at Girton College (and described by the Principal as an outstanding scholar), Llanelli-bred Pegi George was in the Grange Road crowd cheering on the Cambridge team against visitors Cardiff, and after the final whistle she and Gwilliam fell into conversation. This young woman of good Welsh Baptist stock and the serious-minded Varsity lock forward found their attitudes to life mutually compatible, and the relationship took root. It would flourish.

Rugby Blues do not play for the University in their penulti-mate term, when the passing of exams and identifying a suitable career rank foremost in their priorities. However, the big light blue second row forward (with ambitions to play at number eight) was now recognised as one of the outstanding line-out forwards in Europe. Hence the business of playing for Wales would not go away and he contributed to a satisfactory win over England before figuring in sides beaten by Scotland, France and Ireland – the last-named featuring Des O'Brien.

It was at Murrayfield, however, after Wales had lost 6-5 that Gwilliam's professional career was pointed in its first direction. From his erstwhile Varsity match opponents Graham Wilson and Peter Kininmonth, by now members of the victorious Scottish XV, he learned that Trinity College, Glenalmond – known to the educational world simply as Glenalmond – was seeking a junior teacher of history. It seemed that the Headmaster, a Mr R.M. Barlow, had won a Blue for Cambridge in 1925 and would presumably look kindly upon an application from one who had trodden that path and gone on to International ranking. It was duly submitted.

The young Welshman's performance in the history Tripos was deemed adequate, a job offer was confirmed, and that autumn he took the high road northwards from Edinburgh. The Almond is an ice-cold river which joins the Tay at Perth, from where the school bearing its name lies some ten miles up-country. The scenery and ambience of this part of Scotland held appeal for the novice schoolmaster, and the welcome was warm. A distinguished predecessor had been Mark Sugden who made 28 appearances for Ireland in the inter-War years, and like him Gwilliam would be expected to train Glenalmond's First XV who met other top Scottish schools like Loretto, Fettes and Merchiston.

More than half a century on, Gwilliam does not agree that the move could have posed a major threat to his International career and his haul of caps which then stood at six. He recalls that fairly regular outings with Edinburgh Wanderers were wholly sufficient to maintain the technical side of his game, for he believed then, as now, that forwards play too much. As for general fitness, he is quick to recall that the terrain surrounding the school was a constant challenge for intensive road-work, besides being good for the lungs at six hundred feet above sea level. He felt confident, too, that the Welsh selectors knew where he was – teaching at 'the Eton of Scotland'. And, since the school played little or no Rugby in the spring term, if he was picked by Wales there would be no problem in getting leave of absence.

Glenalmond had been founded by the nineteenth century Liberal Prime Minister William Gladstone for the education of ordinands for the Scottish Presbyterian Ministry. No doubt this was another factor which influenced Gwilliam's choice of employer; and the regimen he encountered was suitably stoic. The new history master's working day began at eight o'clock when he left his small apartment for early Assembly attended by the three hundred or so boarders. Lessons occupied the morning, after which the whole school undertook a twenty minute period of physical jerks superintended by Mr Gwilliam, another feature of school life which helped him to maintain a high level of physical fitness. For masters and boys the day was long, ending at around 6.30pm with a chapel service and prep.

Even if they did not always agree with some of his innovative ploys during big games, all his contemporaries agree that Gwilliam's thinking about Rugby was radical and creative. There seems little doubt that in his schoolmastering days at

Glenalmond, Bromsgrove, Dulwich and even Birkenhead whose Headmaster he eventually became, he saw his Rugby-playing pupils as raw material on which he could test pet theories and novel tactics.

Not all of these were original but they were unusual. For example, he had got hold of the book on Rugby brought out by the great New Zealand captain Dave Gallaher who led the First All Blacks on their 1905 European tour. Gallaher played as a 'rover' or eighth back, operating close to the pack and able to exert relentless pressure on the opposing half backs. Gwilliam toyed with this idea at Glenalmond, noting how it could function positively, but probably feeling too junior to introduce it to the school XV. By the time he was running Rugby at Dulwich, however, he had the seniority to use it in matches and it excited much interest, not least among the boys themselves, who were thus encouraged to think afresh about the game instead of taking it for granted that Rugby and its tactics are immutable. Alas, it was never widely adopted, and in the coaching manual which he wrote in 1958 – 'to raise £2,000 for a house' – he acknowledges its limitations: possible confusion behind the scrum, the absence of a key defender close to set-pieces, and the inability of seven men to win a decent share of the ball, especially in wet weather.

An aspect of the game that Gwilliam, although a forward, understood very well and impressed upon his young charges was the quick possession needed by back divisions. His nick-name, 'Bucket', was a reference to his very large hands, which he could use to spiral the ball straight to the midfield, perhaps missing out both half backs. If this could save just one second, he reasoned, a centre could have ten extra yards in which to weave mischief.

Fitness training was mostly orthodox, except that he had taken on board an idea propounded by Tommy Vile, a Newport scrum half who played for Wales and refereed International games after his playing days. Vile thought that running downhill enabled people to gain speed – since their legs had to go faster; and the steep slopes around the school were ideal for trying this theory out on Glenalmond's rising stars. Later, after being privileged to watch the Fourth Springboks train under Danie Craven, Gwilliam also came to believe that shouting encouragement at forwards really did produce a higher work-rate, and now admits to talking non-stop at his packs, especially at lines out. Here his 'minder' was the short, burly prop J.D. Robins, who took so many earfuls of verbal stick when winning his first cap that he thought the skipper had taken a personal dislike to him.

Like one or two others in the Welsh XV originally named to play at Twickenham in 1950 Robins had never met the captain. Even those who knew what he looked like and how he played had had little opportunity to experience the force of his personality. To these men John Gwilliam was merely a team-mate who would drop in on the Welsh scene from Cambridge, either to win another cap or to give the Black and Ambers a hand, before departing across Offa's Dyke. Now, in 1950, it seemed that he was playing for some Scottish club called Edinburgh Wanderers.

The man himself likes to recall the observation at this time of magic-fingered Ray Lewis, the Wales team physiotherapist. Perhaps the subject came up as he lay on the massage table at the 'Round House' in Cross Keys being kneaded by a great servant both of International sides and Newport RFC. As Wales captain, should he be playing in Scotland?

Came the answer, "Being away from here is just right for you. At that distance there's no way you can get involved in endless arguments about selection or Welsh club politics."

Half a century on, however, it will strike the reader as astonishing that a player based six hundred miles distant, scarcely getting enough demanding fixtures, and having to be imported from a great distance to play in Trial games should have enjoyed the continuing favour of the selectors. His track record with Newport was less than impressive. Did not one or two of the Big Five need to drop in announced at a big game to monitor his form? And as for being skipper – how could he possibly have gained enough experience of captaining a Rugby XV, not even having led Cambridge? How did the selectors know he could manage the job? And once they had given it to him was there not a need for constant contact and the exchange of views on team selection and tactics?

Gwilliam's initial response to such questions is sardonic. With a grin he recalls that contact with selectors was non-existent in between matches. Indeed, to find out whether he had been selected for the next match, let alone as captain, he had to catch the sports news on the radio.

In serious vein, however, he simply quotes his war-time experience, beginning with an extended period of training at Sandhurst in setting examples, giving orders and securing obedience. Certainly, those who served in the Forces even as lowly National Servicemen may well agree that the preparation and conditioning of personnel by the British army beats any similar experience that can be imagined in civvy street. But, over and above such training Gwilliam could point to leadership under fire, as controller of a four-tank fighting unit. He had been at one sharp end; International Rugby would be another. Transferring his expertise to a Rugby field would be a challenge, but at least not one which he feared.

Finally, he goes back to Napoleon – again – to exemplify. When the great French field marshal was considering the appointment of a new general the first question he put to his advisers was, "Is he lucky?" John Gwilliam reflects that luck was on his side when he needed it. Which was just as well as the fifties got under way, for that time was about to arrive.

The Welsh selectors, it seemed, had got the message: new blood was urgently needed. Haydn Tanner was only one of a few veterans who retired after the 1949 Five Nations tournament, to be followed by Frank Trott, 'Bunner' Travers and Swansea's Dai Jones. Jack Matthews, Bleddyn Williams and Billy Cleaver each felt that he had more petrol in the tank, as did the prop Cliff Davies and lock forward Rees Stephens. The men chosen to make debuts in January 1950 – six in all – were formidable, durable and full of promise. Two of them, the new scrum half and the tight head prop, had first handled a Rugby ball at Llandaff Cathedral school on the playing field beside Western Avenue in north Cardiff. Both of them would win caps in plenty for their country and tour New Zealand later in the year with the British Isles.

Rex Willis was a great 'minder' of his stand off half who, interestingly, never scored a try in a five-year International career which included three Tests for the Lions. Partly this must have been because he saw an accurate, consistent service as the priority, and would rather die with the ball than expose his partner to undue risks. Secondly, his chosen method of passing was the dive pass, which was swift and accurate but took him out of the game for a few moments and made him unavailable as a support player to his back row. But his reputation for bravery is unsurpassed.

His schoolmate John Robins was a granite-hard prop who whispers that he had played for England in a Services International before going on to study at Loughborough and secure a teaching job on the Wirral. There was Rugby at this time with Sale, where he propped England hooker Eric Evans, and then with Birkenhead Park. It was in the latters' colours that he turned out on Boxing Day, 1949, at Newport where the impression he made led to a fast-track invitation into Wales' Final Trial and selection for Twickenham. Until the eve of the match, reflects Robins, he cannot recall even meeting, let alone playing alongside, the other two members of the front row, another new cap in D.M. Davies, the Somerset Police hooker and the experienced Cliff Davies. Chosen on a wing for the first of his three caps was Trevor Brewer, later of London Welsh but then at Newport.

Undoubtedly, however, the most daring and imaginative selection was that of Lewis Jones, a product of the redoubtable Gowerton Grammar School, who had played some memorable Rugby for Neath before being called up by the Royal Navy. His Rugby base for the next two years would be Devonport Services, and the youngster believed that he would be out of sight, out of mind, as far as the Welsh selectors were concerned.

The latter, however, needed to replace Trott, and despite having played most of his short career in big Rugby at centre

Jones found himself summoned to Welsh Trials each side of Christmas 1949 to play at full back. His opposite number was Glyncorrwg-born Gerwyn Williams, whose time would come, but Jones got the nod for the 21 January encounter.

What was different about his selection was his age; when he arrived in London for a Friday afternoon run-out at Herne Hill he was just eighteen years and nine months old.

The best-laid plans and team selections of Rugby's elders are sometimes dashed. The first mishap of January 1950 for Wales was an injury to her likely pack leader, Rees Stephens, which prevented him from appearing in the England game. In the January final Trial his Neath clubmate Roy John, as yet uncapped, filled the gap in the second row as he would at Twickenham. The Big Five gave the pack leadership to John Gwilliam.

Playing at centre in the same Trial was Bleddyn Williams, captaining the Probables against the Possibles as the heir-apparent to Haydn Tanner. Though managing to finish the game, after a heavy tackle by Malcolm Thomas he had felt a stabbing pain in a knee. By the time he returned to the changing room he well knew that "the Welsh team will take the Twickenham field without me". The damage was indeed serious, since the external ligaments in the knee joint had been torn away from the bone. He made the correct decision, informing the Big Five that he would have to stand down. Ironically it was Thomas who replaced him in the midfield.

It may be that the selectors delayed naming a new captain as long as possible in the faint hope that Stephens, as senior forward in the original selection, would recover during the fortnight leading up to 21 January. He failed to do so (and missed Wales' three subsequent games in addition), so that and until the eve of the match the Welsh were without a designated leader. At this time, John Gwilliam was just beginning a second term at Glenalmond and left Edinburgh at the crack of dawn on the Friday morning to join his team at Herne Hill (a friendly outpost in those days as the home of London Welsh). The new leader, as he thought, of the pack was taken to one side by Vince Griffiths to be told of his second promotion. Gwilliam says that the Chairman of Selectors delivered the news as if the selectors really could not think of anyone else for the job. He said:

> Er, we're making you captain tomorrow. You are quite free to play your own game. But: don't hold the ball in the back row. Don't take it upon yourself to hurl out any of those scrum half type passes. And don't flip the ball back from the line out.

Gwilliam affected dismay. "Those provisos forbade all my limited ideas for winning a Rugby match," he later observed tartly.

Half a century on the third-choice skipper cannot remember whether he lost any sleep that night. If he did so, however, it seems to me that the reason would have had more to do with expectation and impatience than apprehension. Although the Gwilliam who conversed with me in 2001 was in no way immodest – indeed, the opposite, with a slight tendency to self-deprecation – he certainly did not lack self-confidence. He had been "a little bit bossy" at school. In the Army "I had learned to give orders and expect a reaction". As far as the forwards went he was a ring-master who kept up a torrent of exhortation and cracked his whip; but, he claims, "I never told my back divisions what to do. I did and do believe in quick passing, if possible in a single stride, and urged Jack [Matthews] and Bleddyn [Williams] to try it. They looked bemused – but gave it a try!"

He is also at pains to point out that, although he was playing and working a long distance from Wales he could still claim friendship with a number of his players. There had been inter-school games, representative Rugby with teenage friends, enough games for Newport to get himself known and respected on the Welsh circuit, games for Cambridge against Welsh clubs, and also the six times he had already worn the three feathers of Wales at senior level. Thus he could claim more than a passing acquaintance with nearly all the men he was to lead. Although geographically he was detached from his native country, he was no stranger to the troops.

This meant too that he well knew the great skills of his senior lieutenants. Billy Cleaver he names as a true general, who nursed a pack upfield with soaring line-licks or perfectly-placed diagonal shots which turned defences and found touch deep inside their 25. Jack Matthews gave the back line acceleration and impact, Ken Jones was its speed merchant. The pack, too, contained aces. Gwilliam himself already had a big reputation at the line out as one who could touch a crossbar with one hand off a standing leap from the ground. Thus he had blinked with surprise, and delight, at Herne Hill as newcomer Roy John leaped to clap two hands above the crossbar at just on ten feet, six inches off the ground. He remembers the gigantic neck of his loose head prop Cliff Davies. On the other side of a hooker was the technical ability of John Robins, also a reliable goal kicker.

Most of his surviving team-mates – even the wonder-boy Lewis Jones reached seventy in 2001 – recall awareness of the skipper's big presence on the field. Certainly he talked constantly and vaciferously, urging, exhorting and cajoling, but this, they confirm, did not include telling anyone what to do, least of all a back. The crucial thing was that, at all times, they were to do what they did best to the highest possible standard. Only if that level was not attained might they expect a frustrated frown or grimace in their direction.

But there were golden rules of captaincy, too, revealed in his 1958 manual:

> 1.If you win the toss take the wind. Do not be clever and hope there will be more wind, and sun, in the second half.
> 2.Go hard all the time, especially in the last ten minutes.
> 3.Play hard; make sure the rest of the team do too.
> 4.Never let forwards blame backs or backs blame forwards.
> 5.Do not irritate the referee and do not let the other side irritate you.
> 6.Stop to laugh at something in each half; it restores a sense of proportion.

Observation of these maxims were good enough to bring about two Grand Slams from three seasons in 1950 and 1952. They remain worth study by ambitious captains in the new Millennium.

Gwilliam was certainly ambitious. Did he think at the outset that he would make an ideal captain? Modestly he deflects the question towards New Zealand's captain of 1905: "The ideal captain should be possessed of a multiplicity of virtues as seems impossible of association in the person of one individual."

So there.

SIX

John Gwilliam's relationship with Pegi George had intensified since their meeting at Grange Road. The daughter of a Welsh Baptist preacher had seriously contemplated going to China as a missionary after graduation, but the political turbulence accompanying Mao Tse Tung's rise to power led to the abandoning of the ambition, a decision which allowed her to remain close to the man who now became her fiancé. There were visits by him to her family at Llanelli, which in turn prompted invitations to Gwilliam from the Scarlets to play a game or two for them. He remembers being shown Stradey Park for the first time and walking around the pitch with a local guide: "I told him that the surface was excellent, but there was a definite dip and slope in the area outside one of the 25 lines." My guide looked at me aghast. 'But that's where Albert Jenkins used to drop goals from,' he replied reverently."

On 29 December 1949 the Cambridge couple were married and took a honeymoon in Torquay, memories of which include "one of the best turkey dinners I've ever eaten, plus a visit to the pantomime, which we left early because it was somewhat coarse." The bride quickly came face-to-face with Rugby men's priorities, for by her husband's candid admission the nuptials were carefully scheduled to fit between Llanelli's game against London Welsh on Boxing Day and Wales' Final Trial. Then it was back to Glenalmond and an apartment that would now be more companionable, before the newly-weds travelled south again on 20 January, 1950. It is certainly worth speculating, in the light of the developments that afternoon at Herne Hill, that Gwilliam now knew a certain contentment and stability in his domestic situation that would stand him in good stead.

Meanwhile his fellow countrymen were travelling eastwards in force, with or without their entry to the great arena guaranteed. The Welsh Rugby Union had traditionally been loath to release the numbers of stand tickets allocated to them for away games.

Only by discreetly questioning the other Celtic Unions could the Welsh Press come up with a figure of 700 for this day allocated by the RFU, or about seven tickets for each of Wales' member clubs – a Scrooge-like ration, complained several correspondents. Many prospective occupants of stand seats would butter up contacts in London who might have tickets for sale, while for the *hoi polloi* in those days it would be first come, first served at the Twickenham turnstiles.

Thus many fans knew that they were bound to be locked out when the gates closed at one-thirty for the kick off an hour later. But hope has always sprung eternal in the breasts of loyal supporters, some twenty thousand of whom were estimated to have left Wales by special trains on the eve of the match alone. Since the stadium was opened in 1910 getting to it by rail has always been awkward for the Welsh, and remains so today. Fans have first to go into London as far as Paddington, and then cross the city before heading out of it again in a south westerly direction. Even then, a walk awaits them of some twenty minutes from Twickenham station to the Rugby arena. Approaching and leaving 'HQ' by road is also time-consuming. Today, the last few miles from the M3 can take over an hour; afterwards drivers who park in one of the northern car-parks are in for long delays as they struggle to reach the roundabout to access the west-bound lane of the A316.

But such inconvenience cannot remotely compare with the trials and tribulations of the minority who chose to travel by car and coach in the forties and fifties. For the post-M4 and Severn Bridge generation it is worth mile-stoning a journey that was tedious and tortuous. Let us take for example a car-load of Swansea supporters setting off for London. In 1950 the bridge over the River Neath at Briton Ferry had yet to be constructed, so that our motorists started by going northwards via Morriston before turning towards Port Talbot. In the steel town they had to negotiate, in slow succession, a canal bridge, a level crossing, several sets of traffic lights, bus stops galore and the pedestrian crossings used by shoppers in the town centre. Patience had already been stretched near to break-point with two hundred miles still to go.

Pyle lay ahead and the old A48 with its two, sometimes three, lanes. This brought traffic to Cowbridge, to manoeuvre its way along a main street full of parked cars and up the long hill towards Bonvilston and St Nicholas, quite likely in the wake of a lumbering cattle truck. Western Cardiff's roads were adequate but, after what is now the Gabalfa flyover and was then a simple crossroads, motorists had to weave their way through Penylan and Roath before ascending Rumney Hill bound for Newport.

In days, before the Georgetown bridge was built, its narrower predecessor was the next obstacle for drivers, who would join a queue which could be up to a mile long. Having crossed that, cars fairly sprinted as far as Chepstow only to grind to a halt at the next queue, which led all the way down the hill to the set of traffic lights which controlled the Wye bridge. In days before the Severn crossings, this single-lane structure was the only exit from Wales south of Monmouth. As they crawled over it travellers could not help noting the plaque fixed to one of the walls inscribed with the date of its erection – 1815. Up the hill towards Lydney went the supporters from Swansea, having already taken a probable four hours to get as far as England.

The Severn Valley and the A40 drive across the Cotswolds were pleasant enough, Oxford boasted a new by-pass, and if they were lucky travellers would not be delayed in High Wycombe. Though Reading was unpredictable and could be fraught, some turned towards it now, to approach Twickenham from further south. In any case, the out-skirts of London presented a final few tests of map-reading before the Rugby car parks came in sight at the end of a journey that was as tortuous as it was long drawn out – having probably taken a full seven hours to complete.

The fans of the day, however, had lots to talk about to while away the time. For example now, at the outset of the fifties, the question of Wales' future Rugby headquarters had suddenly reared its head. The WRU had revealed ambitious plans to up-date Cardiff Arms Park into a modern stadium which could accommodate 72,000 spectators. In order to recoup the capital expenditure on the project, the Union was beginning to warn that all home Internationals would have to be played within it. Besides volubly emphasising the great Rugby tradition of their town, a strong lobby was pointing out that Swansea's Council intended to modernise the St Helen's arena, which it owned, and raise the capacity to 60,000. The calculations had been based on the continuation of International Rugby in the town; hence many people feared that if the WRU scheme went ahead, and big matches moved to Cardiff, an unbearable financial debt would descend on rate-payers. It was therefore vital that the Union communicated its intentions as soon as possible to Swansea's city fathers.

Other subjects that would have kept tongues wagging naturally included the state of Rugby on the field at the time. In the final Welsh Trial it was agreed by most onlookers that the delivery of the ball from loose play to the half backs still left much to be desired. The Laws on scrummaging and tackle situations, critics felt, were in need of stream-lining and clarifying – though fifty years later the latter issue is one that is only now becoming meaningful thanks to stern refereeing.

But what Welsh critics, and those of other Celtic countries, found outrageous was the horse and cart driven by England's selectors through the International Rugby Board's rule on eligibility passed early in the twentieth century stating that 'no man may play for two countries'. With a fine disregard for it, the XV included by England on 11 January included Ian Botting, who had played nine games for New Zealand in South Africa the previous summer and was now, fortuitously, an undergraduate at Oxford, having taken up residence in October. Two other selections which, it could be argued, were not in the best spirit were Murray Hofmeyr, bred in Northern Transvaal, and Harry Small, his fellow undergraduate, who had learned his Rugby at Witwatersrand University.

In his *Book of English International Rugby* John Griffiths makes no mention of an ethical misdemeanour of which Five

Nations rivals took a dim view. Neither do U.A. Titley and Ross McWhirter in their *Centenary History of the Rugby Football Union*. But J.B.G. Thomas was outspoken: "the selection of Botting is farcical", he thundered. Doubtless he was still hurting at Wales' 5-6 defeat in Edinburgh a year before by a Scottish side led by Doug Keller, who had already played six games for Australia including the Test against Wales. Such blatant indiscretions make the 'Grannygate' affairs of 1999 seem almost innocuous. To the credit of Welsh Rugby, its riposte to the English was to be delivered in the most effective way possible.

As the twin stands of HQ came into sight on the horizon fans who had tickets would finger them anxiously checking for the umpteenth time that they had not been lost or left behind. There may well have been heated comment on the escalation of prices charged for a seat, rising to 15/- compared with the ten shillings of 1949. It seemed that cash was badly needed by the RFU for painting the East Stand and some structural work. The visitors were not impressed. Other ticket anecdotes on the day concerned the cap-to-be Lewis Jones, who lamented that he had not been able to obtain one for his father – and the promise in response from Eric Evans that he would gladly hand over his own and stand on the terrace if one could not be sourced. There was a narrow escape, too, for John Gwilliam who left the inner enclosure via a turnstile bearing a ticket for his father in the car-park. On his return a steward declined to let him back in, saying that many hopefuls had tried to pull the "I'm one of the Welsh team" story, to be sent packing by him. It took a friendly Welsh-born policeman to accredit the captain.

The tunnel at Twickenham has undergone some design changes in recent years, but its location in 1950 was where it is today, close to the west touchline. Behind it are the changing rooms where, on this afternoon, Gwilliam was seeking with some success to establish a cool, focussed atmosphere. England's XV a few doors down the corridor could be excused for being on edge. The selectors' general dissatisfaction was manifested in their awarding of eight new caps for this game.

Hofmeyr, Boobyer plus the two wings, Botting and J.V. Smith were new selections in the back division with Cain, Holmes, H.A. Jones and Small at forward. The side was led by 29-year-old Ivor Ap Reece, aka Preece, who sounded as if he had changed allegiance but had been – impeccably – born at Coventry, with whom he had played for some seasons. His task, on a ground where the Welsh had won only once since its opening in 1910, was to get England's bandwagon going forward again after seven defeats in thirteen post-War games. Ireland, in particular, had given the Saxons grief through a rare trio of wins on the trot, with France and Scotland also drawing blood. After a promising start to peacetime Rugby at Cardiff English teams had lost against Wales in 1949 and been lucky to get a draw the previous January. On this day England Expected; and every member of its Rugby XV felt on trial.

The sun shone bleakly over misty south west London as John Gwilliam took Wales onto the pitch to a crescendo of sound telling the world that the visitors were up for it. The stands and terraces which soared away from the gladiators at ground level were splashed with red; giant dragons swirled lazily on a modest breeze; leeks were waved; and so was all manner of headgear in times when men without a hat were improperly dressed. Even the sad thousands unable to gain entry saw the game, viewing it on television for the first time (for the Wenvoe transmitter was not yet operational) courtesy of local householders.

As they wait for the action to start many players chafe their way through the anthems, often binding themselves onto team-mates to steady themselves. In the case of players at International level, however, such nerves have little to do with apprehension. Rather, they arise from impatience and frustration at not being able to start doing what they have been brought here to do. If they also have to shake hands with a celebrity the delay seems endless.

Thus the experience reported by eighteen year old Lewis Jones is as remarkable as it is candid. He recalls how it was possible for visiting XVs at Twickenham in those days to be over-awed by its impression of grandeur and the feeling that they were playing at the game's true headquarters; and he has owned up since to being deeply affected: "I can feel again that sinking in the pit of the stomach as I stood with the rest of the boys for the playing of the anthems". Imagine the relief, then, of this precocious eighteen-year-old when John Gwilliam, sensing his discomfiture, came to entrust the new yellow ball to his young full back with the directive, "Far downfield as you can, Lewis". A first, authentic act of leadership – the captain signalling his trust. The kick-off went high and deep into England's 25.

But the men in white had no intention of staying there. Eight minutes in they seized the initiative dramatically as Wales sought to move the ball along their ten-yard line. A move between Malcolm Thomas and Trevor Brewer was well anticipated by Smith, who intercepted and scorched forty yards to the corner flag, just ahead of the last-ditch tackles of defenders. As Hofmeyr's splendid conversion sailed overhead the Welsh stood in dismay at the early piercing of their defence. Several correspondents blamed Thomas for an ill-judged pass; but Brewer seems to have carried the can since his next cap did not come until 1955.

The captain must have been as shell-shocked as the next man, but he swiftly set to rallying his men, with both perspiration and inspiration. "Get us back to their 25," he told Billy Cleaver. The stand off half needed no further encouragement, and began to move Wales slowly upfield. Gwilliam and newcomer Roy John leaped magnificently to dominate the battle for possession, allowing Cleaver to plug the touchline. Soon the the home team's 25 was the theatre of action, from which the tight forwards launched drives that impacted like a battering-ram on England's goal line. From one such attacks the ball squirted to Hofmeyr, who under severe pressure, put in an attempted clearance to his left. Despite the heavy screw put on it, the ball swung away from touch some forty metres out, to be caught by Lewis Jones – and Twickenham was about to witness running that produced a try to rank with Obolensky's and, in later years, ones of Sharp, Hancock and St-Andre.

It took the full back no more than half a second to perceive, with the wide-angle sight possessed by many great sportsmen, that the English follow-up had been less than intense, and that he was in space. Quickly he accelerated to top speed, covering twenty yards on long, lean – and always slightly bandy – legs before being confronted by two defenders. They both bought a dummy as Lewis Jones swung back to the right and moved, still at top speed, through a defence that he had sent to panic stations. Not before reaching the England 25 was he finally cornered, when Malcolm Thomas appeared in support to receive the ball and send it on the Bob Evans. The Newport flanker gave a scoring pass to chunky Cliff Davies whose try remained unconverted. It had been a move of great flair and quality which drew a sustained ovation and, afterwards, the unstinted praise of the Press. John Gwilliam recalls being enthralled with it: "I saw it from the best possible position – at the hub of a movement which sort of revolved magically around me."

As the second half got under way Lewis Jones kicked a penalty which put Wales in front, before another of Cleaver's tactical probes set up the try which killed England off. He floated a ball in the direction of Boobyer, who gathered only to become the immediate victim of a heavy tackle by Jack Matthews. Following up, Cleaver carefully tapped the loose ball across England's line for Cale to claim the try. This time the conversion by Jones was successful, after which Wales put up the shutters against a late England rally for an 11-5 win. The Wooden Spoonists of 1949 had become front-runners in the Five Nations' tournament of 1950, and the Twickenham bogy had been knocked off his perch. Gwilliam and Lewis Jones were chaired from the field as the Welsh fans indulged their exuberance. There were other challenges ahead, but this win was the scalp Wales wanted most – and always will.

Vivian Jenkins, himself a superb Wales full back in pre-War days, praised Lewis Jones fulsomely and compared Gwilliam to Richard the Lionheart (perhaps Owain Glyndwr or Llywelyn the Great would have been more apposite, but the thought counted). Another comparison opined: "...he disciplines his forces with the thoroughness and ice-cool detachment of a Cromwell while playing his own not inconsiderable part with cavalier-like relish." Even the *Daily Express* was bowled over. Wrote Pat Marshall, "Englishmen found themselves cheering wildly as Gwilliam's pack whipped the ball back to eager backs." Hm. Pull the other one.

At all events the victory was a memorable one, not least because it re-opened a prospect of the Triple Crown again after seasons of falling at the first fence. In addition, it was a bright start for a side that had come to Twickenham as holders of the Wooden Spoon. The early evening, with its after-the-match dinner at a Mayfair Hotel, began quietly enough before the volume was gradually turned up, and the captain left before the less inhibited merriment began. His mission was to visit patients at the London Hospital at which his new sister-in-law was a nurse. Under wraps he carried a memento which he thought that any Welsh people in the ward might like to see – and even to feel. At the final whistle Billy Cleaver had said to him, "Here you are, skipper. You'd better have this." It was the match ball, which was later signed by both teams. The Gwilliams keep it at their seaside cottage at Moelfre, but since their sons played touch and pass with it as small boys the only signatures that remain legiable are those of Roy John and Jack Matthews.

The verdicts on Wales' new captain were positive. Wrote the *South Wales Echo:*

> On this second memorable occasion for Wales at Twickenham it was Edinburgh Wanderer John Gwilliam who was the outstanding player in a rousing game and... all through the tough struggle in front gave his forwards a splendid lead.

With Wales as her next opponents at Swansea in February's fifty-fourth encounter between the two nations Scotland had a keen interest in what had gone on in London. Andrew Wemyss's Monday morning report in the Scottish edition of the *Daily*

Express – naming Gwilliam, almost proudly, as a member of a Scottish club – was full of grave warnings. In particular there was the "devastating tackling of Jack Matthews who hit some of the Englishmen sickening cracks." Young Lewis Jones had made some "amazing runs" on the Saturday afternoon. The pack "barely shared possession with England's eight... but played with tremendous fire in the loose." One of the very few weak features in Wales' display was the passing in midfield, and Wemyss had talked with Welsh Pressmen who were speculating mournfully that Bleddyn Williams was not expected to be fit enough to put this failing right – something which would have come as a great relief to the newspaper's readers, since the great centre had scored against their team on each of the two occasions when he played at Murrayfield.

In fact, by now Williams was in plaster to assist the recovery of a severely torn ligament. There can have been no more devoted clubman than Bleddyn whose blood, some suspect, runs Blue and Black – and the injury had caused the second half of his first season as Cardiff's captain to be prematurely abandoned (though in twenty-three matches he yet managed to score twenty -three tries).

On the International front he was doomed to miss the remaining Five Nations games, while the knee injury had even-tually proved so serious that his dearest ambition – to make the Lions' tour to New Zealand that summer – was in jeopardy. The boat was scheduled to leave Liverpool on 1 April, which gave the Welsh star just two months to start walking on the leg again and possibly get in some light training. He would be selected and make the travelling deadline by the skin of his teeth, and can be forgiven for railing at the ill-luck that dogged what should have been a career as smooth-running as it was brilliant. From his 1956 autobiography it is clear how frustrated he felt while a Grand Slam season happened without him. Hence he can be forgiven for his lukewarm estimation of the highly successful leader who had, perforce, replaced him. "Gwilliam," he wrote, "was the figure-head of a Welsh team that had almost all the talents necessary to win in modern International Rugby. Whoever had been captain in the side of 1950 would undoubtedly have led a Triple Crown winning unit... this new figure was thrust to the fore by the brilliance of the Welsh team."

It has to be said that such a view was wholly out of agreement with the generality of opinion. Both were statements implying that Gwilliam 'rode' his team's success. 'Brought it about,' thought the great majority at the time. In his autobiography published two years later Lewis Jones made a point of stating, "I will never begin to agree with my friend Bleddyn Williams's criticism of John Gwilliam as a captain, for if ever a leader was capable of commanding respect and discipline by a mere word or gesture it was he... In particular, he led the pack superbly."

The days would come when Bleddyn Williams, too, was captaining Wales to great victories. When that time arrived he would be only too glad to have the commanding presence of Gwilliam leading his forwards.

Although there had been no firm decision about a possible expansion and face-lift for St Helen's, minor improvements had taken place including new terracing and a small temporary stand at the town end, which together raised the arena's capacity to a fully paid-up 41,000, of whom observers said 30,000 were in their places an hour before kick off in February 1950. On the morning of the match tractors moved over the pitch and its surrounds baling up the tons of straw which had given protection from freezing rain during the week. The Swansea playing surface has always been one of the best in the world; how sad that in 2002 its accommodation is long past its sell-by date.

The match programme for the day was two-tone, as usual, cost 3d (one new penny) and contained just eight pages, much of whose space was filled by advertisements. The copy held today by John Gwilliam carries vital statistics of the two teams which help to indicate how the height and bulk of Rugby's top performers have grown in half a century. Gwilliam's pack contained only two men – Hayward and himself – who weighed in at fifteen stones, while props Davies and Robins were thirteen stones and eight pounds, and thirteen stones four respectively. Its two tallest members were each six feet and two inches. Contrast such dimensions with the Welsh XV which met England in February 2001 in which only Martyn Williams was below six feet, and four players weighed seventeen stones or more. The Scottish statistics are not given, but centre Charlie Drummond was evidently the sort of 'big, strong opponent' that Andrew Wemyss thought was needed.

Reports make it clear that the game was not a classic. The action was constantly interrupted by penalty awards, and when the *Football Echo's* reporter Reg Pelling lost count midway through the second half nineteen penalties had been awarded by referee M.J. Dowling from Cork. A number of them were within range of the posts; but Logie Bruce-Lockhart could not kick any for the visitors and only Lewis Jones, sharing the Welsh kicks at goal with John Robins, placed only for Wales. The crowd's delight at the close was genuine, but it was for the victory rather than the manner in which it had been achieved.

The game's personnel were notable for including two British Isles managers of the future, Doug Smith (New Zealand, 1971) and George Burrell (New Zealand, 1977). In 1950 Smith was always in the action on his wing, early on leaving for dead Windsor Major, the twenty-year-old Maesteg speed merchant whose inclusion at Brewer's expense was the only change made by the Welsh selectors from Twickenham. The Scot continued well into the Welsh 25 before "several defenders succeeded in pulling him down". Burrell was praised by several eye-witnesses for his tackling and accurate touch-finding.

It is clear, however, that stalemate was the order of the day, since Gwilliam's aim was to crush the Scots up front while the latter were also resolved to give as good as they got under the expected threat. When the ball was released by the packs, Cleaver kicked for the most part postively and with purpose while Bruce-Lockhart's similar efforts were under pressure and gained little ground. Smith beat Major again as half time drew near (and may have forced his omission from the Belfast game) but in the thirty-ninth minute Cleaver's precise timing of a pass sent Matthews racing through the Scottish midfield towards the left corner. Making as if to veer inside he drew defenders off Malcolm Thomas who took a scoring pass and went thirty yards for an unconverted try. The half time oranges must have tasted sweet.

Lewis Jones at last kicked a penalty before Jack Matthews engineered a second Welsh try. Again a surge of speed took him outside his marker with room to shoot a grub kick towards the Welsh right. It rolled and bounced its way over Scotland's goal-line for Ken Jones to win a desperate race against Burrell and Smith for the touch-down. The score remained unconverted, but shortly before the end Cleaver, safe in the pocket behind a scrum on Scotland's 25, received from Willis and dropped a goal. The crowd surged onto the pitch thinking it was all over – and had to be pushed back by ranks of police; but the time added on by Mr Dowling was merely a stay of execution.

And Mr Wemyss of the *Daily Express?* He thought that Bruce-Lockhart was mainly to blame for Scotland's defeat for failing to escape the heavy marking by Wales' back row – Evans and Cale again – and that Scotland's pack gave up the ghost once they went 9-0 down. He thought Wales were "lively and tactically alert" and would now challenge hard for the Championship title and a Triple Crown. Most Welsh fans shared that opinion, and endless ingenuity was employed in the five weeks that followed to secure a ticket for the showdown in Belfast.

SEVEN

After Scotland there followed a long interval before Wales' journey westwards in pursuit of a Triple Crown. Goodness knows what the modern coaches would make of a five-week gap between the penultimate weekend of a prestigious Rugby competition and the games to determine the winners. The change to pushing through what is now the Six Nations tournament on five successive fortnights certainly maintains momentum and ensures that players remain at full throttle throughout it. The entry of Italy has meant that even the single Saturday off which each of the five nations could once look forward to no longer exists. International coaches approve of this format for the continuity of control which it affords them and, given their way, would probably concertina the competition even more. Millionaire owners of clubs and their Boards are less than convinced. But in 1950 no such people had been thought of, and with a few exceptions Rugby Football was still for fun.

Those exceptions included the Inter Services trophy played for by the the Army, the Navy and the RAF. This tourney caught the imagination in two respects: first, because all adult males had to do 'national service' in one of the three fighting forces so that at any one time each was sure to have on strength some of the most exciting young Rugby players in the land. Secondly, for the first time since the Rugby League was founded the amateurs of the day and Rugby League professionals were allowed to play together, since the Services deemed them all to be simply employees of the War Office. This apart, there was a knock-out tournament involving the Counties of England, while Wales ran a somewhat pallid equivalent. That was all.

Thus to participate in or watch Rugby Football at its fiercest and most competitive no fixtures approached the unrelenting tempo of International matches. Alas, the rigidity of the fixture list at this time meant that every January the two strongest nations in terms of pure statistics, Wales and England, were each other's opponents in their first Five Nations game. Depending on the result one or both of them would forfeit the chance of either a Triple Crown or the Grand Slam (which, by 1950, England had won six times to Wales' three). Yet, happily, spread over three months the Five Nations was still robust enough to sustain spectator interest until its closing stages, for a team which lost its opening game could still run into form and do well enough to emerge in the end as Champions. Even in seasons when the title was definitely out of reach England and Scotland still had the Calcutta Cup to compete for, guaranteed to generate white heat on both sides of the touchline; while at this time every single match was a vital one for French sides and their supporters, bent on proving that they could live on a Rugby pitch with the best in the world.

Meanwhile the Celtic cousins would be slogging it out in what was always Ireland's final outing unless inclement weather had forced postponement of an earlier fixture. As Sean Diffley remarks in *The Men in Green* Wales and Ireland have taken a wicked delight in denying each other Triple Crowns at the last hurdle. Eight times before 1950 Wales had frustrated their opponents' bid for it; while, rather more relevantly to this particular year, the Irish had twice been good enough to return the compliment. On this occasion only honour would be at stake for the latter, since they had been held to a draw in Paris and lost narrowly against England. Nevertheless they could claim to be an improving side, having scored three fine tries in their defeat of Scotland a fortnight earlier.

As for Wales, it was 1911 when a Triple Crown had last been won, let alone a Grand Slam. The names of that vintage included Jack Bancroft, Reggie Gibbs, W.J. Trew and Dickie Owen, and the memory of Gwyn Nicholls was still fresh and able to inspire. That year's Crown had been clinched at Cardiff, but the team of 1950 would be bidding for theirs before 32,000 passionate – and mostly hostile – spectators in Belfast. The venue was Ravenhill which, like St Helen's, was soon to be struck off the list of Test match stadia.

Welsh team spirit suffered what could have been a fatal body-blow on 13 February when the British Isles party to tour Australasia in the summer was named. Although approached to captain the tourists, John Gwilliam had felt unable to accept. The reasons were several: he and Pegi were still relative newly-weds and a first child, to be named Catherine, was on the way. Moreover, he had come to enjoy Glenalmond very much, and as one of the most junior members of staff felt unable to ask for half a year off. The School, too, was not enthusiastic about letting him go, threatening – maybe tongue-in-cheek – that he would have to pay for a locum!

The fact is that, in the light of Gwilliam's unavailability, few in the British Isles could quarrel with the appointment of Karl Mullen as captain. He had been a major influence in Ireland's consistent successes of recent seasons, particularly at forward where the Lions could expect to be tested to the utmost. Six Welsh backs were selected including Bleddyn Williams whose knee had now mended well enough for him to begin training and who would have to demonstrate his fitness to the tour selectors before departure. (Lewis Jones was later summoned to join the squad when George Norton broke an arm playing against Southland at Invercargill).

Seven Welsh forwards also got invitations. They included Rees Stephens who, as we have seen, was unavailable for selection throughout the 1950 Five Nations campaign. He would become a Lion through potential rather than playing record, for his International career showed five defeats and only three wins in the seasons up to 1949. So perhaps lineage had something to do with the selectors' choice: Stephens senior had won caps for Wales before World War I and was now on his way up the WRU's administrative ladder. After two years as a Welsh representative on the International Board he would become President in 1956. He was in a position to put words into the right ears.

But Welsh attention, and sympathy, was directed at the forward who was not wanted on voyage. Like Dai Morris, a key back-row forward in the Welsh Grand Slam side of 1971 who failed to make the New Zealand tour that summer, Ray Cale did not earn selection in 1950; neither initially nor when J.R.C. Matthews (England) withdrew, to be replaced by the Cornishman Vic Roberts. His team-mates were as upset as they were mystified, for they well knew the flanker's quality.

After being dropped by Wales following his first caps from Newbridge, Cale had joined Pontypool and fought his way back to Test level as a blind side flanker. For Wales John Gwilliam packed down next to him and would have been well aware of his in-put at set scrummages; he knew the quality of his protective play at lines out; and, tracking his team-mate around the field, would be left in no doubt of his tireless covering and the close support play which could produce tries like that which he had snapped up at Twickenham. The captain's summation of his calibre, therefore, is "a real tough nut", which in the Gwilliam portfolio of terse, hard-to-earn compliments ranks as the tops. But in that same appraisal there may be the germ of a reason why the British Isles selectors did not choose him.

Although the Twickenham try had revealed a constructive side to Cale's game, there is no doubt that he belonged in a special category of hunter-killer back-row forwards who set out to intimidate opposing half backs. Other names which come to mind include Fergus Slattery, Mark Shaw, Paul Ringer and (before the knee injury which blunted his cutting edge) Richard Webster. The trendy modern phrase for such players is that they are 'in your face'. In the tackle Cale hit opponents like a guided missile; opponents remember equally vividly the malevolence he projected at the edge of their eye-line, as if to promise that their afternoon was not going to be fun. John Gwilliam is on record as saying that in Belfast a few weeks later Cale "showed the power and determination to contain McCarthy and McKay who had run riot for the previous two years". His captain rated him.

Since thirteen Welshmen had been chosen to travel, the outrage felt in the homeland at Cale's omission fell short of the intensity it might otherwise have reached. The immediate reaction of critics like J.B.G. Thomas and Dennis Busher had to be one of restraint. But in due course they owed it to their readers, especially those of Monmouthshire, to come up with a reason for his omission. The word in the end was – and it is repeated by J.B.G.'s son Wayne in his *Century of Welsh Rugby Players* – that Cale was "too aggressive". Absurd, you say. Too aggressive? – to oppose the nation that had produced Kevin Skinner and 'Tiny' White and would soon give the world Colin Meads? It was, however, something of which the Tours Committee of the day, loaded with polite Englishmen, would have been capable.

Life, and the Five Nations tournament, had to go on. Ireland's team contained four relatively inexperienced backs in Uprichard, Phipps, Crowe and the scrum half Carroll. At forward, however, their selectors had remained loyal to the eight which had spearheaded the Triple Crown successes of 1948 and 1949, including a front row described by John Robins as the best he scrummaged against containing Mullen, McKibbin and Clifford. The Welsh would also remember with horror the previous year's 'steal' at Swansea by Jim McCarthy when a kick across the breaking packs to the corner flag found the carrot-haired flanker positioned for the winning score.

That kick was the work of the inimitable Jack Kyle, who was always aware of his back row and well knew the clever anticipation which enabled them to clinch scores that he had initiated. He was also a brilliant runner, whose choice of when to break was always right and who possessed a change of pace that was baffling in its subtlety. Some sceptics thought that such individualistic know-how, and the ability to play to his pack, were mainly needed because of the limitations of Ireland's three quarters of the day. Whatever the motivation: Kyle was still a great player. "When Jack decided to have a go, it was a score", wrote Sean Diffley.

The Welsh selectors had just one position to chew over. Having been found wanting, wings Brewer and, now, Major were side-lined for the time being. Rather than the straightforward choice of a new left wing there now followed a radical restructuring of the back division in order to maximise the available talent. The decision to move Malcolm Thomas to the left wing

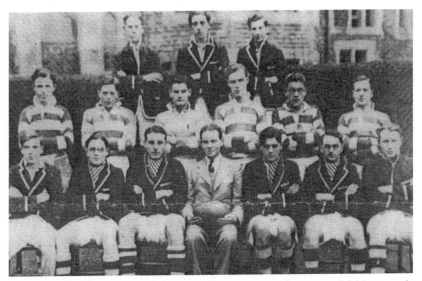

1. The young Gwilliam (seated, third left) as captain of a successful Monmouth School XV in 1940.

2. The maturing Gwilliam: the wartime Tank Commander is back at Cambridge – where the new opponents were Dark Blues.

3. The 1950 Welsh XV which clinched their country's first Triple Crown for 39 years in Belfast. Standing (l-r) Ivor Jones (touch judge), John Robins, Don Hayward, Roy John, Bob Evans, Ray Cale, Billy Cleaver. Seated: Ken Jones, Malcolm Thomas, Lewis Jones, John Gwilliam (capt), Jack Matthews, Cliff Davies, Gerwyn Williams. At front: Rex Willis and Dai Davies.

4. A dive pass on its way to the midfield from Wales scrum half Rex Willis. Skipper John Gwilliam knows the ball is in safe hands.

5. John Gwilliam thunders down the five-yard line as Irish opponents close on him.

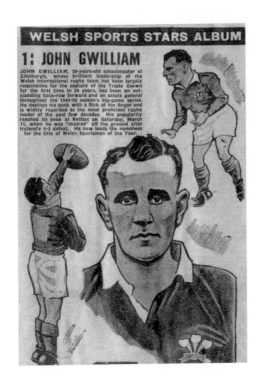

WELSH SPORTS STARS ALBUM

1: JOHN GWILLIAM

JOHN GWILLIAM, 29-years-old schoolmaster at Edinburgh, whose brilliant leadership of the Welsh International rugby team has been largely responsible for the capture of the Triple Crown for the first time in 39 years, has been an outstanding back-row forward and an astute general throughout the 1949-50 season's big-game series. He deploys his pack with a flick of the finger and is widely regarded as the most proficient rugby leader of the past few decades. His popularity reached its peak at Belfast on Saturday, March 11, when he was "chaired" off the ground after Ireland's 6-3 defeat. He now leads the nominees for the title of Welsh Sportsman of the Year.

6. Gwilliam's first season in charge of the Wales XV drew plaudits from all quarters, including the tabloid press.

7. 'Magnifique!' is all France's captain Guy Basquet can tell John Gwilliam after Wales overwhelm France at Cardiff to clinch the Grand Slam of 1950. Memorable three quarter play, worthy of a Golden Era, saw the Welsh through to a 21-0 triumph.

8.

9.

0.

11.

8-11. A main source of quality possession for the great mid-century Welsh sides was the line out. John Gwilliam himself (8) was a formidable performer with one or two hands, but he himself is the first to pay tribute to Neath's Roy John (9) seen here taking ball from the 1951 Springboks at Cardiff and again (10) against England in 1952. For Wales and Neath (11) John could always count on expert support from club-mate Rees Stephens, pictured here with socks characteristically around his ankles.

12. John Gwilliam indulging in one of the reverse passes that so alarmed his teams, yet often delivered rapid ball to the midfield. Billy Williams and the Scots in the background look equally bemused.

13. John Gwilliam hugs the ball and waits for support as he tidies up loose possession.

14 & 15. John Gwilliam was never afraid to put boot to ball, and here he lines up a probing kick to turn the defence at Cardiff Arms Park... and the Irish challenge is just too late.

17. Cardiff RFC's half backs Cliff Morgan and (background) his 'minder' Rex Willis.

16. Billy Cleaver on the burst in Cardiff strip. His tactical flair was highly rated by John Gwilliam in the 1950 Gland Slam season, but his Lions tour the same summer was troubled by career dilemmas.

and play Lewis Jones in the centre brought the latter closer to defenders, with less room to probe and mesmerise them. Gerwyn Williams, however, the other available full back, was arguably a more valuable player than anyone currently competing for the left wing position; hence the award of a first cap for the London Welshman. Not a big man, he was ever liable to be blown away by large, fast wings heading for the goal line; but in all other respects he was an accomplished player who would finish up with fourteen caps.

On 9 March the Welsh party left Cardiff on the first leg of its seventeen-hour journey to Belfast via Holyhead. John Gwilliam had come south to join his team at Crewe, where he remembers a wait to change trains that lasted two hours. He fell into conversation, for the first time it seems, with J.B.G. Thomas and Reg Pelling of the defunct *News Chronicle*, and talked earnestly about 'organisation' in Rugby Football. "If we were properly organised," he assured the two journalists, "Wales could beat anybody – every time." To illustrate how unorganised Welsh teams could be he told J.B.G. and Pelling how, at the eve-of-match run-out two years previously at the same venue, Haydn Tanner had staged a contest featuring Frank Trott, Cleaver and Jack Matthews to decide who would be the team's place-kicker. Whoever it was that won, the solitary try scored by the visitors in defeat next day stayed unconverted. It is fair to say that as captain Gwilliam himself had an organised approach to the game, and held views which would be endorsed in due course by the 'coaching' lobby. But, domiciled a great distance from the home front, he was unable to give the concept the totality of approach which it demanded.

Compared with the altogether more spacious Lansdowne Road, Ravenhill in 1950 was a small, not very elegant stadium first used for International Rugby in 1924. North of Ireland FC played club Rugby there but, set in a soccer-conscious hinterland, it was not noted for pulling big crowds to watch the handling code. However, all vantage-points were occupied, with bright splashes of red along the terracing, as kick-off time arrived and Wales took the field to an ear-bursting roar. Gwilliam had won the toss and the visitors chose to start with the wind behind them.

The game was vital, and tense, and as hard-fought as might have been expected. The formula that had brought unprecedented Irish successes in the immediate post-War years would be perse- vered with by the men in green who, like Scotland, were determined that the true mettle of the vaunted Welsh pack should be put to the test. Equally, Gwilliam's forward-based tactics were based on the belief that opposition eights – even this one – could be so battered by his men as to run out of strength and stamina. He was to be proved right, though not until the eighty ninth minute. And, anyway, for fanatical, success-starved supporters 6- 3 was enough, even at the end of a game that was scrappy throughout. Those who are dyed-in-the-wool would prefer a 3-0 win to defeat by 28 points to 27 in a spectacular game.

Thus the neutral match report by Jim Swanton in the *Daily Telegraph* can claim to be among the most candid about the game's quality. Having been careful to describe Wales as "the best of the five countries" he turns to an assessment of the early forward exchanges:

> The two packs were mostly locked in a frenzied embrace, occasionally staggering laterally to and fro across the field. A succession of collapsed scrums, for which each side in turn was extremely lucky not to be penalised, made wearisome interludes.

Later, after Norton's second half penalty to cancel out the first Welsh try scored by Ken Jones, he wrote:

> The struggle from now to the end grew, if possible, in inten- sity as the two packs tired. Neither, though, ever threatened to crack. Ireland now had much more of things, Cleaver once appearing providentially to kick away as McCarthy was about to drop on the ball for a try.

Besides that near miss other excitement seems to have depended on players' mistakes. Most obviously these were made by the kickers, including Lewis Jones who sent two down-wind penalty chances wide in the first quarter. The Irish centres were guilty of knock-ons and forward passes and one of them, Phipps, missed with a drop goal attempt from the middle distance. Ironically, it was the old master himself who made the crucial mistake when eyes were turning repeatedly to the clock.

The moment of truth came with a minute of proper time remaining. Carroll whipped a swift pass away from a scrum on Ireland's 25, only for Kyle to spill the vital possession under a challenge from his opposite number. Cleaver smartly released a pass to Lewis Jones, who accelerated away to the left towards Malcolm Thomas, now pursued by a horde of Irish coverers all of whom he outstripped with the exception of Ireland's full back. Came the moment of truth: down went Thomas, diving for the line; flat-out went Norton, into the tackle; over went the corner flag, under touch judge Ossie Glasgow's nose

And down stayed his flag. There were only moments left for the conversion attempt before referee R.A. Beattie of Scotland blew for full time and the combatants were engulfed by a host of overjoyed fans. Wales had waited a long time for their latest Triple Crown, and Ireland had made them compete right to the wire. Belfast was a lovely place to be that night; and although defeated the Irish, as ever, were more than ready to help their vanquishers celebrate the night away. With one game still to play, moreover, Wales were now assured of the Championship title.

Air travel by Rugby groups in the southern hemisphere was relatively common by the middle of the twentieth century, since the distances between centres of population were so great. In Europe, however, teams from the Five Nations travelled by boat, train and ferry when the Channel or the Celtic Sea needed to be crossed. Cardiff's 1945 outing to Nantes alluded to in Chapter Three may well have been the first flight to a fixture ever undertaken by a European Rugby club or nation. It was, it should be added, a one-off, which owed more than a little to constructive collusion between RAF St Athan and a certain Flying Officer Bleddyn Williams.

There had therefore been much excitement when a travel agency advertised an excursion by air from South Wales to Ireland run by a firm called Fair-flight Ltd for fans wanting to see the vital game in Belfast. At £10.5s (ten pounds and twenty five pence) the 'packages' sold steadily, including as they did a flight to Collinstown Airport, Dublin, and back from Llandow air-strip in the Vale of Glamorgan, two overnight stays in a Dublin hotel, a return trip by coach to Belfast's Ravenhill ground and a ticket for the game. The Avro Tudor V which would carry them had played a part in the Berlin air-lift a year earlier, and its chief pilot who took the aircraft out of Wales on Friday, 10 March, was highly experienced. On board all told were its crew of five plus seventy eight fans from all parts of South Wales, notably Glynneath, the Ammanford area and the Western Valley of Gwent. Among them were a Llanelli ship's chandler Handel Rogers, his brother in law Gwyn Anthony and an acquaintance called Mel Thomas. With tragic prescience J.B.G. Thomas had called them collectively the "select few supporters who are going by air."

Spirits were high on the post-match journey back to Dublin. An impromptu glee party from Risca sang to passengers, and at the hotel conversation flourished into the early hours as the afternoon's highlights were analysed and endlessly re-lived. While some fans slept late in the morning, others went out to buy souvenirs and presents from shops that opened on Sunday, noting enviously the cornucopia of goods on offer, for at home food rationing still prevailed. Colourful hand-baggage bulging with souvenirs, confectionery and duty free drinks was piled on the racks above the seats as passengers boarded the aircraft for its return flight, due to leave at ten past two and touch down at Llandow just under an hour later.

The places occupied by Handel Rogers and his two companions on the outward leg were already occupied for the return trip, obliging them to look elsewhere. Choosing the three back seats of the passenger cabin they settled down to a journey in what seemed to be near-perfect conditions. Having flown often before, as a maintenance fitter with the RAF during the War, Rogers was aware of a strong tail-wind above Cardigan Bay which was speeding their return, but not something to cause concern. Soon, viewing the Welsh countryside below and thinking how beautiful it looked in the sunshine, he was reflecting on what had been a perfect weekend as the pilot took the aircraft into a wide banking manoeuvre that would bring it down above Siginstone to the east of the air-strip and into what would now be a head-wind.

The catastrophe which then occurred was ascribed by an enquiry to 'causes unknown'. But Rogers, in 2001 half way through his eighties, believes there was a navigational error. His theory is that the pilot had underestimated the force of the wind, and realised in the final moments that he was doomed to strike the ground before the runway, possibly as much as 750 yards short – hence the last desperate attempt to gain a height which would enable his aircraft to touch down safely on tarmac. It failed in this aim, stalling instead and nose-diving into a ploughed field. This account of events is borne out by an eye-witness quoted in the *Western Mail,* an RAF sergeant called Mettam who had seen at close range the flight's last moments, while in photographs carried by the newspaper the perimeter hedge can be seen only yards from the wreckage.

On impact the aircraft broke into three segments; the crew and seventy-five Rugby fans died, most of them instantly. Handel Rogers says that many were victims of whiplash; for these were days before seats in airliners included head-supports. Just behind his row, however, was the back wall of the cabin and he puts his survival down to that and also what were called in those days safety 'straps', not belts. He thinks that despite instructions from the stewardess Mel Thomas was actually in the toilet at the moment of impact; its confined space may have saved his life.

Rogers and his brother-in-law had leaned forward, closed their eyes and used hands and arms to protect their heads. After the "horrendous sounds" as the aircraft tore itself apart died away, they found themselves staring at grass; the second rupture in the fuselage had occurred immediately in front of their row. Rogers first tried to find a shoe that had been torn from his foot as the seats in front of them broke away. He called out to fellow passengers to ask if anyone had seen it. The enquiry was met by an eery silence, broken only by the wind gusting through the wreckage.

The occupants of all other seats were dead or dying in what was the worst civil aviation disaster so far in the history of flying. Llandow eclipsed the fifty-five victims of a crash at Washington's airport the previous November and the forty killed in what had been the United Kingdom's biggest catastrophe, at Prestwick in 1948.

Flotillas of ambulances from all parts of Glamorgan were swiftly at the scene to evacuate ten of the "terribly injured" passengers, but none survived to walk from the scene save Handel Rogers (carrying, would you believe, a tea-set bought as a present, which amazingly had survived the impact unscathed) and his companions. They were taken to the RAF hospital at St Athan, where Thomas was to remain on the critical list for some time. The other two were discharged after a fortnight under observation. His religious beliefs encouraged Rogers to think that his survival was down to divine intervention and that he had been spared for some good reason. Thus in later years he put time and energy into serving both Llanelli RFC and the Rugby football fraternity at large through the Welsh Rugby Union, whose President he became in 1976 – to be saluted with a Grand Slam by the National XV.

John and Pegi Gwilliam had returned to Scotland by ferry from Belfast on the Saturday night, travelling on immediately to Glenalmond and retiring immediately to catch up with some lost sleep. It was none too pleasant to be telephoned in the afternoon by a Fleet Street reporter asking if it was true that Bert Gwilliam had been on the stricken aircraft. It was a relief to be able to say that he had travelled by sea; but his son and daughter-in-law were devastated at the tidings they were hearing.

A few years later John Gwilliam, along with Jack Matthews and Ken Jones, attended a service at Llandow to unveil a memorial stone commemorating a weekend when grief followed joy. At Ravenhill Welsh Rugby had triumphed mightily, but her longed-for and well-deserved trophy turned out to be a Crown of Thorns. Two weeks later in Cardiff France's players remained at attention alongside their hosts after the playing of the anthems before the final Five Nations game began. Five buglers in uniform sounded the Last Post – a sombre note during a season that should have brought only joy.

In 1950 French Rugby teams were still objects of British sportsmen's curiosity, a presence in the game almost as exotic as tourists from the great Rugby-playing Dominions who came to Europe once a decade. Part of the reason was that, whichever means of travel opponents chose, the cost for supporters of trips to Paris was prohibitive; few went to Colombes. More significantly France and her clubs upset the International Board in the nineteen twenties by allegedly paying generous salaries and bloated expenses to top players. At the end of the 1930-31 season this led to her expulsion from International Board membership. Hence there had been no more contact between the Home Countries and French Rugby until 1945.

Getting round the problem by allowing the clubs to find jobs for star players France re-entered the Championship in 1947, restoring it to a 'Five Nations' tournament. Back-to-back wins over Wales in 1948 and 1949 confirmed her status as an up-and-coming force in world Rugby. The names of top French players began to be as well known to the British as their counterparts in the Home Countries, with distance lending them an extra romantic appeal. Lourdes hotelier Jean Prat was well into a career which would see him play fifty-one Tests in the back row and earn the title 'M'sieu Rugby'. Andre Alvarez and Michel Pomathios were elegant attacking backs. Guy Basquet was an all-action number eight forward with good hands. There were a terrifying pair of locks: Georges Soro and Alban Moga each tipped the scales at seventeen stones in an era when an average second row forward weighed in at three stones less. Wales was doubtless relieved at the latter pair's retirement.

Said the *Western Mail* gallantly on 25 March: *Les joueurs Français peuvent assure que le peuple Gallois leur offre de tout coeur, le plus cordiale acceuil!* That welcome did not, however, extend to sourcing tickets to some 500 supporters who had made the trip without them. The French had been warned that entry to Cardiff Arms Park would be 'all ticket' – still a relatively new concept. The usually cheerful Chief Constable W.J. Price repeatedly said that 52,000 was the capacity agreed between his Force and the WRU and there could be no concessions. The French Consul at Cardiff, M. Henri Langlais, broadcast an appeal to Welshmen to give up their tickets, but the response it drew was negligible. Of course not: everyone wanted to be present to cheer the Champions – a status earned by three straight victories.

But now a Grand Slam beckoned. Statisticians pointed out that after fourteen years Wales might go through a season unbeaten (instead of France, New Zealand were beaten instead in 1935). There was general agreement that this Welsh team were up for it. Studied carefully, pre-match photographs can betray a mood; and in the one published by the *Western Mail* Gwilliam and his men are nothing if not relaxed. Even the captain's features convey the faint suggestion of a smile. Lewis Jones, Don Hayward and R.T. Evans all look positively happy; but the broadest grin is worn by Ray Cale standing at the rear and harbouring the private knowledge that he was about to cash in his chips. That was sad in one way; but Cale was obviously tickled pink at the thought of the cheque St Helen's Rugby League club had agree to pay him to turn professional.

Interestingly D.R. Gent picked up this happiness theme in his newspaper report on the Monday morning, commenting: "In the second half Wales took the game almost light-heartedly, so much were they on top". Lewis Jones, on the day evidently keen to run, sparked a great combined movement at fifteen minutes which, unusually, involved the captain. A recycled ball reached Gwilliam who, doubtless startled to be featuring in the wide open spaces, nonetheless found the presence of mind to project a pass to the midfield which travelled an estimated twenty five yards and narrowly failed to unlock the visitors' defence. Soon Jack Matthews did the trick however, intercepting and going between the posts for a try converted by Jones. The latter's penalty was also the first score of the second half.

The Welsh display now got better and better. Ken Jones was sent in for two tries, the second following another movement featuring the skipper, and the whole team joined in what was almost exhibition Rugby in the final ten minutes. What most critics judged the best action of the game rounded things off, with Lewis Jones hiding the ball from the French behind his back before presenting Roy John with a clear run beneath the bar to effect a joyous climax. This fourth try of the match was the lock's sole score for Wales in a career that brought him nineteen caps, while conversions by Lewis Jones lifted the winning score to twenty one points. The clean sweep by Wales was her fourth since France's entry into competition in 1908. After a while the sheer exultation died away to be replaced by deep, deep satisfaction.

EIGHT

Just seven days after that last great Welsh triumph the *Ceramic* left Liverpool bound for Wellington, New Zealand, with a thirty-strong complement of British Lions on board. The controlling duo were Surgeon Captain L.B. Osborne, the manager, and skipper Karl Mullen of Old Belvedere whose post-war track record included leading Ireland to two Triple Crowns and a Grand Slam. Remarkably, he was still only 24.

John Gwilliam is on record as stating that "captaincy of a successful representative side... should begin when a player is comparatively young in years and experience... An outstanding recent example is Karl Mullen." Some contemporary observers had urged the tour selectors to work harder to change Gwilliam's mind – and that of his School – about leading the tour. But the man whom the British media thought should have been at the helm was now back on the Scottish moors, inculcating history into his Glenalmond pupils. And perhaps his allusion to Mullen was an oblique way of telling the Irishman, "No hard feelings – good luck".

When Gwilliam waved them goodbye, then, what was lost to the Lions and their cause? What did his maturing qualities as an International player and captain amount to?

First of all, the tourists went without a man who was emerging as one of the great natural captains of twentieth century Rugby. J.B.G. Thomas and others frequently called his approach 'school-masterly'; but on the contrary his fondness for quoting the example of generals and field marshals indicates a substantial militaristic – that is, authoritative and combative – strain in his make-up. In conversation he still likes to use terms straight out of tank tactics: for example, a team should remain 'hull down' until it has taken a good look at 'the terrain'. When he talks of preferring to play at number eight to lock 'because you can get your head up to see what is going on' you are put in mind of a commander poking his head above the turret and surveying the landscape through powerful field glasses.

He is a man who, throughout his life I guess, has aimed to radiate an air of confidence which is not easily dispelled. If sometimes, in conversation, an awkward question is put to him, far from seeming flustered his first reaction is to raise his eyebrows, as if to register surprise that an interrogator could not have worked out the answer for himself. Half a century ago it would have been: "John Gwilliam, can your team beat England?" "Hah. Of course. We will." Such confidence amounts to reassurance, and in the build-up to a great challenge or ordeal it is a wonderful, infectious, commodity. The eyes of team-mates struggling to mask trepidation under pressure suddenly brighten. They have got a message from him.

It seems certain that he was exceedingly loyal to his teams and generous in his summation of them. At the end of the 1950 Five Nations campaign he picked out men to praise, in particular Cleaver and the tactical control which he delivered on demand. Perhaps he was closest to his fellow forwards, notably Roy John whose consistent dominance at the throw-in made lines-out a reliable platform off which the next surge could develop. The captain loves to recall the spirited in-put of Cliff Davies, he of the eighteen-plus inch neck, who insisted that changing room doors should be opened wide before Wales went down the tunnel so that cowering opponents next door could hear the Welsh battle hymns. He enjoyed the humour radiated by Dai Davies, his hooker from Somerset Police, behind whom Don Hayward was a taciturn strong man. As for the flankers who packed down beside him, he has always said that the tackling of Cale and R.T. Evans was an inspiration throughout the ten-week campaign. The latter took some time to accept Gwilliam's views on intensive backing-up to ensure the continuity of attack, only to accept the concept wholeheartedly – and his own vital role in it.

After his men demonstrated the following year that they were, after all, mere mortals (won one, drawn one, lost two) Gwilliam would be stripped of the captaincy and his place in the team. He took these blows on the chin and although, as we shall see, the banishment was scarcely justified there were no tantrums. Many years later he told me, dismissive as ever, "Remember, we weren't paid a fee to play, so being dropped was not the blow it can be in 2002."

For the most part these were the virtues which made the character of John Gwilliam a robust one. There is one other observation to make, in the light of his church-going and sober life-style. The meek may indeed be blessed; but the Welsh captain was in no way 'piously humble and submissive' (OED). You did not live with opponents like Agar, du Rand, Mias, 'Tiny' White and O'Brien without having the necessary competitive streak embedded in your make-up: the desire to generate apprehension in an opponent and give him grief. Or to take his best shot and laugh it off. Gwilliam could mix it. He was tough. He was also tall: this is a physical attribute which allows a man to look down on the majority of his fellows. It follows that they cannot do otherwise than look up to him.

Besides leadership, the other set of attributes which the British Isles had perforce left behind them was Gwilliam's on-field Rugby skills. There seems no doubt that, even before being made Welsh captain, he had become one of the two or three best line out forwards in the world during his spell in the National XV's second row. Photographs in his well-kept career albums show him taking balls with one or both hands as appropriate and reaching great heights along the touch-lines. From there, now and then, he let fly that hair-raising pass from touchline out to the midfield so deplored by his half backs. Though outrageous, it was more than once able to send his centres into space. Occasionally he would put in a nifty screw-kick or lead a combined dribble; and sometimes, to the consternation of both teams, run in attack, taking and giving expertly with good hands. A burly, not too elegant mover he was more like John Scott or Dean Richards as a number eight than Alun Pask or Hennie Muller; but once under way and aimed at towards midfield defenders his sheer bulk could cause panic in an opposing back-line. He never scored a try, or indeed any points, for Wales, but by his own admission once dropped a scoring pass given him by Glyn Davies in a game at Cardiff against England.

I think finally that, although Glenalmond was a mighty long way from Welsh Rugby's heartland, to be able to retire there after each representative match was indeed a bonus for John Gwilliam. Ray Lewis had assured him that thereby he could keep his nose away from the washing of dirty linen. True, no doubt. But further, to the men he led those absences generated a certain aura, or mystique, which stimulated fascination. This was succeeded by a desire to understand him, which in turn led to the determination to please him. In short, there was neither the time nor the opportunity for negative attitudes to develop towards the emigre in charge.

This, then, was the major figure without whom the British Isles sought to accomplish a winning mission in the southern hemisphere. Down Under, many of his contemporaries would argue, his presence was sorely missed.

Back home, in the wake of *Ceramic's* steady progress across the Atlantic and through the Panama Canal the domestic season slowly died away. John Gwilliam brought a Select XV featuring Glyn Davies and the rising star R.C.C. Thomas to Pontypridd for a charity game. An eighteen-year-old called Russell Robins shone in a home victory by 11-6 and gave tacit notice that he would one day succeed his opposite number in the Wales back row. Maesteg beat Neath 29-4 to complete a memorable unbeaten season in which they won thirty eight matches and drew six. Though pressed to captain Pontypool, Ray Cale took his expected departure for St Helens. Laudably, Cardiff City AFC went to Belfast to play Distillery in a game which raised money for families of the Llandow victims. Before it closed the Fund begun by the *Western Mail* was nudging £40,000, a stupendous amount for the period which now, half a century on, equates to an estimated £800,000. Cardiff RFC had contributed generously, too.

The club would also vote for Billy Cleaver as skipper for 1950-51. Down Under and far away, this captain-apparent was by now cruising towards rain-swept Wellington after the Lions' voyage. Cleaver was among twenty-one fellow Britons and nine Irishmen, all of whom should have been stirring company. For him, however, the longevity of his leave of absence from the National Coal Board was a great concern. The career dilemma which had troubled him all the way from Merseyside would not go away. It is worth setting down the details, for in those days it dogged every amateur who sought time off to travel with a representative side.

The Blue and Blacks were very much Cleaver's club. He had begun playing for Cardiff as a student in the early war-time days, and continued to do so as an employee within the newly-nationalised coal industry. His Saturday routine was to rise at five a.m. in order to reach the pit-head and go underground by six. There would follow a mile-and-a-half walk to the coal face where his task was measuring and checking the work of the colliers, who were on piece-work. Next he had to enter up the company books, and locate the manager to counter-sign his computations. Then the walk home; a discarding of black-dusted clothing; a soak in the tub (these were days before pit-head baths); an urgent walk, or run, through the village to the bus-stop. A journey to Pontypridd, followed by a change of bus and the final lap to Westgate Street and Cardiff Arms Park – just in time for kick-off, with a bit of luck.

Cleaver was a high-flier who, after a gruelling apprenticeship, was just twenty six when he was appointed manager of North Celynen and Graig Fawr collieries at Newbridge, where two thousand men were employed. Now, in far distant New Zealand, what continued to worry him as the team bus drove the Lions away from Wellington's magnificent harbour were the new regulations drawn up by the Government to control the mining industry. These specified that no colliery could operate without the presence of a fully qualified manager for more than three months. The tour was was scheduled to last for six months and one week and the Cardiffian was acutely aware that in his absence he would be the sole nominee for the captaincy of his club, a time-consuming responsibility outside his job. Problems, problems.

It would be 1971 before Lions tours truly captured the imagination of the mass media in Britain. In 1950 television was just struggling back into existence after a war-time hibernation, so that pictorial coverage of the 1950 Tests relayed into British sitting rooms was totally out of the question. Radio reportage, however, had spread its wings, and as the summer of 1950 opened there was live commentary on the West Indians' tour, the Derby, Bruce Woodcock versus Lee Savold and English Soccer being humiliated by the USA in a World Cup tie. The 'Welsh Home Service' also covered the National Eisteddfod and Cricket between Glamorgan and Pembrokeshire. It is probable that reportage from New Zealand was carried in the five minutes of sports tit-bits broadcast at 6.25 each evening on the coat-tails of 'News from Wales'.

As for print journalism, the All Black Bob Scott's autobiography confirms that there was only one Fleet Street writer Down Under in 1950. Gallant Dai Gent funded his own trip as a contract freelance, contributing mainly to the *Sunday Times*, but otherwise the British Press was full of material 'from Our Own Correspondent' (which in newspaper parlance does not mean 'our own' at all but any local hack hired for *ad hoc* coverage and probably serving several newspapers). This lack of interest was further evidenced by match reports, and especially previews, which filled no more than one third of one column. Even J.B.G. Thomas could not persuade his editor to 'splash' Lions material on sports pages dominated by Test cricket, Wooller's Glamorgan and the ring performances of Eddie Thomas. Bemoaning all this a reader wrote in begging for Rugby Football (outside Wales) to "emerge from its private world". However, the *Western Mail* did print the neat *double entendre* of Surgeon-Captain L.B. Osborne, the British Isles tour manager, when asked by the Kiwi Press what impression he hoped his men would make in the coming months: "I sincerely hope," he replied, "that New Zealand will be sad when it is time for us to go home."

The Lions were whisked around the Wellington region at speed, calling at Parliament House where one of the welcoming speeches was delivered in Welsh by an emigre from Carmarthenshire. Endless rigmaroles of civic receptions, social evenings and visits to schools confronted them. The tourists stayed patiently on their best behaviour, signing autographs and listening politely to fans who demanded to know whether they knew a distant uncle in Britain. The distance between North Island and 'Home' (the word used about Britain by New Zealanders until well into the second half of the last century), and the expense and rarity of opportunities to go back, made them greedy for any tit-bits about the Old Country.

On board ship the Lions had been able to exercise, polish up their passing, and even scrummage a little. Now at last, crossing the strait to South Island for the first fixture against Nelson-Marlborough, they could again practice in space, on turf. Bleddyn Williams took the chance to show that his recovery had been satisfactory. Considering that he had been required to prove his fitness to the selectors in March, the Welshman was entitled to some quiet indignation that Scotland's Doug Smith had been allowed to leave Britain with an arm in plaster, an injury which was to keep him out of action until the eighteenth game of the tour.

The tourists kicked off with three successive wins and eighty points at Nelson, Buller and Greymouth. In 1949 the Wallabies had won a two-Test series in the 'land of the long white cloud' while New Zealand's first-choices were away in South Africa but, with respect to Australia, British Rugby men were what the crowds wanted to watch. Their appetite for top level action was every bit as keen as that of the Europeans – and they had been obliged to wait an extra five years since the War to see any. Hence capacity crowds were at every venue to watch and assess living legends like Bleddyn Williams, Angus Black, Jackie Kyle, Roy John and Gordon Rimmer.

On the trains of the day refreshments were not served, and the Lions disembarked at selected stations to eat off trestle tables set up on platforms. Local farmers noted the tour schedule, and would leave livestock behind to journey from the hills by tractor or horseback. Unfailingly they were delighted to find that the Lions were very approachable – 'matey' – and willingly signed autographs.

As has often been the experience of touring sides in New Zealand the run of success hit the buffers at Dunedin. Otago is where All Black rucking was born, and bravely though the Lions forwards competed the new technique baffled them. The Province's coaches, notably Vic Kavanagh, had carefully analysed what happened at tackle situations and how to exploit it. Essentially, they had developed the idea that a tackled ball-carrier went to ground and immediately placed the ball on the turf. The role of advancing team-mates was to bind tightly to form a loose equivalent of a set scrum, engaging any opponents in their way. The object then was to surge powerfully and in unison over the ball, not necessarily touching it with a foot. The opposition was thus brushed aside, often ending up on their backs in disarray after a manoeuvre carried out ruthlessly without pity. Grateful scrum halves – or half backs, as New Zealand calls them – found possession under their noses with all the time and space needed to use it profitably.

A story wonderfully told by Brian Price, a Lion sixteen years later, indicates how long it took the northern hemisphere to respond to rucking. It seems that Ken – D.K. – Jones announced to team-mates before the 1966 game against Otago that he had discovered how to nullify the technique – it boiled down to a special way of falling when tackled with the ball. Team mates watched hopefully when their hero raced onto early possession before being put on the ground by his opposite number. It was the Province's back row, however, which next arrived on the loose ball, immediately initiating a ruck. And Ken bach? "He looked like a pair of pyjamas whirling round in a washing-machine," was Big Brian's recall.

So the fury of Otago's pack and its rucking decided the outcome, spearheaded by a front row comprising three men who had toured South Africa the previous year with four fellow-tourists in other positions plus six All Blacks of a different vintage. A 23-9 defeat was administered to the shell-shocked tourists, for whom Kyle scored a single try against three by Otago. A crucial moment for the Brits came at ten minutes, when Bleddyn Williams injured a leg. He stayed on the field for the remainder of the game, but the Lions' attacking machine was obviously disrupted, as was the selection process for the first Test the following Saturday, for which the centre was unavailable. Happily the injury was muscular, not a recurrence of the ligament problem, and Williams recovered before very long.

The Otago game, viewed as a Test trial, had been a wake-up call to the Lions, but their gloom deepened at a midweek defeat by Southland at Invercargill. Eight of the Test side had to play, indicating the length of the tourists' injury list, but only seven came through safely. Full back George Norton broke an arm in the second half, which brought to an end his usefulness and paved the way for 'utility' back Cleaver to step into his boots in three Tests. 'Utility' was a term introduced to sport by baseballers in the United States for a versatile team member. In wartime Britain it had meant something that was not in the luxury category and boasted no frills. Cleaver, I guess, did not mind the term.

In mid-May the utility back heard from Cardiff that he had indeed been elected captain for the club's 1950-51 season. Given the position in which he found himself he could not afford to agonise over the news, but he did worry about the feasibility of serving both Club and Coal Board. Remarkably, he refused to allow career anxiety to affect his form, and was duly named at full back for the first Test, one of six Welshmen in a team that read: Cleaver, Ken Jones, Jack Matthews, Ivor Preece, Ranald Macdonald, Jackie Kyle, A.W. Black, John Robins, Karl Mullen (capt), Tom Clifford, Don Hayward, Roy John, Bill McKay, R.T. Evans and Peter Kininmonth. Dai Gent cabled the *Western Mail* to report that Lewis Jones had been sent for as Norton's replacement.

The All Blacks, meanwhile were spitting blood. The post-War

era had begun catastrophically for them with a 0-4 whitewash in the latest Test series against the nation which was their arch-opponent – South Africa. In his book *Rugby's Greatest Rivalry* (1996) Paul Dobson says:

> In 1949 the All Blacks came to South Africa with high hopes, regarded in New Zealand as a great side. White-washed and bitter... the tourists went back to their islands to seeth and nurse their wrath, feeding it and developing it into a powerful force, ready to be unleashed.

Two considerations had steeled New Zealand's ambition before they arrived on the veldt. One was the painful memory that the Springboks had won the last series in their country, in 1937, whereas the All Blacks had yet to win in the Republic. The second was memories of the Kiwis who had enjoyed such huge success in the UK during 1945-46. Half a dozen of those proven winners, including skipper Fred Allen, went to South Africa full of confidence – which was cruelly dashed. In *100 Years of All Black Rugby* Chester and McMillan use more temperate language than Dobson, claiming that the series could easily have been drawn, or even won 3-1.

For the record the Test defeats were 11-15 (Cape Town), 6-12 (Johannesburg), 3-9 (Durban) and 8-11 (Port Elizabeth). On their return home at the end of September the tourists were given an official state welcome and cocktail reception, but they knew that the public's general verdict on them was, 'Must Try Harder'.

All candidates for Test selection against the Lions took a few weeks off before going into highly-committed and intensive training through the six months leading up to 27 May 1950. By that day the evidence suggests that informed critics in New Zealand favoured a home win. The British Isles had begun brightly, it was felt, before falling to top-class Provincial opposi-tion. History, too, was on the All Blacks' side: in eight previous encounters the British had won only once. Moreover, the present tourists had six players unavailable for selection through injury.

There is some evidence that the All Blacks players, too, felt, if not complacent, extremely confident about the outcome in front of 35,000 fans at Carisbrook Park, Dunedin. They were undoubtedly rocked by J.D. Robins' early penalty (though he was later narrowly wide with two or three kickable chances), and every time the Lions' three quarters were able to run possession the New Zealand back division went to panic stations.

There was more of the same as the second half got under way, with Kyle foxing Bob Scott and 'Brownie' Cherrington on his way to a brilliant unconverted try. 6-0 behind, the All Black giant at last stirred, with Beatty and Roper combining for the latter to cross for an unconverted try. Then the Lions restored their six point margin when Ken Jones accelerated sensationally in pursuit of Black's diagonal kick to beat full back Scott to the corner flag. Clifford was now place-kicking, no more successfully than Robins; but even at 9-3 the Lions were still two scores ahead.

New Zealand dug deep to close the gap with a dominant display in the final quarter. Until then Scott had earned cat-calls from the South Islanders – 'Go back to Auckland' they hollered as he missed with drop goal attempts and the occasional place kick. Now, from thirty-five yards' range he put over a penalty that encouraged his side to launch a blistering final offensive. From a scrum on the visitors' line the formidable New Zealand captain Ron Elvidge stormed through three tackles near the corner to tie the scores. Scott missed the conversion but, as he later remarked, he was glad he did so – "The British Isles deserved the game".

From then on the Lions prowled successfully around the regions of New Zealand, winning every provincial game including one against the Maoris but losing the next three Tests. This depressing hat-trick of reverses began in the leafy suburbs of Christchurch where the All Blacks went 8-0 up in half an hour. The damage was done by Pat Crowley, who dived beneath the tourists' second row for a first, unconverted, try and soon afterwards by Roper who got possession on the wing after the Lions' defenders had been perfectly drawn one by one and scorched the final ten yards for a try converted by Haig.

In between the two winning All Black scores the Lions lost fast-moving flanker Bill McKay who had been carried to the touchline unconscious after suffering a crack on the head. In days before replacements were allowed this was a major setback, but the gallant fourteen rallied energetically and, say the reports, more than held their own. Kyle broke the home defence with astonishing acceleration in the second half which could have yielded a big dividend had not the sheer audacity of his running left his team-mates out of range of a scoring pass. This and other vigorous attacks were put in despite a revealing statistic: New Zealand won forty-six line outs to twenty five. The reality now was that, while the home side was getting its act together and players were rediscovering belief in themselves, the tourists were injury-ridden and beginning to be travel-weary. Only victories in the last two Tests could win them the series.

Besides visiting a farm where they saw a sheep with five legs the Lions made an immediate impression upon North Island, notably at Gisborne. Here the bad news was that Lane and Dai Davies were injured, Lane seriously, in the clash with an East Coast XV, while the good news concerned a 27-3 win in which Lewis Jones made his debut. He played well within himself, which was sensible considering that he had flown into Auckland only the previous day. After injuring a shoulder in the first game of the tour Rees Stephens came back for this match, too late alas to mount a serious challenge for a Test place, while skipper-for-the-day Jack Matthews was the man who orchestrated the victory. For much of his career he was ever-so-slightly in the shadow of his fellow-centre Williams; but the New Zealanders, who love a hard man, rated him very highly indeed. Newly-retired Fred Allen, busy learning how to watch a game analytically before plunging into the coaching business, named Dr Jack as "the greatest head-on tackler I ever saw":

> The secret of his success at this most difficult of all the tack-les was his surging acceleration into the victim's body. He went rather high, aiming about the stomach or the short ribs, and so avoided trouble with the runner's knees which are

usually the daunting obstacle to front-on tackles. His acceleration deprived the ball-carrier of any chance to fend him
off. It was thrilling to watch this technique so well displayed.

The 12-6 victory over Wellington that came next was clear-
cut, the Lions running in four tries against one plus a penalty
goal by their opponents. Ken Jones (who was injured later in the
game and could not play in the Third Test) went in for one try,
Jim McCarthy crossed for another, but this particular afternoon
belonged to Bleddyn Williams, who got two. Since praise of
Doctor Jack has been recorded it is worth including a cameo
impression of his partner. What follows was written by Dai Gent,
himself a midfield back:

> At a scrum 30 yards out the tourists gave a clean heel to
> Rimmer, who missed out Kyle and sent the ball straight to
> the advancing Williams. Directly in front of him were three
> defenders, and as he approached them he had 25 yards to
> go. Now, as I have often seen him do, he squared his shoul-
> ders, tossed his head back, and accelerated through this
> bunch of opponents for a fine try.

Those who read such lines nod, musing, 'Just like Barry' or
'Jonathan could go like that' or 'Mmm. Watkins'. A rare gift, from
a golden seam of magical Welsh midfield players.

However, still dogged by injuries the brilliant Lions back division was again shackled by New Zealand, losing the Third Test,
and hence the rubber, by 6-3. It did not help that Mullen was
unavailable for, well though Dai Davies performed, a touring
side desperately needs its captain. A selection that seems to have
failed saw Roy John at number eight, where he had not played at
International level. His build, height and line-out capability were
not in question; just his positional play.

This game is memorable for the heroic contribution of New
Zealand's captain Elvidge, who returned to the fray after treatment with an eyebrow stitched and his chest badly bruised. It
was he who broke a threatened 3-3 deadlock and grabbed an
unconverted winning try.

It was about this time that Billy Cleaver learned that the amount of time he had spent away from his managerial post at Newbridge broke regulations. Accordingly his job had been given by the NCB to another manager. As a married man with a growing family, Cleaver decided that he could not risk any further damage to his career prospects and sadly wrote to Cardiff RFC saying that his job must come first. He would not, after all, be able to accept the captaincy and was retiring from the game. He was just twenty-eight years of age; the decision was a drastic one; and it is interesting to speculate whether a chat with the NCB's personnel department before making up his mind might have paid a dividend by permitting him one more season. Cardiff's reaction was 'shock', and the club's – somewhat reactionary – historian Danny Davies expressed no sympathy for Cleaver's dilemma in his *History*. But the stand off would be welcomed back to Cardiff Arms Park one last time when he turned out in the autumn of 1951 for a Lions team which beat Cardiff 14-12 in a 75th anniversary celebration game. Cleaver was scrum half to Jackie Kyle.

There now followed six wins in succession at various North Island venues, climaxing at Eden Park. The 32-9 victory over Auckland pleased the Lions no end in the light of the Test displays the opposing captain, Crowley, had been giving at open side flanker. It was one of four matches in which twenty points or more were run up. Undeniably a side which knows it cannot win a rubber is likely to experience a mood of resignation and, more significant, relaxation which allowed free, even abandoned, play of a very high standard. Capacity crowds lapped up the entertainment.

At the same venue on 29 July there followed the last Test of the series in New Zealand, which was by all accounts a thriller. With nothing to salvage except pride, the Lions clearly gave it their all. Adjustments made to the team affected the front row, where Cliff Davies and the Scot Grahame Budge came in at the expense of Clifford and Robins. Roy John reverted to lock, squeezing out Don Hayward, while Kininmonth was restored to

the middle of the back row. Behind the scrum Willis was introduced at scrum half, Lane replaced Malcolm Thomas and young
Lewis Jones was selected at full back instead of Cleaver. Given
his career problem it may be that at last, within himself, Cleaver
was out of sorts.

What 60,000 spectators at Eden Park saw that afternoon was
called by the All Black captain Peter Johnstone the most exciting
match he had ever played in. It is interesting that with Mullen still
injured Bleddyn Williams continued to lead the tourists, and he
recalls that "we took every risk and tried every ruse". At
Wellington, heavy rain and a soggy, slippery pitch had robbed the
Third Test of speed and sure-footed action; but on this final day
good conditions allowed the Cardiff midfielder to exercise a liber-
ating influence on the game and get the Lions playing his way. It
would be another two years before Wales would benefit from him
as leader: the Cavalier, perhaps, to Gwilliam's Roundhead.

New Zealand took the lead after a rousing foot-rush finished
with a touch-down by Wilson which Scott converted. Before half
time the full back had also dropped a goal, the Lions' only reply
being a penalty goal by Lewis Jones: 3-8 to the All Blacks at half
time with the British Isles down but emphatically not out.
Bleddyn Williams had nearly crossed twice: first he was charged
into a corner flag in the act of scoring by a posse of defenders;
and later Roy John galloped through a host of tacklers and gave
the skipper a scoring pass, only for Peter Henderson to speed in
and crunch him to the ground just short of the line. It was the
same Henderson whose second half try put his team just out of
reach and sparked a stupendous final quarter's attacking Rugby
by the tourists. It contained one of the finest tries the game had
ever seen, celebrated enthusiastically by the *Weekly News* Rugby
Correspondent on 2 August:

> Kyle took the pass and out it went to second five eighth; but
> in place of Bleddyn Williams Lewis Jones took the transfer
> right before his own posts. A neat but audacious side-step to
> his left – and he had made his gap. Into top gear in an
> instant, the brilliant youngster raced downfield glancing to

his right to see if Ken Jones was in position – he was.
Approaching [New Zealand full back] Scott, Lewis Jones
slowed ever so slightly to make sure of his pass... but was
very careful and floated an upward ball to Ken Jones. Away
went the latter from the All Black ten-yard line with
Henderson and Roper in full cry behind him. How the
crowd roared madly as Ken Jones brought the goal-line ever-
nearer with his terrific speed. There was no doubt about it:
if ever there was a great try, this was it.

There were Maoris to play, and two Tests to play in Australia,
but in the memory of many Lions that 8-11 defeat was the
climax of their tour, leaving a pleasant afterglow Down Under.
Writing in 1984 the New Zealand historians Chester and
McMillan said that the tourists of 1950 remained one of the
most popular sides ever to have toured their country. Tribute is
paid to their exemplary conduct and the attractive nature of the
game they played. But: "the team lacked the forward power to
contain the All Black pack".

In his autobiography Bob Scott goes into more detail:

> The application to tight play by our forwards, the utter reck-
> lessness with which they made their runs, their charges into
> the rucks and their falling on the ball gave us a good head
> start. Our men got down lower... they used their weight
> more efficiently, their style was more virile... only at
> Auckland did the British Isles forwards really approach the
> All Black standard.

Beginning in 1950, those are characteristics which, with a
blip or two, have enabled New Zealand and her small population
to be a dominant force in world Rugby. In that year the tourists
from Britain were blitzed by a forward style in which All Black
players subsumed virtuoso ambitions to the ideal of an all-
enveloping unity – the 'black blanket' – with huge forward
momentum born of correct body-angles. Forwards therefore are
cogs in a supreme machine-tool; with one or two exceptions backs
are efficient finishers of tactical opportunities created for them.

What follows from this is that when their country is visited by
tour squads which include masters of creative back play New

Zealand fans' enjoyment of the game experiences a new dimension. No particular ambitions are harboured to mimic Welsh
back divisions or French flair; but when they witness it such
alternative Rugby is enjoyed and applauded by all. Even hard
cases like Colin Meads will shake hands vigorously, and
graciously, with fifteen free spirits who prove themselves a better
side than his.

The Lions defeated a Maori XV in the last game before their
move to Australia. Here, with Rugby Union still a peripheral
sport, the tourists won five matches including two Tests before
going down to New South Wales in their very last serious game.
The 1950 Lions had earned their languid homeward voyage
across the Indian Ocean after laying their bodies on the line in
the southern hemisphere. They stopped off for a fun game at
Colombo, capital of the island once known as Ceylon and now
called Sri Lanka. Billy Cleaver ran the line, and was asked at the
close what the final score was. "Lions forty four, Ceylon three",
he replied, "but a draw would have been a fairer result".

Then it was onwards on board the *Strathnavar* to complete a
circumnavigation of the world. As they lounged in the boat deck
sunshine, Welsh members of the party could reassure themselves
that even in defeat the back division and its lining of gold had
shimmered magically in the wintry sunshine. There had been
Bleddyn Williams's unfailing eye for openings, Matthews's cast-
iron defence, the searing and sustained speed of Ken Jones,
Malcolm Thomas's all-round brilliance, the tactical astuteness of
Willis and Cleaver, seasoned with Lewis Jones's amazing antics.

What, they wondered, might have been the impact of the two
outstanding men who did not travel. In the Test series New
Zealand's total of points was 34; the Lions scored 20. Surely
Gwilliam and Cale between them would have done more than
merely close the gap?

NINE

The 1950 British Isles party got back to Europe on 7 October. When their disembarkation was delayed a little Ken Jones, Newport's captain for the new season, R.T. Evans, his vice captain, and team-mate Malcolm Thomas persuaded the *Strathnaver*'s radio room to pick up commentary from Rodney Parade on the first of their club's traditional four clashes per season with Cardiff. On air was G.V. Wynne Jones, describing the damage Black and Amber stand off half Roy Burnett was doing to the Cardiff defence, and explaining to listeners that five of the visitors' top players were still at sea with the returning British Lions. After the third such apologia – from a commentator who was a member of the Cardiff club! – R.T. remarked to Ken Jones, "When is he going to say that Newport's captain, vice captain, plus Malcolm Thomas are on the same ship?" Never mind: their team won 8-3, and they knew only too certainly that they were back in familiar climes full of local rivalries.

Although the tourists had lost the series in New Zealand, knowledgeable supporters felt that they had given a good account of themselves. The Welsh input had been immense and now, at successive railway stations across South Wales, crowds who had bought platform tickets thronged to welcome their thirteen heroes back to the homeland (including John Robins, who intended visiting his parents in Cardiff before returning to Birkenhead). In the days that followed, great clubs and small villages alike feted their representatives at special ceremonies. Lewis Jones remembers being presented with a fountain pen by Gorseinon Council – carefully chosen, for at that time any gift deemed too expensive by the Welsh Rugby Union would have professionalised him (prematurely, that is).

Spurred by youth's insatiable appetite for activity, National Servicemen Jones and Malcolm Thomas were quickly back on duty at Plymouth and in the Devonport Services' line-up, while the Newport men re-appeared at Rodney Parade on 21 October. At Cardiff, where Cleaver was no longer on the books, lock forward Bill Tamplin had been chosen as replacement captain. The club's other Lions rested up until 4 November and the home game against Bridgend, when the Arms Park regulars extended cordial greetings to their four stars. Contrast the latters' freedom of choice, as amateurs, with the speed at which the professionals of 2001 were bundled back into stern league competition following their stressful tour of Australia.

Exactly a week after the Lions' arrival at Tilbury John and Pegi Gwilliam were celebrating the arrival of their first child at Glenalmond. Catherine's birthday is not readily forgotten by the family, since 14 October was a Saturday and she was born at 3.40 pm exactly – at the interval, recalls her father. Perhaps it was during a half-term trip to Monmouth and Llanelli for the baby to be introduced to her grandparents that Gwilliam came across members of his Wales team who had been Down Under, and listened to what they had to pass on about the New Zealand game. He and Able Seaman Lewis Jones, who had chosen to play for the Scarlets when on leave, would doubtless have enjoyed a chin-wag, for it appears that the skipper enjoyed the teenager's company and the freshness which he exuded. At any rate, Gwilliam certainly wanted to hear about the harsh lessons that had been learned Down Under.

As far as general team play was concerned, for instance, information about 'rucking' was valuable. Both backs and forwards needed to study this brand-new and highly efficient method of recycling possession from tackle situations which had taken the 1950 Lions by surprise. Gwilliam also learned about "a tendency to obstruct in midfield... sometimes accidental but very difficult for a referee to spot". Certainly running at an angle to the ball-carrier by a decoy player has become commonplace in the last twenty years, and refereeing has met its challenge. Now, if the latter player moves in front of the former, the side in possession does not receive the benefit of the doubt; instead the referee blows for "crossing" and penalises the attackers.

Other insight brought back by the tourists concerned the line out move used against the tourists by New Zealand on their own throw. As the ball came in the two props drove forward, converging in a protective wedge on the far side of their jumper and spoiling the other side's capacity to compete for the ball. This too has been made illegal by the rulers of the game.

But perhaps the most important tidings that men like prop John Robins could bring to Gwilliam concerned the new approach employed by New Zealand's forwards at scrums. The All Blacks themselves, it will be remembered, had been shunted all over the field by South Africa's forwards a year earlier. To their credit, they had pocketed their pride and taken advice from the great Springbok mentor Danie Craven who cultivated a friendly relationship with the tourists and even travelled occasionally on their team coach. Since the Lions' visit to the Republic in 1938, think-tanks had been hyper-active on the veldt, with particular attention being paid to the scrummage. As a result, consigning '3-2-3' to history, the 'Boks had adopted a 3-4-1 format, which required key players to push in new ways. Notably, the binding of the front row had become more elastic, with the props pushing straight ahead and giving a wiry hooker space for profitable contortions of his frame. The responsibility for maintaining the props' alignment was then delegated to the flankers. It was essential for both to push inwards in order that the scrum should not disintegrate. This posture had additional benefits: it protected the scrum half from harassment by his opposite number and flankers, while when South Africa's back row forwards broke they were one stride, at least, nearer to the enemy half backs. Also, the number eight – in those days the great Hennie Muller – could afford to play a much looser game, supporting his backs more closely in attack and threatening the opposition more immediately in defence.

New Zealand had been won over to this method of packing at set scrums and several of her provincial sides used it against the Lions. Having shared the shattering experience at the sharp end in South Africa, Test hooker Evelyn Catley took the new scrummaging into a fresh dimension. Before opponents' put-in, he had mastered the art of withdrawing his arm from the loose head prop's back until, technically, he was not binding. Now he could so twist his body as to get his feet as close to the ball as those of the opposing hooker, and was often able to strike successfully against the head. As one who played three Tests in the Lions' front row Robins could describe these antics vividly to John Gwilliam. Any doubts the latter may have harboured about 3-4-1, non-binding hookers and – most importantly 'rucking' – were brushed aside when a 'White' pack led by him in one of the WRU's autumn Trials was taken apart by a Reds side containing six forwards who had been with the Lions.

On tour Robins does not remember the Lions totally abandoning 3-2-3, and its occasional 3-3-2 variant, which had been used at the scrummage in Britain since the game's early formalisation. However, having reached home the players must have enthused about 3-4-1 and the Catley method, for the new gospel they preached was acted upon, first by their clubs and not long afterwards by Europe's national XVs. Advised and tutored by Robins, Birkenhead Park took to it keenly. So did an up-and-coming England hooker at nearby Sale called Eric Evans who shrewdly calculated the beneficial effect it would have on both his club's game and his own. The reaction of John Gwilliam, too, was positive.

But before long there was a domestic Championship to be contested, with a Triple Crown and Grand Slam the targets again. John Gwilliam was one of thirteen members of the all-conquering 1950 side who would again be available for selection, with Rees Stephens and Bleddyn Williams waiting impatiently in the wings.

The autumn of 1950 was windy and extremely wet, conditions in which it is never pleasurable to play Rugby. Without the resting Lions the club scene in Wales was anaemic; nor was there a major touring side in the UK that year to beef up the season. Hence the media needed to be more than usually inventive to keep readers and listeners happy. J.B.G. Thomas launched a slightly artificial *Western Mail* debate about the captaincy between 'the Gwilliam style' and the approach of Bleddyn Williams, now perceived as a challenger for the captaincy after leading the Lions capably when Mullen was injured. J.B.G. hypothesised that Gwilliam discouraged his backs to attack until the opposition 25 had been reached, whereas Bleddyn was of the 'attack from anywhere' school. But bearing in mind that during 1950 a free spirit like Lewis Jones had managed to contrive spectacular tries from long range under each captain their standpoints could not have been all that far apart.

Another lobby, with the *News Chronicle's* Reg Pelling at its head, wondered why the Welsh selectors persevered with Trials, suggesting instead that club form was a more reliable and consistent guide to players' cap claims. Often the pre-Christmas season included two or even three such Trials, which polarised opinion among the candidates. The young bloods' aim was to make a big impression on the selectors at any cost, while established players needed only slight headaches to withdraw lest their reputations should be tarnished, unnecessarily in their opinion. As a result the first two pre-Christmas Trials invariably required re-shuffles and adjustments. In fairness to the selectors of the day it should be remembered that there was little or no television coverage at this time, let alone sophisticated VCR capability whereby the performances of a wide number of contenders could be put under scrutiny and assessed. Trials, then, were a necessary inconvenience. And they drew big crowds.

However, assuming that key men could hit their good form of the previous season the selectors' task that spring did not seem unduly onerous. Shaping a back division might have been a more complex task had Bleddyn Williams remained available, but his bad luck in his own country continued with an injury which kept him out of the first two Five Nations games. The team named by the Big Five to play England at Swansea was that which had won in Paris the previous year, with Glyn Davies and Llanelli's Peter Evans in for the retired Cleaver and the departed Cale.

January 20 1951 was, of course, one of Welsh Rugby's 22-carat days. People said afterwards that the England side had to be one of the worst they had ever fielded; but that is unfair to the visitors' ten new caps who found themselves thrown in against giants of the game (especially as the experienced Kendall-Carpenter, given the captaincy, had to withdraw before the kick-off). At the end of the day Wales had won a fifth consecutive game, her 23-5 win building a points difference of 73 against 13.

Not for the first time it was Jack Matthews who demoralised the opposition with the power of physical contact. Early on the Doctor decided to test the mettle of new England cap Lionel Oakley, his opposite number, by offering himself as a sitting duck. The Englishman went in for the crash tackle; Matthews shielded the ball, bracing himself for the impact. "Then" wrote Peter Moss in the *Mirror*, "Oakley disintegrated as a breaker shatters on a sea wall."

But the visitors kept defending bravely, despite leaking two scores. Shining this time in attack, Matthews careered through defenders left floundering behind his outside burst for a try converted by Lewis Jones. One would-be tackler who failed to regain his feet after the score was England scrum half Gordon Rimmer. Mindful of his medical ethics Matthews gave him a quick, friendly consultation before heading back to the Welsh half. Nice gesture – and Rimmer returned to the field after attention on the touchline. The next try was set up by Glyn Davies, whose break was built on by Peter and R.T. Evans with help from Cliff Davies, and when the ball was worked to the Welsh left Malcolm Thomas took possession, put his head back and covered an estimated seventy yards to the England line. At half time the Welsh lead was 8-0.

Eye-witnesses concur that the second half belonged to Lewis Jones. Two glorious breaks by him soon created a try for Ken Jones followed by a second for Matthews – this was when a touch judge waiting to flag the conversion, famously heard one of the visitors ask despairingly, "This man's made of iron – how are we expected to stop him?" Jones's personal *piece de resistance* was saved for the final quarter when the young maestro intercepted an English pass in his 25 and set off on a sixty-yard sprint which brought the packed grandstand to its feet. As always his fellow Devonport Serviceman Malcolm Thomas was perfectly positioned for the scoring pass. Rimmer made England's consolation try with a long pass which sent in Rittson-Thomas.

Now the superlatives were tossed like confetti onto the home team. "Superbly directed by Gwilliam the Welsh forwards went from strength to strength," wrote H.L.V. Day in the *Sunday Chronicle*. "Scintillating," said one billboard. "Magnificent," screamed a headline. "A glorious Welsh scoring spree," wrote Rugby historian John Griffiths in his *Book of English International Rugby*, though other English historians like U.A. Titley and O.L. Owen deem only the score-line worth a mention (so it must indeed have hurt). But in the *Daily Express* Pat Marshall left readers in no doubt of Wales' quality, dwelling interestingly on a new ingredient that was becoming an essential ingredient of successful international Rugby – continuity:

> Whenever a Welshman was tackled he flipped the ball back with never a hindward glance – there was always a man at hand to carry on the movement. If a Welshman missed a tackle, which was rare, a team-mate would cover him... that was the difference between the two sides: England were fifteen individuals, Wales a team. England lacked leadership and a big personality; Wales had John Gwilliam – the leader, the tactician, the master.

This had evidently been the kind of Rugby Wales had been expecting, and expected, to play since the First Golden Era before World War I. Supporters approved, selectors tried hard not to claim too much praise, players walked on air. Now to unseat the Murrayfield bogy.

A general theme in amid all the euphoria was that Cilfynydd-born Glyn Davies had at last come of age as a midfield general and would now use the game in Edinburgh to make the stand off half position his own rather than appearing as an alternative to Cleaver. He had been a nearly-man for a number of seasons since playing in a 'Victory International' with his teenage scrum half partner Wynford – no relation – while still a sixth former at Pontypridd

County School. As a small spectator at Cardiff High School's Harlequins ground I remember seeing the two of them taking our First XV apart 21-3 in 1945, with the eighteen-year-old Glyn Davies quite unstoppable. Bleddyn Williams once said that "Glyn should have joined Cardiff RFC as soon as he left Cambridge – we'd have looked after him". Then he paused and added thoughtfully, "Hm. Then we wouldn't have had Cliff Morgan".

Young Davies had enjoyed mixed fortunes in Edinburgh. A remarkable 22-8 Welsh win there in 1947 prompted J.B.G. Thomas to write of him:

> Here is another Willie Davies: a clean, straight runner whose thrustful incisions could not be sealed by Scotland... his success fully justified the selectors' trust and gave birth to what might prove to be a new era in Welsh midfield play.

Then came the 1949 season when Davies evidently reached great heights in a win over England only to encounter a Scottish back row at Murrayfield which had targeted him and Tanner, a skipper who was by now in his Rugby dotage. The sheep farmer Douglas Elliott, in particular, subjected Davies to huge tackles throughout, leading critics to suggest that the stand off had been ill-served by his captain. At all events, he was dropped, missing the great 1950 season, but now reclaimed the number six jersey (as it then was) for the 1951 game against England after Cleaver's retirement. On form, it is clear that he could create critical space in the midfield for hard runners like Matthews, who needed only half a yard to get behind defenders.

The Welsh mood was noisily confident, with an estimated 20,000 supporters on the sidelines. As spectators poured into the great stadium their bulk swept away the main gates and turn-stiles, making the final attendance figure hard to determine. Scottish estimates put it at 75,000, Welsh statistician John Billot quotes 81,000 – a record for British Rugby – while Scotland's hooker on the day Norman Mair thinks that it could have been as high as 90,000. At all events, Murrayfield was a cauldron just waiting to reach boiling point as the teams followed by referee

M.J. Dowling of Ireland took the field.

For their part, the Scots were feeling hard-done-by and cheat-ed after a 13 January defeat at Colombes. Tom Gray, they believed, had kicked a penalty which in all likelihood would have won the game by a point only for their own touch judge, Wilson Shaw, to disallow it because the sun was in his eyes. Impatient after their long lay-off, during which Wales had conquered England, they would take the field as snarling under-dogs who could not wait to sink their teeth into the visitors. Before a quarter of an hour had gone by the referee had twice called up the packs at scrums, issu-ing a severe warning the second time to John Gwilliam and his men. At half time the Scottish lead was a slender 3-0, and it seems that Welsh enterprise had won the crowd's praise. There was an air of expectancy as the second half began, as if it was only a matter of time before the floodgates were opened.

They were – but not by the favourites. The man who turned the tide was Scotland's captain Peter Kininmonth, who had played three Tests in New Zealand the previous summer. He it was, not a nimble-booted stand off half or a full back who, kicked with aplomb, but a back row forward, who had the nerve to drop one of the most outrageous goals in International Rugby's eighty-year history from which Wales simply could not recover. Canny Scots supporters were not as surprised as the remainder of the Rugby world, being aware that Kininmonth's formative seasons in the game at Sedbergh School were spent as a full back or in the midfield where he was known as a reliable kicker from the hand. Not until he came to work in London and joined Richmond was he moved to the back five of the pack, proceed-ing to win his Blue at number eight.

At Murrayfield, he seized the chance that arose when Welsh full back Gerwyn Williams, a left footed kicker, missed touch on the grandstand side with his weaker right foot. Kininmonth had time to steady himself before – 'almost casually', say reports – swinging the foot that sent the ball over the bar from forty yards' range. It was a huge blow to Welsh confidence, and at regular intervals through the remainder of the match the vistors defence was pierced for thirteen more points including three tries. In the end Scotland were rampant; their supporters delirious.

Though Norman Mair was on three losing sides that season, and never played subsequently for Scotland, he had the consolation of figuring as hooker in one of the greatest upsets of a Rugby Union applecart. He admits that Kininmonth's masterstroke convinced the home side that they could and would win; but he also believes that on the day they were far superior: faster and surer onto the ball and physically more intimidating. John Gwilliam's view is: "Before, and possibly after, the game Wales were a better side; but in the interim – that is, when it counted – Scotland were the more spirited team, which gained confidence as the game progressed while we deteriorated." Mair, who had played local Rugby with and against John Gwilliam in Edinburgh and had a very high regard for his captaincy, concurs. In the second half he remembers the Welsh captain going up and down the line outs trying to rouse his men, but for once even he could draw no response. His forwards' fire had gone out.

The other crucial area of the game was at half back and featured the ruthless gunning-down of Glyn Davies. The undisputed champion of Swansea was being hunted – again – at Murrayfield – by Scotland's open side flanker Douglas Elliott, who Bleddyn Williams says could have swung the 1950 tour in the Lions' favour had not farming commitments kept him at home. Elliott was giving the Pontypridd man, still a slight 23-year-old, a grievous afternoon in days when the back row could break early and there were no touch judges to flag slightly late tackles. As the second half progressed Gwilliam switched Davies to the centre and brought Lewis Jones to stand off half, a move which drew heavy criticism from partisan critics in east Wales who perceived it as a defeatist tactical adjustment which, they said, accelerated Welsh demoralisation. Today Gwilliam dismisses the point, just stating tersely, "Glyn's mobility was affected – he'd had one big bump too many". It was an injury which caused Davies to limp out of International Rugby.

The morning after was almost as bad in some respects than

the match itself. The captain went back to Glenalmond after the match where, doubtless, the reception was polite even to the point of sympathy. His team and the camp followers retreated sadly southwards, some of them on excursion trains that were muted and gloomy, others via the main A6 road which preceded today's M6. This route, which climbed steadily and often steeply between Penrith and Tebay to cross the mountains, was the one used on the Sunday morning by John Robins and a friend heading back towards Merseyside in the former's sports car. They decided to stop for coffee at the cafe which stood at the road's highest point. Recalls the prop with a wry smile:

> I only wish we hadn't. On entering the place we at once realised that a whole crowd of Welsh supporters had chosen to break their journey there as well. Inevitably, I was recognised, and the whole room fell silent. I just wished the floor would open up and swallow me.

But domiciled outside Wales Robins, along with the skipper, was spared the white heat of the post-mortem that kept tongues wagging furiously back home. It is fair to say that the Rugby community was traumatised. J.B.G. Thomas later wrote that in the corridors of power the selectors were haunted for a full twelve months as they sought to account for their side's fall from grace. Half a century on the Gwilliam perspective – from the heart of the action – seems as good as any: the Welsh had an off day while Scotland touched sublime heights. Rugby can be as simple as that.

What can be stated as a matter of fact is that the Big Five identified not one but three fall guys, who turned out to be Glyn Davies, Lewis Jones and the flanker Allen Forward. Though dropped for the next game against Ireland the latter two came back in due course. But at just 23, with eleven caps to his name, Glyn Davies's day was done: huge promise, already fulfilling itself, was cruelly rebuffed. In retrospect it was probably his further bad luck that Cliff Morgan was now judged ripe enough for International Rugby and was about to enjoy a very good debut.

The selectors' tactic at the time, however, was glaringly short-termist. Thoughtful people wondered why on earth Davies had been encouraged during over half a decade as Cleaver's successor if he was to be discarded at the first suspicion of fallibility.

Their selection for the match against Ireland at Cardiff evidenced other knee-jerk reactions by the Big Five. Having axed Lewis Jones they needed a place kicker to take the long-range attempts which were out of Robins's range. So, moving Roy John to the back row, where he had shown in New Zealand that he was ill at ease, they capped the massive Newport lock Ben Edwards. He obligingly slotted the second-minute goal which was just enough to get a draw for Wales by matching Kyle's unconverted try, a result which meant that Ireland were champions, just missing a third post-War Triple Crown. The selectors showed their gratitude by dropping Edwards for the final game at Colombes, when John was moved back to the second row. Sadly, Edwards remained a one-cap wonder.

The other absentee in Paris was John Gwilliam, omitted after seven games in charge of the Welsh side, of which five had been won, one drawn and one lost. It was the sort of record with which later captains might have been well satisfied, but evidently the Big Five expected their skipper-in-exile to deliver success every time they parachuted him in. As it was, under Rees Stephens Wales went down to only their fourth defeat by France. Looking on was Bleddyn Williams, also dropped after the Irish game, who recalls tersely, "Our men were no match for the speedier French second half offensive."

Gwilliam took his omission on the chin, and can even smile about it fifty years on as he recalls a charity match near Bristol which featured a number of Welshmen. They included himself and his hooker of the last two international seasons, Dai Davies, a Somerset Police officer but born at Penygraig. Davies, already nearly changed into his playing kit, glanced up as the tall forward entered the changing room. "Aha," he announced. "Here comes the Fallen Angel." Says Gwilliam: "A great example of the traditional humour, and nonconformist make-up, of the Rhondda!"

The golden era was dulled a little, then, at the close of the 1951 Five Nations campaign. To the captain, however, being demoted and apparently side-lined indefinitely was not the chilling circumstance it would be in, say, 2001 when lucrative match fees were at stake. Further, he had come to savour the Glenalmond ambience, and there was a small daughter to enjoy. Summer was an attractive season in the fresh air out on the Scottish moors. There was more time available for dipping into his favourite historian Lecky's eight volumes of English history. All in all, any well-balanced – amateur – person would not be particularly impatient for autumn to arrive bringing with it the resumption of Rugby commitments.

And yet... the season which September would usher in would bring a huge challenge mounted by the mighty Springboks, set to tour in the UK for the first time in two decades. The prospect of tangling with them would set the blood racing again, especially as South Africa had won their three previous matches against Wales. A first challenge for John Gwilliam would be the reclaiming of a place in the National XV, preferably as captain. And if he managed that, could he beat South Africa? And then lead Wales to a ninth Triple Crown? And another Grand Slam?

TEN

In the autumn of 1951 the Fourth Springboks reached Wales after two pipe-opening games on England's south coast. This first incursion would comprise three games, beginning at Pontypool and ending at Llanelli five days later with a first appearance at the Arms Park against Cardiff to be sandwiched in between on Saturday, 20 October. As a member of the School First XV squad at the time I joined sixth form Rugby players from all over the city for a coffee function at the Park Hotel (now known as the Thistle) attended by five members of the South African tour party who circulated and conversed pleasantly with their wide-eyed young guests. They told us about their country, and spoke of their attitude to the Rugby game.

Rather like the American military personnel with whose presence small boys had become familiar when they were based here before D-Day, the South Africans struck me as physically bigger and healthier-looking than the British, certainly the Welsh. The group we met (whose names now escape me) were without exception well over the six foot mark – tall for those days – and the shape and size of their upper-bodies were emphasised by the cut of the dark green blazers which they wore. These were trimmed with bright yellow braid to replicate the fashion common in British grammar schools of the day. The other point about their appearance concerns the tourists' browned skin. Those were days before Brits dashed down to Spain to collect a quick tan or could darken their complexions out of a bottle. To me these South African players looked unusually well-fed, brimming with virility.

It is, of course, the case that their country had not been directly menaced in World War II and did not know food rationing. The South African Sixth Division served with distinction in the Western Desert under Auchinleck and Montgomery; but it seems that the Republic's way of life was not particularly troubled by the deadly struggle going on along Africa's Mediterranean coast and further north in Europe. However, identifying opponents who might provide the Springboks with Test-standard opposition was impossible, so that South Africa had gone from the Lions' visit of 1938 to 1949 and the inward tour by New Zealand without playing serious Rugby at International level. Their 4-0 whitewash of the All Blacks in the latter year thus delighted and surprised them.

But now the Springboks faced a tour of Britain, Ireland and France, the first to be undertaken since 1932 when all the Tests had been won. News coming back to Wales indicated that the thoroughness of South Africa's preparations defied belief. The build-up had begun at the University of Cape Town, where no fewer than 129 players were accommodated for a week-long series of Trials. These arduous games ended on 14 July when a thirty-strong touring party was announced. Managed by Frank Mellish, coached by Danie Craven and captained by Basil Kenyon it was to play thirty-one games, of which the last four would be in France. Some South Africans regretted that the fixture-list did not include Tests against an all-British side such as the touring Lions. Afterwards they were relieved that it had not.

Wales was certainly the deep end. As scrum half of the Third Springboks two decades earlier Danie Craven recalled that although his side was strong and successful Welsh clubs had been among the very hardest opponents encountered. A Heads of the Valleys fixture against Abertillery & Cross Keys found the big boys from the southern hemisphere pushed to the brink before escaping with a 10-9 success. In 1951 a Pontypool & Newbridge combination could not set so severe a test; but the tourists did suffer damage at Pontypool Park when skipper Basil Kenyon took a knock from an opponent's elbow at the edge of his right eye. The retina was detached and before October was out the burly sheep farmer had been advised by a London specialist not to play any contact sport again if he wished to save his sight. Kenyon took the sensible decision. Hennie Muller assumed the captaincy.

Muller bemoaned the loss – partly because he admitted that he did not like the captaincy job. But, more important, he said at the time that the heavy turf in the UK seemed to suit Kenyon and the inspirational Rugby he was playing would be sorely missed. The Springbok players understood how Muller felt and seamlessly transferred their loyalty to him.

The tourists ground their way to victory at Pontypool Park watched by a task force from Cardiff. The latter held a final training session next day, Friday, on the eve of their club's game against South Africa. In no way were these men – or this club – fazed by the prospect of meeting the mighty Springboks. South Africa had won at Cardiff Arms Park in 1912 and 1931, but in 1906 an inspired Gwyn Nicholls had devastated the visitors' defence on New Year's Day in a memorable Blue and Black victory by 17-0, which remained until recent times the biggest losing margin ever suffered, anywhere, by South Africa.

The Cardiff XV named on the eve of the 1951 match was among the strongest in its history. Every member of the back division had been or would be capped, in addition to six of the forwards. Collins was one of the two odd men out, the other being Arthur Hull who was to win acclaim by rejoining the pack for the second half after spending the interval having damaged ribs attended to. Six of the team had been in New Zealand with the Lions, while the fast-developing Cliff Morgan was well into his second season as Billy Cleaver's successor. Despite this galaxy of talent a series of injuries to key players meant that four defeats had been suffered in the first seven weeks of the season, by Neath, Aberavon, a British Lions XV (in the 75th anniversary romp which featured Cleaver) and the Wasps. Nevertheless the now injury-free XV which would represent Cardiff in this fixture was formidable.

South Africa's selection was close to a Test side. Muller, Lategan and Brewis had starred against the 1949 All Blacks. There had been much hard thinking about the kicking options and the composition of the front row, for prop Aaron 'Okey' Geffin was rated among the best place kickers ever to represent his country. But that responsibility was given to 21-year old full back Johnny Buchler, and Bekker went in at loose head.

The visitors' evident quality, and post-War successes, had quickly built interest in the tour to a stupendous level. Everybody was talking about them, everybody wanted to see them play, and even practice: they themselves were open-minded and interested parties were allowed along the touch-lines to watch training sessions. How good were they, people wondered? Forwards like Allen Forward and Don Hayward, who had been in the XV beaten at Pontypool Park, were pressed for comment by the media.

Partly this fascination was down to the Springboks' rarity value. The post-War Australian tourists were not in world Rugby's Premiership. By the autumn of 1951, therefore, sixteen years had elapsed since the last tour of Britain by a major Rugby power, the 1935 New Zealanders. Association Football had been quick to resume a variety of overseas fixtures after the War, and a World Cup tournament was staged in 1950. There had been the London Olympiad. Don Bradman brought a world-beating squad of cricketers to the UK in 1948. In contrast, Rugby Football had been relatively slow in getting its act together. Here, at last, was curtain up.

Another factor was South Africa's record of dominance. Their entry onto the International sporting stage, as learners, had taken place as early as 1891, only for progress to be inter-rupted by the Boer War and its aftermath. Once they had begun touring regularly and participating in Test series their playing record quickly nosed ahead of the seven major rivals – the Home Countries, France and the southern hemisphere Dominions. Of forty-seven Test matches played up to 1949 (against both indi-vidual nations and the British Isles) they had lost only nine, winning thirty-three and drawing the remaining five. The chal-lenge they presented in Wales was a huge one.

These were the kind of reasons why 53,000 spectators crammed the Arms Park to watch Cardiff RFC – a mere club side, if a very special one – take on the acknowledged pace-setters of Test Rugby. Although Cardiff's anniversary season had not begun in all-conquering style, the pre-match feeling around the city was that the Blue and Blacks were in with a chance. These tourists might be hugely efficient and physically formidable; but when the chips were down could they contain the home side's superlative back-line? First impressions suggested that their own play behind the scrum might be technically correct while lacking vision. If Cardiff did not yield kicks at goal to Buchler how would the Springboks score enough points to win the game?

Any South African who was on the field or in the crowd that day finds that final question – put retrospectively – a difficult one to deal with. "The Springboks marvelled that they ever managed to win," wrote Chris Greyvenstein in his *Springbok Rugby*, published in 1995. "They lost the scrums 18-26 and line-outs 15-18. Fifteen penalties were awarded against them compared with nine against Cardiff. With one minute to go Cardiff were in the lead at 9-8. The crowd had begun singing them home."

On a still afternoon the drama had begun in the first minute when the wing 'Chum' Ochse pulled down Cardiff's captain Jack Matthews inches from a score. Some minutes later came an incident which, almost certainly, affected the course of the game. Dr Jack was involved again, charging down a clearance from the visitors' scrum half Oelofse and falling on the ball over South Africa's line. The referee, Mr Joynson of Caerleon ruled a knock-on and gave the tourists a drop-out 25, a decision which would have been correct in previous years. But under a law change made during the close season, a player could now escape being called back for a knock-on if this occurred when charging down a kick. The referee was, categorically, wrong. It would scarcely be in order to suggest that an event so early in the match cost Cardiff a victory, but it left them feeling frustrated and undermined.

The other factor which affected the outcome was the off-day experienced by the home team's place kicker Bill Tamplin who missed with five penalty shots at goal and a conversion attempt. *The South African Rugby Annual* commented tersely, "Had Cardiff taken full advantage of the 15 penalties awarded them they must have won."

Tamplin did kick two penalties, but was unable to convert the single try conjured up by the home team's backs on the half hour. It manifested the creativity for which Welsh backs were noted until the 1980s, being direct and clever but not complex. From a scrum Alun Thomas came infield off his wing to check the Springbok back row momentarily before spinning a perfect pass that forced Cliff Morgan to engage top gear and reach out for the ball. Matthews was the next handler who, as he was challenged, fed co-centre Bleddyn Williams at his elbow to deceive van Schoor and dive in for a memorable score. For South Africa Ochse had got a first try, converted by Buchler, and in due course an unconverted try by Oelofse (whose charge-down of Morgan's attempted clearance replicated the earlier, disallowed, effort by Matthews) cut Cardiff's lead to 9-8.

This, then, was how things stood with eighty minutes up and South Africa living on borrowed time. At a line out on the Springbok right, Muller asked the referee how much extra time he would play. From stand off half Brewis overheard Mr Joynson reply that this would be the final set-piece of the game. "Get me the ball, whatever happens," he screamed at Muller. The Springbok pack obliged. Cardiff historian Danny Davies witnessed what followed from close range:

> Brewis now kicked sharply towards the left corner flag. The position to me, as touch judge on the opposite side of the field, did not appear to be dangerous. But the South African left wing J.K. Ochse had taken off like a bomb to follow up the kick he expected, and Alun Thomas had to turn awkwardly and chase him. From a position in front of our posts Trott could now be seen trying desperately to cut off Ochse, but he lacked speed and the South African scored the try and ensured victory for his side to the immense relief of his team and officials.
>
> It has been stated that [the Manager] Mr Mellish got through fifty cigarettes during the match... but he acknowledged that the Springboks were a trifle lucky. Later in the season the visitors presented the club with a Springbok head as a sporting gesture to the best losers on tour.

Sad Cardiff. But historian Greyvenstein paid the Welshmen a tremendous compliment when he wrote that the victory was one of the "veritable Everests in South African Rugby history". They certainly deserved to conquer this peak for, remember, they scored three tries to one.

The Springboks beat Llanelli 20-11 before moving out of Wales and heading north. Apart from a quick dart back to beat Aberavon and Neath 22-0 they would not return to the Principality until December, and their absence was keenly felt by the admirers they had made across South Wales. Internal affairs were re-focussed upon by the Welsh media, the *South Wales Argus* leading the way with a spicy revelation about Lewis Jones. It seems that the gifted youngster, still only twenty-one years of age, had accepted the managership of a new luxury coach firm based at Newport. Would he turn out for the Black and Ambers? Newport RFC said that if he wanted to join the club "he would have to make a formal application which would be considered by the committee in the usual way". Lewis Jones was quoted as saying that "as far as possible he would try to play with Llanelli" (his National Service at Devonport having now been completed).

Compensation for the disappointed Uskside club was the assurance by the powerful centre Malcolm Thomas that he had turned down a £5,000 offer to turn professional. Leeds Rugby League side had made an approach, but Thomas had refused to talk business with them. He was duly named at centre for the Probables in the WRU's First Trial at Abertillery Park on 10 November. His side was packed with Welsh 'greats' – but so were the 'Possibles'. Lewis Jones and Bleddyn Williams were paired at centre. John Robins was at loose-head. Clem Thomas, capped in 1949 at twenty years of age and then discarded, was a flanker. J.A. Gwilliam (Edinburgh Wanderers) was named at number eight and thereby challenged to win back his place in the Wales XV plus the captaincy. The Probables' Rees Stephens needed to look out.

Before travelling to Wales to box his corner John Gwilliam had been kept busy by Scottish involvements. In conditions described as 'arctic', North of Scotland went down to the Springboks on 29 November by just 14-3. This was, to put it diplomatically, considerably better than the performance of their national XV the previous Saturday, whose margin of defeat in the Test was 44-0, staggering for those days and still a huge differential today. The score-line, including nine tries, possibly triggered what has become an old chestnut down the years, with the Scottish fans telling their taxi driver on the way home from Murrayfield, "Aye, and we were damn lucky to get the nil".

In the North's pack at Aberdeen all the reports say that the Welsh guest was 'an outstanding leader', sharing the home team's honours with its scrum half W.D. Allardyce. *The Bulletin* and *Scots Pictorial* reported that the North played very good 'wet ball' Rugby and were ultimately beaten as much by their opponents' stamina as any marked superiority in skill. A.C. Parker of the *Cape Argus* observed how superior had been the tackling of the regional side compared with Murrayfield, speculating that the presence of Gwilliam had influenced the markedly improved performance of the regional XV. The demoted Welsh captain headed for the Abertillery Park Trial of 10 November with his tail up.

The old authority was still there; the brilliance at the lines out; and the willingness to risk an occasional unorthodoxy. The Welsh selectors liked what they saw and Gwilliam was restored to the Reds and the captaincy for the 8 December Final Trial, which duly produced the required result. It did not follow from this, however, that the debate over selection was clear-cut, since a number of men in several positions had hit a streak of form at the same time. Given Gwilliam's obvious fitness and commitment, what to do then with Neath's authoritative Rees Stephens? OK: pair him with Roy John in the second row. But brawny Don Hayward had been playing there. Right: move the Newbridge man up to prop to partner Swansea's Billy 'Stoker' Williams, another six-footer. Partly the vital statistics of this front row, in which Dai Davies would hook, was in order to match, and hopefully subdue, opponents perceived to be a cornerstone of Springbok dominance.

The props who had occupied the front row through a not unsuccessful period were thus sidelined. Cliff Davies was, in any case, close to retirement and would not come back; nor did he play for Cardiff after this particular season. The omission of John Robins (after a last-minute eight from nine decision) was a harder bullet to bite on, especially following a Lions tour when he had seen off New Zealand's best props. Technically expert, however, he did not possess the physique the selectors thought desirable at this particular time. Interestingly, he declined to throw in his International towel and although drawing a blank in 1952 was to make three further appearances for Wales in 1953.

The pack was completed by the selection of Allen Forward and Len Blyth on the flanks. The latter scorned the day off traditionally enjoyed by a man about to win his first cap, and led Swansea in the club's epic game with the tourists on 15 December. He nearly paid the penalty, spending ten minutes off the field having an injury attended to in a game which was narrowly lost. One of the two loose forwards, it has to be said, might have given way to R.T. Evans had the Newport flanker not suffered an injury on 3 November which ended his career. Two tacklers fell awkwardly across his knee; a cruciate ligament was ruptured; medicine then was not what it is today; and this great hunter-killer, who would have matched Muller's marauding instincts in the Test, had to call it a day.

Behind the scrum the form shown by Bleddyn Williams, for once enjoying spell of injury-free Rugby, had been welcomed by the selectors. He was inked in at centre alongside Malcolm Thomas, while after some procrastination Lewis Jones was given the left wing berth and Ken Jones the other side. Gerwyn Williams would be the full back; but after five seasons loyal service and seventeen caps there was no place for Jack Matthews. The 'iron doctor' had played his last representative Rugby, but enjoyed a couple more winters with Cardiff RFC before moving into retirement – and, it should be added, serving the game in Wales in numerous non-combatant roles.

The chosen side looked a good one. Besides solidity and

maturity it contained youthful get-up-and-go. Some of the backs possessed qualities amounting to genius. There was every chance that the colours of the mighty visitors could be lowered in a game hyped as the "World Championship play-off". The newspapers reported that fifteen shilling tickets (£0.75p) were on sale from the touts at £10 each.

The South African team which took the field for a 2.45 kick-off showed one change from that which had beaten Ireland, Barnard coming into the second row for Dinkelmann. At open-side flanker was a man who had become a great favourite of the crowds, readily identifiable for his shiny bald scalp and predatory ambitions in the back row. Johannes Christiaan van Wyk – nick-named 'Basie' – had hit tremendous form as the tour progressed and, packing down in the back row with Fry and Muller, more or less made up for the loss of Basil Kenyon.

However, just as it had been Osler who piloted the Third Springboks to success, so again in 1951 South Africa's key man was at stand off half. This time the name was Brewis, known to his team-mates as Hannes. Nervous of the strike power of the Welsh backs the tourists had decided to play a total forward game in which South Africa would rarely move the ball outside the opposition 25. Brewis's line kicks took his forwards unfailingly up the touch lines despite his being constantly in the sights of Allen Forward and Len Blyth, while it was also the dropped goal by him which clinched the result.

However, far from being a battle which the Springboks could win comfortably the forward clash was unending and immense. With neither of the two eights willing to give ground, it evolved into a kind of stalemate, which nevertheless managed to be enthralling – rather as a boxing match can bring ringside crowds to their feet when all finesse is abandoned by two opponents who just hit each other hard and often in desperation for a victory. But at Cardiff Arms Park on 22 December 1951 there were no knock-down blows until the first half was almost at an end. By this juncture at least one South African onlooker has written that the visitors were "starved of possession". If that is true, it seems that the Springbok game plan, which assumed supremacy at forward, had gone awry.

For it implies that Brewis's tactics were committing his forwards to a doomed tussle with a Welsh pack who were playing out of their skins. Every time he found touch, opponents Roy John and Gwilliam would gain possession off the resultant Welsh throw. If South Africa won a throw, with one of their forwards taking the ball the chances were that the home team's vigour and aggression would turn the possession into a maul, from which clean ball could not be guaranteed.

It was somewhat against the run of play, then, that a second try of the tour at Cardiff by 'Chum' Ochse made sure that Wales would trail at half time. First, his forwards won a set scrum deep in Welsh territory where for the first time in the game Brewis ran with the ball, wrong-footing Cliff Morgan and causing Bleddyn Williams to check his stride. Lategan came to accept possession at top speed, immediately turning the Welsh defence and drawing the sprinter-wing Ken Jones in from the touch-line. A lofted pass finally found Ochse in just enough space near the left touchline to justify going for the flag rather than swinging the ball blindly back inside. With Jones and full back Gerwyn Williams clinging to him the wing just made the touch-down.

Maybe the occasion got to Okey Geffin, for he could not convert on a still afternoon and had already missed three first half penalty attempts, one of them from a mere thirty yards. Unfortunately for Wales chances were also missed by Lewis Jones. Nevertheless the 55,000 spectators, who included an estimated 1,000 tour-followers, well knew at the interval as the sides huddled and sucked their oranges that the game could go either way. Three times beaten in three matches against South Africa during the first half of the century, could the home side reverse a negative trend?

Alas for Wales, the second half mirrored features from the first forty minutes. Scrum half Du Toit and his partner Brewis continued to plug the touchlines and, the great Hennie Muller has written, "It is my considered opinion that had we tried to move the ball through our three quarters we would have lost the match by a fair number of points. This would have played right into the hands of the Welsh backs."

It became more and more clear that South Africa were unlikely to score a second try, and Brewis spent the final quarter of the game trying to drop a goal that would wrap things up. He was tantalisingly close with one shot before, with some ten minutes left, he sighted the posts from thirty yards' range and hit a climbing kick that dropped just inside an upright. 6-0, with full-time approaching fast.

Wales played the second half where they left off after the first forty minutes – at full pelt, with Cliff Morgan sending the Springboks to panic stations with a blind-side break that saw the defence melt away with the exception of full back Buchler. His deflection of the young stand off's attempted chip ahead undoubtedly prevented a try.

But the home side came good in the seventy-eighth minute with a score the Springboks remembered – especially skipper Muller:

> They won a line out just inside our half and the ball reached the strong-running Bleddyn Williams, who beat me and Ryk van Schoor hands down by turning and working a scissors with Malcolm Thomas. I had cut across very fast and sat down on my haunches as the centres changed direction. Except for our full back the line was wide open and Thomas, drawing his tackle, put Williams over for a splendid try ten yards in from the corner flag.

That was the end of the scoring, for a straightforward conversion attempt by Lewis Jones missed narrowly and very soon after the re-start Irish referee N.H. Lambert ended the game. The world title had stayed in the southern hemisphere.

No sooner had the players trudged wearily up the tunnel than the post-mortems began – in the pubs and clubs surrounding Cardiff Arms Park, in clubhouses and, most rigorously, in the Press box. Here the scribes and their acolytes began trying to make sense of what had happened down on the pitch. The script had suggested that although the Welsh forwards might have to give best their backs would win the day in brilliant fashion. Of the thirty participants out on the field, not one appeared to have learned his lines.

Not only did the Welsh forwards dominate the exchanges, they were stronger and fitter in the final moments. The much-vaunted back division, however, ensured that the day would be lost. South Africa scored a memorable and matchless try which the veteran centre Rhys Gabe, by now a Pressbox critic, said was made by Lategan helped by the shadow tackling of his opponents.

And then there was the display of Cliff Morgan.

In his third International the Tonyrefail-bred stand off half had decided on a kicking game, based on the old Cleaver capability so valued by John Gwilliam. In his third International match and aged just twenty one, he tried his hardest – only to be thwarted by an equally inexperienced South African full back. Johnny Buchler chose this December day to achieve maturity.

Morgan is probably bored to tears with discussing his form that day and confirming, initially to journalists and later to historians, that the tactical game he opted for was flawed by kicking that was less than International class. If he grub-kicked past the South African midfield the bounce favoured Buchler; if his kick was high-trajectory and diagonal it drifted infield for the visitors' full back to gather and punish Wales with touch-finders that travelled twenty, thirty and even forty yards upfield. In other words, the Springboks were not being put under pressure – or if they were their full back was lifting it. The Welsh midfield were only too aware of what was going on and were hugely frustrated.

Fifty years on, however, the balance can be re-dressed a little. In his book *Tot Siens to Test Rugby* – not widely circulated in the British Isles – the late Hennie Muller revealed how the Welsh threat was nullified by the close targeting of their half backs by South Africa's back row:

> Stephen Fry marked Rex Willis, easily the best scrum half
> we played against on tour... van Wyk and I tore down onto

Morgan, Basie on the inside with me on the outside ready to swing towards the inside centre if he passed out. Not unnaturally the young stand off half looked for damage limitation, and at both line outs and scrums began to stand directly behind Willis and the pack in order to gain the maximum protection.

In fact, Morgan was in a cleft-stick. He could not use the ball to set his line moving; if he did choose to pass out he had to stand still rather than challenge the two world-class loose forwards bent on cutting him down. Therefore he took the kicking option, hurriedly and without variation. Buchler seemed magnetised as the ball repeatedly came to him, firing it consistently back over the heads of the advancing Welsh attackers. In the *Daily Mail* Roy McKelvie wrote, "Buchler missed touch only once in a match of over sixty line outs."

Morgan denies that he was under orders to kick, saying that it was his decision to do so. The question arises, however: when it was perceived that his approach was not working why did helpful advice not materialise from senior players nearby – including John Gwilliam, who very well recognised the importance of quick ball reaching the midfield? Bleddyn Williams thought that if Wales' three quarter line was given fast, clean ball from the half backs huge problems could be caused to the visitors' three quarters. Why therefore did not one or both of the two veterans instruct the youngster to move the ball into space – even from a standing start? And why did Wales not use her back row to vary tactics and halt the marauding of the Springbok loose forwards?

Sadly, however, and slowly the passion subsided in Wales, who had still to beat South Africa in a Test match. The tourists went on to win their final twelve games of their tour (including the defeat of Newport), returning to Cardiff to beat the Barbarians 17-3 in the second of what were becoming exceedingly popular 'farewell' games.

They left a Europe that was slightly stunned by this reminder of how well-drilled southern hemisphere sides could visit the British Isles (and fast-improving France) and consistently come out on top. This Springbok invasion had resulted in a 5-0 Test record in their favour. They were an attritional team, who scored after subduing opponents (which the great Welsh sides of the seventies also did). But, even disregarding the sad events at Murrayfield, the Fourth Springboks rank among the most dangerous sides to come here. Some of my (senior) media friends still say that they were the best tourists of the twentieth century. On that I reserve judgement. However, they had a certain capacity to survive – soaking up pressure, appearing to be on the ropes, and then suddenly contriving the moments that won matches.

A couple of years after this I played a number of games at Oxford under Paul Johnstone who had arrived there on a Rhodes Scholarship and become the University's captain of Rugby. It was my good fortune to enjoy close contact with this expert and elusive wing three quarter (who also appeared at stand of half for South Africa). I had been reasonably well-drilled in Wales; but even compared with that, Johnstone's version of the Rugby he wanted his Blue team to play was chock full of unimagined insight into the minutiae of the game.

It would be another quarter of a century before the Europeans, led by France, could match such comprehension and begin mounting a serious challenge to the men from the Veldt. As for Wales, not until 1999 was a first-ever win scored against South Africa.

But meanwhile, the Five Nations tournament of 1952 lay in waiting. What did it have in store for the Welsh? Another Murrayfield? Or 1950 all over again?

ELEVEN

Rhys Gabe had been one of Gwyn Nicholls's legendary heroes who took away the 1905 All Blacks' unbeaten record. A master at Howard Gardens High School, after retirement from active Rugby he was in demand from sports editors and was able to to blend some freelance writing with his classroom labours. Readers of the *Western Mail* in particular looked forward to his Monday morning comments on the big match of the weekend. He did not waste words, and when sternness was needed could readily supply that.

So the headline above his short essay after the match against South Africa was an imperative: "Pick this Welsh team v England", it commanded. Although Gabe was critical of the backs' tactics (and the kicking by both sides that dominated play) he was full of praise for the "heroic" Welsh forwards: "they matched their heavier opponents for toughness and fitness and called the tune as the game drew to a close". The selectors acknowledged this vote of confidence by the veteran. With the England game still four weeks away they speedily named an unchanged team for it.

Thus the two men moved up from the second row to meet the 'Boks pack retained their places at prop. In their day W.O. 'Stoker' Williams and Don Hayward were dubbed 'jumbo' forwards, and indeed both were taller and heavier than contemporaries John Robins and Cliff Davies. Their pairing in the game against South Africa had been an inspired selection, for they were key components of a pack which more than held its own. But was not the front row a place where experience and technique were all-important? Surely, by repeating a one-off experiment the Big Five were perpetuating a huge gamble.

Fifty years later John Gwilliam effectively laughed off the idea that the two front row men suffered by lacking technical expertise: "They were big, enormously powerful forwards who pushed their weight and refused to give ground. In their case that was all that was needed." However, 'Stoker', now moving robustly through his

151

seventies, says: "The skipper hasn't got it quite right. I cannot remember whether he knew this, but when it was announced that I was being converted to the front row Cliff Davies was so concerned that he rang me up and arranged to call in at St Helen's to give me a crash-course in propping. That's when I learned all about 'boring in' and 'dropping' and how to get my head under an opponent's neck. That was definitely technique!"

As for the late Don Hayward, I was lucky enough to meet him on a trip to New Zealand in 1984. A railway engineer, he had switched to Rugby League, emigrated to play Down Under, and became a butcher when he retired running a shop in the heart of Wellington. In the company of a film crew I chatted with him about life – and Rugby – in the southern hemisphere. What I remember most vividly was the sheer size of his forearms as he cut into joints of beef; they were as thick as an average man's shins. His hands, too, were enormous, just made for ripping possession out of the middle of a maul.

Although Twickenham's chief Bogy had been unseated two years earlier a private hobgoblin still troubled Bleddyn Williams. At the Herne Hill run-out on the eve of the match against England the great centre succumbed to a dose of flu, mild yet bad enough for him conscientiously to withdraw in favour of a fully fit replacement. Williams had played for Wales at 'HQ' in 1948 but thenceforth in a career which lasted until 1955 he missed every game there for one reason or another. In 1952 he was doomed to be a reluctant onlooker in the grandstand.

Not for the first time the five selectors were now guilty of a palpable *faux pas*. In London as midfield reserve was the experienced but as yet uncapped Alun Thomas, once of Swansea but by now with Cardiff. Before his regrettably early death Thomas specifically recalled in the company of friends how he was advised on the Friday evening that he would play in Williams's place. By the Saturday morning, however, rumours were circulating in the camp that Jack Matthews had been telephoned in Cardiff the night before and told to get an early night, catch the 8.30 am train to Paddington and get himself to Twickenham.

The following morning, unbelievably, Thomas was excluded from the team talk. Not until half an hour before kick-off was his selection confirmed to him – round about the time that Matthews, fresh from the train, was being told that he was not wanted after all. The good doctor was (and still is) livid about his treatment, and half a century later still remembers the egg on five faces.

The stakes were high as referee Lambert of Ireland started this first game of the 1952 campaign for each nation at 2.30 pm in front of 73,000 spectators. Only outright victory would allow one of the two to go forward in search of a Triple Crown and the Grand Slam. Would England succumb for a fourth year running to Welsh determination? Indeed, could the home team improve on a record that had featured only two Five Nations wins in the last two seasons. On the other hand, in a stadium which John Gwilliam says the Welsh find "dark and menacing" could the invaders manage to reproduce their South African form against the *Saison?*

Scarcely had the action got under way, in a slight breeze and on turf that was treacherously slippery in parts, than the visitors suffered a major setback. Chasing a loose ball left wing Lewis Jones suddenly pulled up at what he called an "excruciating" stab of pain in his thigh. Helping him to the touchline trainer Ray Lewis diagnosed a pulled muscle. Making the damage bearable would present a huge challenge to Mr 'magic fingers', while to hold the fort without the wing was a mighty challenge to the fourteen men left on the field.

On the day, even the Jones boy himself would have been at full stretch to fend off England's burly wing Ted Woodward. As it was poor Len Blyth, taken out of the pack to cover Wales' left flank, was on a hiding to nothing faced with an opponent who was a sprint champion despite weighing fifteen stones. Inside the first twenty minutes the High Wycombe butcher had been responsible for two tries.

First he had run cleverly onto a nifty chip ahead from Lew Cannell which turned the Welsh defence. When challenged he found the other England centre on his elbow, the dependable Albert Agar, whom he sent racing in for an unconverted try.

Twickenham's faithful were still congratulating themselves when Woodward struck again, this time on the end of an orthodox three quarter movement. He had ample space to out-flank Blyth before brushing aside full back Gerwyn Williams to score his team's second – unconverted – try at the flag. At 6-0 up England were building a threatening lead, and Welsh depression deepened when Gwilliam suffered a crack on his knee which needed attention and caused him to limp for a few minutes. Then, suddenly, the re-entry into the fray of Lewis Jones, thigh heavily strapped, was a flicker of light at the end of what had seemed to be a very long tunnel. Until the skipper could establish what his wing could, and could not, do as a result of the injury Blyth was left to support him near the touch-line.

This was daring captaincy, since many people who were at the game or in it recall that for the first quarter the Welsh pack was on the ropes. Both England's tries had come from possession won at the line out where locks Matthews and Wilkins, well supported by Kendall-Carpenter, were in the ascendant. But now Wales' skipper built on the surge in morale which followed the wing's return with an outburst of torrid words which suddenly whipped his seven-man pack to a fury.

Maybe, from a few yards away, Cliff Morgan heard the clarion call, for he chose this moment to turn the game, and thereby come of age in world Rugby.

Still only twenty-one the Rhondda youngster carried with him awareness of great Welsh stand off halves who had preceded him. He knew about old-timers like Bush and Bowcott. He had watched and been excited by the style of Cliff Jones, who came from a nearby hillside above the Valley. He knew that he could not be the same kind of player half as Cleaver. He clung to the hope, however, that he could approach the class of the man he still thinks (in 2002) was the best stand off half he ever saw – his immediate predecessor in the Welsh XV, Glyn Davies. Incidentally, one of his beliefs is that good handling is not exactly about hands, however 'soft', but feet and balance. Twinkle-toes, that is. Work it out.

On this day, 19 January 1952, Cliff Morgan decided that he, too, would be numbered among these men. The situation called for immediate action to wipe out a disturbing deficit. An extra percentage of effort was needed to compensate for the team-mate who was carrying an injury. Most important, the composure and machine-like functioning of the English had to be disturbed by something clear-cut, cunning, and Celtic, to force them onto the back foot.

What encouraged Morgan was that he was under a captain who would tolerate the risk. He had first come into contact with John Gwilliam in a fixture Cardiff RFC played at Grange Road against Cambridge. From subsequent Trials and run-outs he had found that:

> As a captain on the field John was always talking, changing directions and tactics. Thus even behind the scrum you became aware of him as an encouraging Presence. He would back you to the hilt if you tried out something imaginative. He did so himself from time to time, for instance with that amazing spin pass from the set-piece which could reach the outside centre... he talked to his men as if we were pupils. Well, perhaps we were!

Morgan's main attacking weapon was an astonishing burst of speed over an initial fifteen yards. Now, as the Twickenham encounter moved into its second quarter, he took off, checking the England back row near the Welsh 25 before accelerating away from Lew Cannell and the veteran N.M. Hall into clear space. Agar soon crowded him from the right as he approached Hook, but the ever-alert Ken Jones had veered sharply infield so that he was now on Morgan's left. Here, just after crossing half way, he took the decisive pass with no Englishman in front of him. Frantic defenders were still menacing from the rear and sides, and the Newport Express needed every last ounce of his Olympic pace to go beneath the bar for a memorable try – created and finished by two of the fastest men Rugby Football has known. Malcolm Thomas converted, and from looking like a one-horse race the game was anybody's once more.

As the second half opened the seven Welsh forwards took another battering as England sought to retrieve momentum and re-take the initiative. Once more a tactical decision by Gwilliam was an inspired one: as if to suggest that, back to full strength, his pack would be more than a match for their opponents he brought back Blyth from the wing. Accompanying this was the decision to confine the play, as far as possible, to the Welsh left, thus minimising the exposure to risk of Lewis Jones.

But it was a totally unexpected intervention by the limping wing that put Wales ahead for the first and final time. Out of the blue he came infield to arrive on Cliff Morgan's elbow, receiving a pass thirty yards from the English line. Here there came just enough suggestion of a dummy to check the defenders – had Jones been kidding them? Would he, could he, make a break? The indecision was just enough for the two Thomases in midfield to take and move possession to right wing Ken Jones. He, too, showed finesse as he cut inside Winn and outside Hook to score at the flag. Since the conversion attempt failed Wales' lead was contained at two points, and the pressure was still very much upon them, since any kind of score by England would have wiped out so slender a lead. There were still thirty minutes to go; the opposition remained full of heart and capable of winning the game.

But Wales, too, still had petrol in the tank, and John Gwilliam fondly remembers even his props Williams and Hayward raising a gallop in midfield – and even leaving him stranded in their wake as he called for a pass. Once the pair caught England's scrum half Gordon Rimmer in midfield, ruthlessly dispossessing him as he writhed in their embrace. But as the game moved into injury time with his side still training 6-8 it was Rimmer who came closest to thwarting the visitors with a burst down the right touchline and a well-aimed cross kick that fell just short of the Welsh line close to the posts. Stands and terraces erupted as bath's Alec Lewis seized the bounce and swooped in to touch down at the posts. Gwilliam recalls how his head sank in dejection. "Well," he told himself, "that's it. No Grand Slam. No more International Rugby for John Gwilliam. The captain bites the dust."

Then, as the home supporters' cheers turned to groans, he looked up – to realise with vast relief that Mr Lambert's whistle had gone, not for a try, but against Lewis for being offside. Malcolm Thomas was given the kick which, from an awkward position beneath the Welsh crossbar, he thumped up to the ten-yard line. Moments later another blast on the whistle ended the game, and for the second time in successive visits Wales had won at HQ. Another quest for the Grand Slam had opened in stirring style.

Writing nearly twenty years later Ken Jones, whose two tries sealed the victory, could still vividly recall Gwilliam's leadership in-put, especially through the seemingly endless second half:

> He never stopped bullying, cajoling, pleading and praising until our pack was so fired-up that it would have taken sledgehammers to subdue them... determinedly as 'Squire' Wilkins, Bob Stirling and Don White fought they could not dominate a magnificent eight led by the finest of post-War Welsh captains.

Not for the first time Gwilliam had re-kindled Welsh fire to scorch the doughtiest of opponents. Only at Murrayfield had his entreaties failed to rally his men to stave off defeat.

Rhys Gabe's mature viewpoint was quoted at the start of this chapter. Let us cap it with the verdict of Gwilliam's predecessor as captain, the equally distinguished Haydn Tanner from the era before and after World War II. Gabe had advised the Welsh selectors to stay with the side that had so nearly undone South Africa; now Tanner added his weighty opinion in a Monday morning column accompanying J.B.G.'s match report on the defeat of England:

> This victory was as good as any that has been gained by a Welsh XV. To succeed at Twickenham is enough in itself, but to win with virtually fourteen men after being six points in arrears was great work... I feel I must mention the two prop forwards, Hayward and Billy Williams. These two were always in the thick of the fray and were continually forcing their way through the English defence from the loose mauls.

These words are doubly significant coming from one who was beyond doubt a match-winner but must often have felt, both before the War and afterwards that the sides led by him suffered from forward play which may have been totally committed but was short on unity and direction. What he witnessed at Twickenham, we may surmise, was the result of lessons learned by the four members of the Welsh pack who, together with their scrum half Willis, had been in New Zealand eighteen months earlier. These had now been thoroughly digested and put to use against the Springboks as part of a concerted and highly effective approach.

A modern reader can be forgiven for scepticism about the sustained finishing power now being displayed by the Welsh. The Grand Slam of 1950 had included wins of 11-5, 12-0 and 6-3 before the clinching 21-0 victory over France. But did these victories, plus the latest 8-6 defeat of England, deserve 'Golden Era' status as some journalists were beginning to accord the Gwilliam years? The answer, I would argue, is Yes. Not all the scores and victory margins are gigantic, but that is because of totally different circumstances and the nature of the game in 1952.

First, in days before the Australian Dispensation Law, it was not too difficult for a side that was having a hard time to close a game down and stem opponents' momentum through non-stop touch-finders (as indeed the Springboks had done under pressure in Cardiff). Second, defenders could lie right up on a side that was winning constant possession and engulf its attacking backs. Tries counted only three points.

And fourthly, adding the bonus points for a conversion could not be guaranteed – these pages have already shown how even the best kickers of the day like Geffin, Hook and Lewis Jones found the heavy balls difficult to score with from long range.

The Gowerton star's injured hamstring did not mend well enough in the weeks that followed to allow Lewis Jones to be considered for the game with Scotland at Cardiff. Bleddyn Williams, however, had recovered his place at centre with Alun

Thomas moving out to the left wing. Otherwise the players were those who had vanquished England and the fans, though they remembered all too well the previous season's disaster at Murrayfield, bought tickets like hot cakes. A year ago they had streamed back southwards full of gloom; Twickenham suggested that 1952 would bring a different outcome. The sweet scent of revenge was in the air.

'Stoker' Williams, who did his National Service in the Navy, had never met a tank commander before. But by now, having played twice under John Gwilliam he was familiar with his virtues at close range. These started with the power and thrust that invariably came up through the scrum from the back five, and were enhanced by the heights that the skipper reached at the line out. Further, like his team-mates, the prop had become aware of Gwilliam's religious principles. At an eve-of-International run-out he remembers letting fly some strong language, far from unusual in forward exchanges. Immediately the captain took him a few yards distant from the practice maul.

Here, just out of earshot of team mates he smacked a large fist into his large palm. "That I can do without," he snapped. "No more, got it?" 'Stoker' meekly acquiesced. Front row forwards are nurtured and shaped in a hard school whose earthy outbursts and invective have been seasoned with short, colourful words. But if the skipper thought that its vocabulary was not appropriate to the top echelon of this gentlemen's sport, then so be it. 'Stoker' would curb his tongue. "Gwilliam ran the show," he recalls half a century later. "I was prepared to go along with that. He had my respect. I did not want to be at odds with him."

But he still wonders whether the captain's devout principles worked against him in the forward exchanges which, especially at the higher levels, are calculated to bully and subdue. His troops suspected that he was in some ways too nice a man. When an opponent whacked him Gwilliam might blink but was not known for hitting back, preferring to convey the impression that punching or stamping was beneath contempt – and that, in any case, the blow had not hurt him. Two feet away from him a true battle might be raging, the unarmed combat between opposing packs that is normal loose play, especially in a game's opening skirmishes. 'W.O.' and Don Hayward were no different from most tight forwards of most vintages. The best ones do have a mean streak, aiming constantly to give opponents pain and suffering by fair means or, if unavoidable, foul.

John Gwilliam, who does not perfectly fit such an exemplar, agrees that he was never sent off. "But I was warned once," he claims with some enthusiasm. "It was in some game or other at Llanelli. I suppose I must have caught an opponent with my elbow at a loose maul, and it was so freakish that I actually laughed out loud. But the referee decided it was foul play, and he gave me a short sharp lecture."

Says 'Stoker' with a grin, "That may be true, but I cannot imagine him giving me the sort of pre-match advice that Dr Jack Matthews of all people handed on before my first cap at Colombes in 1951. He had temporarily replaced John Gwilliam as our captain, and in his team talk he pointed at my boots and said that they would be my best friends that afternoon! Not a bad comment from a back, stationed at a safe distance from the hurly-burly!"

In Cardiff on 2 February the Welsh mood, in recession twelve months earlier, was once again buoyant and bubbly. Ticket sales had reached a record 56,000, prompting Secretary Eric Evans to register concern about behaviour and control. A relatively recent memory was of the 1936 championship battle between Wales and Ireland at this same venue when hundreds of locked-out fans rushed the barriers in attempts to get in and many of those who succeeded spilled onto the field of play. This year, too, the determination to be in the crowd was huge, but good discipline on the day allayed the Secretary's fears.

Further, in 1952 heights of expectation turned out to be overblown. Qualified approval was the reaction of most Welsh reporters after a match that was short on consistent entertainment. The victory was secured for Wales by place kicking by Malcolm Thomas which yielded eight points in an 11-0 win. In

18. Bleddyn Williams hurtles over Ryk van Schoor to claim Cardiff's try in their epic struggle against the Springboks. The Blue and Blacks looked set to win until the game's eighty-first minute...

19. ...and this was the try by electric-heeled 'Chum' Ochse that cost them the game. Cardiff full back Frank Trott is the hapless defender.

20. Burly Cliff Davies, he of the eighteen-inch neck, dribbles menacingly down the touchline against Ireland. A fine musical repertoir earned him the title 'Bard of Kenfig'.

21. The start of Wales' second Grand Slam campaign of the Gwilliam Seasons. Newport flier Ken Jones has ample space to cross for his second try of the Twickenham clash.

22. Cliff Morgan has got round the Irish back row and starts the move which Ken Jones finished to clinch a ninth Triple Crown for Wales, this time in Dublin. Scrum half Billy Williams, at left, has given him early ball; and Alun Thomas, at right, is aware that something is 'on'.

23. Swansea could not repeat their 1935 win over New Zealand, but this side of 1953 fought a valiant 6-6 draw. Standing (l-r) J. Faull, E.J. Rees, D. Jones, L. Blyth, D. Bruce-Thomas, B. Jenkins, H. Phillips. Seated: W. Bratton, R.C.C. Thomas, W.D. Johnson (capt), W.O. Williams, T. Petheridge, T. Williams. At front: G. Morgan, J. Marker.

24. The Cardiff side of 1953 led by Bleddyn Williams which registered the club's first victory over New Zealand. Standing (l-r): Gareth Griffiths, John Llewellyn, Eddie Thomas, Malcolm Collins, John Nelson, J.D. Evans, Seated: C.D. Williams, Stan Bowes, Rex Willis, Sid Judd, Bleddyn Williams, Cliff Morgan, Alun Thomas, Gwyn Rowlands, Geoff Beckingham.

25. Bleddyn Williams took the reins from John Gwilliam in 1953 for a highly successful run as Wales captain. The picture shows his perfect balance and technique.

26. All Black half back V.D. Bevans releases possession to his backs in his team's victory over Llanelli in 1953.

27. 1953 All Black captain Bob Stuart (centre) tries in vain to halt a powerful blind-side sortie for Wales by 'Stoker' Williams. Not for nothing was the prop rated as one of Wales's 'jumbo' forwards.

28. Clem Thomas (15) cannot prevent New Zealand's R.A. White feeding flanker McCaw at right with Cliff Morgan (6) bent on harrassment. This was to be the last time in the twentieth century that a huge Cardiff Arms Park would see Wales beat the All Blacks.

29. This was the winning team: back row (l-r) Clem Thomas, Sid Judd, Rees Stephens, Roy John, John Gwilliam, Courtenay Meredith; middle row (l-r) 'Stoker' Williams, Gareth Griffiths, Bleddyn Williams (capt), Ken Jones, Dai Davies; at front: Gwyn Rowlands, Rex Willis, Cliff Morgan, Gerwyn Williams. The referee is Dr Peter Cooper (England), the touch-judge former Llanelli 'great' Ivor Jones.

30. & 31. Cliff Morgan on the burst for the Lions against South Africa at Johannesburg in 1955. The cover is left for dead and even his old adversary Basie van Wyk (lower picture) cannot lay a hand on him as he goes under the bar.

modern parlance Ken Jones would have been a strong candidate for a man-of-the-match award, with a splendid try plus a terrific tackle on Kininmonth which prevented a score as Scotland's captain neared the Welsh corner flag.

Since January 1950 John Gwilliam had been getting rave reviews in the Cardiff Press. At bottom, I suspect, J.B.G. would initially have preferred Bleddyn Williams, but once he realised that Gwilliam could cope he gave him very fair written support (remember, the 'Ponty' connection). On this occasion he rapped the captain's knuckles:

> The line out work was not efficient. There was far too much tapping-back, particularly by Gwilliam. He also passed a little wildly at times. Great leader though he is, he appears to enjoy the pleasure of the flourish.

We have noted before that Gwilliam was always ready to launch long throws into the Welsh midfield if he thought the situation merited them. On this particular afternoon perhaps they were overdone; if so, the reason must have been to take pressure off scrum half Rex Willis. Despite fracturing his jaw early in the second half this bravest of players refused to leave the field for treatment. J.B.G.'s report, though not published until a day and a half later, does not reflect the gravity of the injury.

Interestingly, a word used of Wales' perceived lack-lustre by more than one Rugby writer was 'stale'. In those amateur days a player could be 'stale' if he had started training too early, or played too many games in a particular month, or recently been on a long close-season tour. Club committees and International selectors alike accepted that staleness could affect form and nodded in sympathy. Now, 'stale' appears to have gone the way of 'scrum cap', 'yards' and 'dribbling', dropping out of Rugby's vocabulary. The 'employers', who pay the new professionals, do not recognise 'being stale' as an excuse for unsatisfactory levels of performance. Their hirelings are paid to reach full throttle without fail under their terms of employment. Sub-standard work is unacceptable, for whatever reason.

If Cliff Morgan had played, as opposed to commentating, in the television age – when video tape made archiving straightforward – tries by him would have been re-run at least as often as great scores by the moderns, including Gareth Edwards. As it is the visual recall of his genius must, perforce, be via photography. Two pictures featuring him, centre foreground, are among my favourite Rugby studies, and they are remarkably similar. One shows him straining to beat the defence and score a memorable Test try for the Lions at Ellis Park, Johannesburg in 1955.

The other (facing page XXX) shows him at Lansdowne Road in March 1952, igniting one of the attacks that brought Wales the Triple Crown. Besides being a fine action picture it highlights superb skill. Billy Williams ('W.A.', from Newport, standing in for the still-sidelined Rex Willis) has sent out a pass which has tempted Irish flanker McCarthy (with hooped socks) to think that he can take Morgan behind the advantage line. But the Welshman's line of running looks certain to send him beyond his opponent's grasp. Gwilliam and Clem Thomas are moving off a scrum which is just breaking up. The give-away is the position of Williams, whose hands show that he has barely completed his flick-pass. Such is Morgan's speed off the mark that he is about to lose McCarthy and is already plotting how to outwit Kyle (not shown), while wing Alun Thomas is accelerating and hoping for a slice of the action. Shadows cast on the players and the turf by the low winter sun heighten the picture's dramatic effect, conveying a sense of virility and boundless energy. These were qualities which kept Wales on course for an outright Championship title, a Triple Crown and a Grand Slam.

As always happens (in the good years) Welsh supporters had descended upon the opposition's capital city in numbers, many camp followers lacking one of the 42,000 tickets that had been issued. Wild rumours swirled around Dublin suggesting that visitors who could not get through the turnstiles would tunnel their way into the Lansdowne Road arena – the film *Colditz* about escaping prisoners-of-war had recently been released. But the only great escape during this weekend was that of the brand-new match ball which, just before half-time, was kicked into the midst of a red and green congress of supporters, never to return for throwing in.

The late Clem Thomas exerted a major influence on this game, starting at the kick-off. This Cambridge Blue had been capped (prematurely, as it turned out) in a losing side at Colombes in 1949, since when he had constantly challenged unsuccessfully for a return to the colours. In this second International game he had pent-up frustration in plenty to release, warning Kyle of his presence at an early stage, and subjecting the Irishman to heavy tackling throughout the eighty minutes. Jackie would win another twenty caps, but on this day the threat he usually posed was neutralised.

After opening the score through a penalty placed by Lewis Jones, the Welsh had to wait twenty-five minutes before their superior forward power moved them further ahead. Gwilliam had just given Ken Jones a scoring pass which, alas, was forward when Roy John, Clem Thomas and finally Rees Stephens roared up to the opposition's line for an unconverted try.

Irish Pressmen pin-pointed the thirty-seventh minute of the game as the moment of doom for their side. A dazzling break-out from his 25 saw Cliff Morgan head for the half way line at top speed, eliminating all defenders with the exception of left wing Major George Phipps (Rosslyn Park and the Army) who forced him to pass. The recipient, Ken Jones, duly scorched the remaining fifty yards for the touch-down. So, it was all over bar some second-half shouting which greeted Murphy's penalty goal. Clem Thomas's try, set up by Roy John and converted by Lewis Jones, merely adjusted the points difference to a correct margin. Paul Mcsweeney in the *Irish Times* lamented, "Only in one post-War game, against Australia in 1947, has Ireland been more out-played. John Gwilliam is a very great captain who kept his men at high pressure from kick-off to the final whistle."

The net result was a ninth Triple Crown, the second under Gwilliam. In those days every Welsh Triple Crown had to be clinched with a final victory over Ireland – always a tall order.

But the Welsh pack had dominated an elderly Irish eight, and effectively ended the International career of Karl Mullen (oddly, since the scrummage ball was the only sure possession Ireland had taken, including two strikes against the head). So, as in 1950 a Grand Slam was again on the cards, with France needing to escape defeat in Swansea to deny Wales another four-from-four season.

The Tricolours' team named on 12 March contained a good deal of fresh blood – particularly in the midfield – as well as old hands like Pomathios, Prat, Basquet and Dufau who had been in the side which had beaten Wales at Colombes a year earlier. So, far from being over-confident, John Gwilliam was a wary skipper. He was not a member of the 1951 side, but nevertheless well knew what the French opposition would amount to. Fifty years on, with typical understatement, he says that "France were always a bit difficult to play against... at the scrums their back row came around the edge of our pack to kick the ball. If that wasn't within reach they kicked your shins, or even your ribs, instead. They might even bite you; Basquet once put his teeth into me very painfully and bit a chunk of flesh from the area of my ribs (England's Eric Evans did that too). Out in the backs Pomathios was a brilliant wing, very elusive, and like a steam train when he got into space."

Gwilliam is quick to add, however, that his team of 1952 was a potent blend of old heads and young legs. The new, big props had proved their worth; John and Stephens could dominate the line out with help from the captain; Morgan had become a match-winner; young three quarters like Malcolm Thomas and Lewis Jones were coming to the boil; while the re-born Clem Thomas was a flanker who could match most midfield opponents for pace and curtail their manoeuvres.

In the event, this team of many talents was good enough to see off the French invaders in a game which never quite burst into glory. Alun Thomas dropped an early goal, but before the interval Pomathios went in for a try converted by Jean Prat. As the second half opened, in these days before replacements were allowed, the Tricolours' scrum half Dufau was taken to hospital with a broken collar bone after a heavy tackle. Throughout an evenly-contested forty minutes, however, France refused to give up the ghost, and it took two penalty goals kicked by Lewis Jones to bring Wales the victory and a Championship clean sweep.

Thus did John Gwilliam secure his place among the great Rugby captains of the twentieth century. His two Grand Slams of 1950 and 1952 would be the glittering centrepieces of nine victories from twelve games in charge. Five decades earlier Gwyn Nicholls won eight from ten, while later Bleddyn Williams and John Dawes, with shorter periods in charge, would each win five from five.

From Swansea the captain returned to Perthshire and his history periods. Schoolmastering suited him, and he was relieved that nothing had forced him off this mainstream career path. It seems that the nearest he had come to professionalising himself and succumbing to Rugby League blandishments was when Newport visited Wasps in 1949. The Press had reported, "Scouts from Bradford Northern will be at the game to watch John Gwilliam."

The presumed object of their attention was flattered: "I felt that my true worth was about to be recognised", he recalls, "though I knew in my heart that given the nature of the Northern code no League club would want a *line out* forward – who spent most of the game disguising his lack of mobility". Nonetheless, at the end of an impressive win for Newport by a clear thirty points, two little men from Bradford stood waiting on the touch line. Gwilliam was filled with anticipation. Alas; they ignored him and made a bee-line for the Black and Ambers' scrum half Haydn Thomas whom they offered £3,500 to turn professional – which, not surprisingly, he accepted.

However, Gwilliam was about to make a career move, and gave notice to Glenalmond that the coming summer term would be his last there. The school was sad to be informed that its enthusiastic young history master, who had now become a world-class Rugby player, would be leaving Scotland. The affection felt for the family can be deduced from the half holiday given on 1 November 1950 to mark the birth of Catherine to Mr and Mrs Gwilliam. The *Glenalmond Chronicle* for September 1952 reported the announcement made by the Warden, Mr Barlow:

> Mr Gwilliam is leaving us this term, much to our regret he takes our best wishes with him, and if we must lose a master who has twice led his country to the Triple Crown we can at any rate count ourselves fortunate to have had him here, even for just three short years.

Gwilliam himself is explicit about his feeling that at his time of life that much time spent at any one educational establishment was ample. The Glenalmond experience had been "very good", both for developing his skills as a schoolmaster and for the style of Rugby he managed to inculcate into his school teams. The extra three quarter system employed in some fixtures was effective, and few tries were conceded.

Truth to tell, the family had become more than a little fed up with the travel involved whenever John needed to reach the wider world. Captaining Wales at one of the Five Nations venues, including Cardiff and Swansea, necessitated journeys that seemed endless. This tedium was especially trying to a lonely passenger on the train back to Scotland while his teams celebrated success in convivial company. Even taking babies to be admired by grandparents in Llanelli or Lydney was a tiring mission.

The aim, then, was a return to South Wales or southern England. The Welshman's availability became known on the educational network, and Oundle and Sedbergh were among public schools who offered him a post. However, his choice fell upon Bromsgrove, between Worcester and Birmingham. Its headmaster, a certain D.J. Walters, had been at Oxford; but his heart had never left Neath, of which town he was a native.

TWELVE

The news that John Gwilliam was about to leave Glenalmond for the English Midlands set tongues a-wagging in the homeland. Bromsgrove School, hardly more than a name in South Wales, was not far from the border. For a start the skipper might become more influential in the Welsh game, rather than parachuting in to take command of the National XV a day or so before big games and rushing off the morning after to catch his train back to Edinburgh.

The clubs, too, pricked up their ears. Given his in-law connections and occasional appearances in the past for the Scarlets, Llanelli thought they might be in with a chance of enlisting him. It was quickly brought home to them that the regular travelling to and from Stradey Park would have been almost as demanding as the commuting to and from Perthshire which the big man was intent on putting behind him. Pontypool were interested, but at this time were scarcely the force that they were later to become and could not provide the regular calibre of opposition which might have appealed to Gwilliam. There was great interest at Newport, whose officials eagerly checked the distance between Rodney Parade and the satellite towns of Birmingham and decided that the same man whom they had launched into big-time Rugby might be tempted back to Gwent. They were exceedingly disappointed when it was announced that the Wales captain would be joining Gloucester RFC.

Once again distance influenced the decision. Journeys which can now be completed comfortably in an hour or so by motorway could take three or four hours in those days (as we have seen with the trip to Twickenham). Llanelli was indeed out of the question, and Gwilliam also found himself disinclined to stomach regular journeys between Worcestershire and Uskside in his little Ford 8. In contrast he could reach Kingsholm in just over the hour.

Nowadays he talks very affectionately of his period with the West Country side, which would last for three seasons. Back-numbers of the local Press make it clear that the club could not believe its good fortune when the distinguished recruit came on strength – a forward as tough as anything produced in that part of the world and able to cover both lock and number eight positions. The Welsh presence in and around Gloucester has always been strong, and the newcomer was guaranteed vociferous support from 'the Shed'. He swiftly made friends off the field, particularly relishing his conversations with the former England back row forward Tom Voyce who scored five tries in twenty-seven cap appearances during England's Golden Era in the twenties. In addition, since most of the big Welsh clubs were on Gloucester's fixture list there was frequent contact between Gwilliam and his own International team-mates – who sometimes got whacked, as when a full-strength Cardiff XV lost 8-0 at Kingsholm in February 1953.

Rugby-wise, therefore, a smooth transfer had been effected from the carefree knock-about of Edinburgh district Rugby to the calculated ferocity of a top West Country pack. It suited the newcomer well as, happily, so did Bromsgrove. He was firmly in charge of Rugby, but is quick to acknowledge the support of Nigel Creese who had played for Oxford and captained Moseley with considerable success. Their first season in harness was "sticky", recalls Gwilliam, but after that the two settled into a combination that began to get good results.

As headmaster, Walters was keen to tempt the offspring of his fellow-countrymen across the border. One of these was the son of a Neath fruiterer called Dunn whose skills, almost fifty years later, can still win high praise from his team coach. Schoolmasters do cherish the memory of outstanding boys and, in Gwilliam's recall, Dunn was one of those talents which appears but seldom, never to be forgotten: "An outside half or centre, he looked exactly like Lewis Jones, played in the same elusive way, and could kick goals like the man from Gowerton". It seems that he was a match-winner who gave Bromsgrove teams a cutting edge. So why did the wider Rugby world never hear of this prodigy? Alas, he badly damaged a knee in his last game before leaving school, and never again touched the same heights of athleticism. Now, evidently, he grows tomatoes in Guernsey – and it is not just for Rugby that John Gwilliam remembers him, since his next career move would be indirectly determined by Master Dunn. Not for a while, however.

If John Gwilliam and his family had come south and were contentedly playing themselves in at Bromsgrove, one of Welsh Rugby's brightest stars and potentially a key component of successful International teams for the foreseeable future was going in the opposite direction. The Northern Union's scouts, healthily loathed by the Welsh Rugby public, had lured Lewis Jones to Leeds.

They had been pursuing the pride of west Wales ever since his sensational entry into Test Rugby in January 1950 at Twickenham. Their early overtures had been briskly rejected for, as their prey himself has recalled, Lewis Jones shared the general dislike of the professional game which had lured away many of Wales' brightest young starlets during the first half of the twentieth century. He pictured it as, "a game for thugs administered for thugs... in which violence and sharp practice existed in exactly equal proportions" – in fairness, a view which he later retracted.

The chase had begun at Devonport, when Jones was still in the Royal Navy, with a visit from two callers bent on meeting him in the NAAFI to open negotiations. Their target was summoned to appear before the Commanding Officer, who told him: "I've had a couple of fellows here looking for you who said they were from a Rugby League club. But you can relax. I had them escorted out and turfed overboard... For your own good, my boy." Another 'scout' was actually ejected from the family house at Gorseinon, though Lewis Jones is quick to say that he and his father did not mind the legitimate calls paid by accredited club representatives; it was the frequent invasions of privacy by freelance touts that they objected to.

Pressure steadily mounted, from the Leeds club in particular, whose team manager, Kenneth Dalby, Jones had met, and liked, at Lords when playing cricket for the Navy against the Army.

Every big Rugby match in which the young star took part fuelled the Yorkshiremen's determination to tempt him north, with the Leeds agent, W.J. Jones (formerly Llanelli and Oldham) becoming a regular caller at Lime Street, Llanelli. The family's caution, even opposition, to the largesse being promised to Lewis was partly influenced by the fact that Llanelli RFC's current captain was now Alun Jones, who clearly stood to be embarrassed if Leeds signed his younger brother.

What finally won Lewis Jones over was ambition. Every avenue he went down in South Wales seemed to lead nowhere, including work as a lorry driver at Carmarthen Bay Power Station. He had also met the young woman that he wanted to marry, one Maureen Williams, and this was a prime reason for wishing to better himself. Once he had made up his mind, after a long meeting with the Leeds directors at Gorseinon, there was no going back and on 7 November 1952 one of the twentieth century's major talents was lost to Wales. He was coy about the fee at the time, but it was later revealed as a very satisfying £6,000.

Interestingly, I bumped into him at Stradey Park in autumn 2000, and in the course of some small talk he said, "This is the first visit I've paid to this ground since I joined Leeds." He left me to judge whether that was down to the Llanelli club's attitude or his own preference.

For a time Welsh spirits were low, and the usual rancour towards northern England pervaded the air. But as the captain-apparent for the new season John Gwilliam was not particularly upset: "You have to remember the huge contribution Lewis had made to our International teams during the previous three seasons," he says today. "It under-pinned Welsh success, and his form with the Lions had impressed Kiwi crowds. Very well: he was distancing himself from us but, you might say, he was in credit." Gwilliam thinks that the most upset member of the Welsh squad of the day was probably Malcolm Thomas, whose friendship with Jones had begun at Devonport and steadily grown.

But with the dawn of a New Year, and the Five Nations challenge looming large it was time to look ahead. One outstanding player had ruled himself out, but Bleddyn Williams was now fit and raring to go (and about to experience the greatest days of his career). Gwilliam was still in charge, his pack strengthened by the return of an old warrior in John Robins and the formidable young Cardiff flanker, Sid Judd. The promising Gareth Griffiths, fresh out of the Rhondda, was set to win his first cap, while as long as Wales had Cliff Morgan on board all opposing back rows had better look out.

Cliff Morgan. Er, yes. Or rather, no.

An injury meant that inside half Willis was unavailable for the England game and, according to Terry Godwin in *The International Rugby Championship*, the Big Five felt that Morgan "would not be as effective without Willis". So, replacing the latter with W.A. Williams, they took one more step that seemed logical and selected Williams's club partner Roy Burnett at stand off half. Burnett was a dazzling runner who, on his day, could cut a defence to shreds. However, most critics and onlookers (beyond the confines of Rodney Parade) tended to agree that clever marking by a quick-breaking flanker could all-too-easily force him to run across-field, crowding his centres. A year earlier England's Don White had found Cliff Morgan too hot to handle, but at Cardiff in 1953 he would dominate Burnett; and, in consequence, says John Griffiths in his *Book of English International Rugby*, the Welsh back division looked "unusually lethargic".

The year 1953 was undoubtedly a colourful one, not least because a new Queen was on the throne, soon to be crowned. For much of his reign George VI had needed to wear a sombre face during Dunkirks and Alameins; Elizabeth II was a young woman who could afford to be a smiling monarch as a peaceful equilibrium, occasionally rocked by the Cold War, settled over the world. There was hyperbole, and talk of twentieth century 'round tables' from which 'New Elizabethans' could be sent to perform valorous deeds which seems absurd in retrospect. But undeniably there was a freshness in the air and some momentous happenings would accrue to Britain's sport and leisure sector: a Cup Final medal for Stanley Matthews, the first sub-four-minute mile by Roger Bannister, the conquest of Everest by New Zealand's Ed Hillary and Sherpa Tensing.

And before the Five Nations Championship opened at Cardiff Arms Park on 17 January the Welsh were promising with one voice that they too would mark Coronation year with a memorable Five Nations campaign – hopefully leading to a third Grand Slam. Gwilliam's team would be on its own patch; England's challengers were old gents like Cannell, Hall, Kendall-Carpenter and Stirling. No contest, thought many of the 56,000 spectators before the kick-off, laughing at the mock battle of leeks brandished by fans on the north terrace and applauding the raiders who darted past stewards and police to scatter daffodils at the centre.

The St Alban's Band Military Band under conductor John Williams whiled away the long wait, and the stadium sang to his baton. In 1953 there was no need for imported male voice choirs with microphones, and even words of the National Anthem spelt out on jumbo TV screens (and in the match programmes); for now, the great hymns of Welsh nonconformity still dominated the song-sheets of Wales. Matches might have become all-ticket, but to secure a good vantage point holders of the cheapest tickets needed to enter Cardiff Arms Park a good ninety minutes before kick-off – there to sing their hearts out to while away the waiting. Just as, in later years, the Dax band and others were to be a cheeky fanfare of malevolence at Parc des Princes, so in Cardiff a little nuclei of famous male voice choirs used to gather along the Arms Park tribunes and roar a tonal challenge to invaders. Beneath the North Terrace were the changing rooms; and if it was said that the Arms Park was worth a ten-point start to Wales it was because visiting XVs could hear the crowd baying for blood in harmony.

The difference at the death, and the Welsh defeat, was just a converted try which came in the first quarter of the game. New full back Terry Davies had given his team the lead from forty five yards with a penalty at eleven minutes after the experienced Don White was spotted by referee Dowling failing to release at a ruck.

The fans howled their glee, and looked forward to the next score. Unfortunately for them it came from England.

Since 1952 some crucial circumstances had changed in England's favour. Don Hayward, whose commanding and weighty presence in the Wales front row, had opted for the professional game. Clem Thomas was also absent. The half back partnership was raw – whereas in contrast the visitors had introduced a new stand off half who would cause opponents big problems in the next few seasons: Martin Regan.

The young man from Liverpool RFC now stole the lead for England by slipping the Swansea policeman Dil Johnson, winning a solitary cap. The latter, wrote J.B.G. Thomas, "did not supply the hard tackling necessary to subdue Regan", his implication being that Clem Thomas might have provided this ingredient. Regan sent a long pass to Bazley who, it has to be said, turned Ken Jones inside out before sending Cannell in for a memorable try. Though disappointed, the capacity 56,000 crowd managed to sound applause for what had been a beautifully-executed score and remained quiet as Hall went through the routine of converting the try. The day of the Yob had not yet arrived.

John Gwilliam admits to a failure to rouse his men on this day, and it is clear that despite scrummaging solidly the possession taken at the line out by England was of a higher quality than Gwilliam's pack could deliver; the captain recalls, "It seemed difficult to fire ourselves up on this particular day". The Welsh often looked nonplussed before the short-passing raids lifted from South Africa's text-book of attack and executed with flair by the English forwards on the day. It did not help the home team's cause that penalty shots at goal were going missing.

As a pulsating second half went its torrid way Wales stayed in touch despite giving away penalty chances to England which Hall missed. It took a change of kicker to apply the killer blow, Woodward scoring his first points with the boot for his country from forty-five yards out after Wales scrum half Billy Williams had been caught offside in too much of a hurry to harass Sykes at the base of England's scrum. The crowd fell silent, to be brought back to life as Wales threw everything into attack over the final quarter. John Gwilliam had delivered what those who heard it ranked among his most rasping half-time talks, whose effect did not kick in until too late.

It did not help that the three place-kickers used by Gwilliam in the second half – Davies, Robins and Malcolm Thomas – could not find the target despite penalty chances from not too far out. Now, inevitably, the immense effort made by England for most of the game lost momentum in the fourth quarter as Wales strove to pull the game out of the fire. They nearly did so, moving the ball briskly to the midfield with only minutes left. Bleddyn Williams was allowed no more than a yard's latitude before he took the tackle and unloaded to Malcolm Thomas. The latter's Newport team-mate Ken Jones was beside him as the attack reached the England 25, perfectly positioned to take a scoring pass that was high but far from out of reach. Alas: the Welsh hero of so many post-War Tests put a slightly high pass on the deck and the visitors held on for victory. At the final whistle they leaped high with delight. A major fortress had been stormed.

Though disappointed and deflated the crowd was well aware how excellent had been the Englishmen's defence on this hostile terrian ruled by Europe's pacemakers of the last three seasons. The match reports record, approvingly, the applause accorded to the visitors as they left the battlefield. Now the winners went to the hot baths along the old, narrow walk-way which once led around to the rear of the North Stand with slaps on the back and praised ringing in their ears.

Welsh attitudes to English Rugby at Test level will surely one day prompt a major thesis by an anthropologist or social historian. Alliances, and support, are deep atavistic emotions, which can sway and bend with circumstances. They are capable of many permutations.

For instance, before the contest we have just noted – and indeed before any English incursion into Wales – you would imagine that a combination of Edward I, Genghis Khan and Saddam Hussein had invaded our capital city, to be booed lustily during the first hour of the game or at any time up to the final whistle – if they led. Nothing remotely resembling such behaviour is paraded if the visitors are Ireland, Scotland or even France. But the latter have done us little or no harm, whereas Angles, Saxons and – especially – the loutish, cruel Normans have seized our territories, tortured and killed our Princes, put up castles (the nuclear submarines of their day), taken our coal, refused to pay for the water they pipe eastwards and suffocated us with cultural beneficence (that is, the English language).

Dear, dear, you reflect. Fancy harbouring racial memories like these. Well, the English do not exactly forget the arrow in Harold's eye, the rout of Henry IV, Prestonpans, Saratoga, Ypres, Dunkirk and the Blitz.

The point being, in a Rugby context: the symbolic action-replay with the oval ball is a renewed catharsis for the Welsh. After the final whistle, whatever the result, onlookers return to normality and if the winners have played well and resisted stoutly then they are to be acclaimed: no hard feelings, chaps (until next time).

But such stances and attitudes merit further discussion. They are reminiscent of Tory politician Norman Tebbit's 'Who do you cheer for?' question (or challenge) to immigrants long ago. For example, if England are to play Ireland or Scotland we hope that the latter two Celtic countries will win. When they meet France we are inclined to support England (unless a win by France will keep the title out of the Saxons' reach). Finally, if England are matched with any of the great southern hemisphere nations Welsh support swings to our near-eastern neighbours, as representatives of the northern hemisphere. I am not sure whether these allegiances are typical of my countrymen. Maybe reading this, you would approve of England defeating Ireland but not South Africa. Hm.

Anybody would think that Wales had been blasted out of sight in January 1953 instead of playing a little below par against an England XV that was heavily motivated by failures against the home nation in the recent past. For the Wales XV announced by the selectors to play at Murrayfield in February turned upside-down the side which England had crushed in Cardiff. Willis and Morgan were back, Malcolm Thomas was unavailable (allowing his namesake Alun to win a fifth cap). Clem Thomas returned at open side flanker and the hugely-promising Russell Robins stole John Gwilliam's place at number eight for a first cap.

As usual the radio was the media through which Gwilliam heard about his demotion. There were no messages of thanks for the results he, and the teams led by him, had delivered to a nation hungry for success on the Rugby field. There were no kind homilies about the unprecedented triumphs under him, and a success rate unparalleled since the Golden Era when Gwyn Nicholls had reigned supreme. And yet, today, he does not look back with acrimony at his summary dismissal.

He says, "I had too many other things on my mind to be upset. I was easing myself into the job at Bromsgrove, and had a family to look after which included the impending arrival of a second child, David on 12 March 1953."

What sort of men were the selectors at this time, who felt able to cast a highly successful leader into the wilderness? John Gwilliam had been their captain for a majority of the games between 1950 and 1953. He had led their XVs expertly, despite having little or no influence upon or input to the sides they had selected (partly because of the geography which separated him from Wales). Now, half a century on, Gwilliam dismisses them summarily. "Their names," he recalls, "were Vince Griffiths, Arthur Cornish, Enoch Rees (a writer of Mills & Boon type romances), Dai Hopkin Thomas and Dai Jones of Blaina. You took them with a pinch of salt."

But they dropped him. He is among a fair number of contemporary players and administrators of the day who survive, but have not the foggiest idea why the skipper got turfed out. Happenings within selectorial meetings are not minuted or carefully archived in any enduring way. The teams selected by the Big Five are the only evidence available of how things went in conclave.

The fact is that in the spring of 1953 Wales went to Murrayfield – the graveyard of 1951 – minus John Gwilliam and managed without him. Even though scrum half Willis hurt his shoulder and missed most of the second half Bleddyn Williams, in his first match as captain of Wales, delivered a 12-0 victory. Newcomers to Test Rugby Courtenay Meredith (Neath) and Russell Robins (Pontypridd) acquitted themselves well. Significantly, in his *History of Welsh International Rugby* John Billot calls Rees Stephens "a grand pack-leader".

Arguably, therefore, it could be argued that the new-look Wales appeared capable of succeeding without the captain who had been dropped. Certainly many fans would not have disagreed with an article in the *Western Mail* by J.B.G. Thomas whose headline read the 'End of the Gwilliam Era'. That was certainly how it was perceived. But the old canon counselling that you do not change a winning team was now thrown overboard by the Big Five as they named their side to play Ireland, tossing out the newcomers who had made an impact in Edinburgh; John Robins, now playing for Bradford, displaced Courtenay Meredith in the front row and the youthful Russell Robins bowed out to make room at number eight for John Gwilliam. Today Robins recalls that the Whites, in which he played, had beaten the Reds in two Trials in the previous autumn, which may have accelerated his promotion. He is also candid enough to concede that, at twenty years of age, he had much to learn; his good days lay a year or two ahead.

For Gwilliam it had been a roller-coaster ride; he had been harshly expelled – and almost immediately restored to a position of influence in the Welsh pack for the game at Swansea. Had his laid-back approach to International Rugby upset one or two of the more straight-laced selectors? Were they just out to teach him a lesson? Were they disappointed that his career move had taken him to the English Midlands rather than bringing him back to the homeland – where his presence might have signalled a firmer commitment to the Cause? All this may be too sophisticated; maybe the Big Five just thought that John Gwilliam had not been playing well; but was now playing better. At any rate, J.B.G. Thomas wrote, "It is vexing that Welsh Rugby men sometimes lack generous minds".

The days immediately before 14 March 1953 were not an ideal preparation for an International Rugby match in which an old-timer planned to remind the Rugby world of his quality. Things did not go smoothly. Baby David arrived on the Thursday night, and the following afternoon his father set off for St Helens without his boots. This meant a journey back to Bromsgrove, an apologetic telephone call to the Welsh Rugby Union, and finally catching a train on the Saturday morning. The journey was, in any case, long and tedious, and the last straw came when it pulled into Neath behind a queue of excursion trains all heading for the match and having to take their turn. Gwilliam finally got off at Swansea station just after two o'clock (kick-off was at three pm), discovering to his horror that all taxis were fully booked. It took a resourceful policeman on point duty to avert a disaster by stopping the traffic and requisitioning a car to take him to St Helens. Here, he recalls, the accommodation for changing compared most unfavourably with the spacious rooms at Twickenham and Murrayfield (and, by the way, they haven't changed in the fifty years since Gwilliam last pulled on his boots there). However, he had made it, albeit by the skin of his teeth.

His presence was important to Wales in the face of a no-holds-barred opening by Ireland, who had clearly decided to let their new young forwards off the leash and attack the Welsh pack supported by Jackie Kyle's tactical kicking. The stand off half was probably well content with this role, for marking him once again was the same Clem Thomas who had subdued him in Dublin a year earlier.

Forward battles are the beating heart of Rugby Football and beloved of the connoisseur. However, they do not provide spectacle; reports of the action write this game down as "rather dull". Only once did the home team break clear of Ireland's suffocating tactics, as the match moved into its second quarter. Roy John brought off a rare dummy at a line out and found enough unguarded space at the front to race away down the five-yard corridor before passing to his club-mate Stephens. The next handler, who must have reacted quickly indeed at the rear end of the line out, was none other than John Gwilliam. After a few strides, at exactly the right time, he gave a scoring pass to Gareth Griffiths who crossed near the corner flag in front of the popular bank. Terry Davies kicked a fine goal which, in the end, proved to be a match-winning conversion when Pedlow's try for the visitors went unconverted.

The win kept the Championship alive – for just one more week. Although England had been held to 9-9 in Dublin they had since beaten France and could only be overtaken if they lost to Scotland on 21 March. Alas for Welsh hopes, the Calcutta Cup remained at Twickenham and England clinched their title, just one point short of a Grand Slam. At the end of the month Gareth Griffiths underlined the promise shown in his first season of representative Rugby by scoring two tries in Paris where the Tricolours' lone penalty goal did not stave off defeat.

England had been held to 9-9 by Ireland in Dublin, and the defeat there of France (who had beaten Scotland) meant that a Grand Slam for any of the Five Nations was not a possibility in the 1953 Championship. The feat that Gwilliam had brought off – twice – as Wales skipper was, and remains, a rare accomplishment. By 2002 Wales had still registered only eight Slams, France six, Scotland three and Ireland just one. Top of the class are England; but even they went through eight decades of the twentieth century with a mere eleven Slams to their credit. The *fin de siecle* beating of breasts and gnashing of teeth as the red rose fell successively to Wales, Scotland, Ireland and, in 2002, France was a manifestation on England's part of hubris: to win Grand Slams is part of the Saxons' Rugby destiny, and if they fail the fates must be confused.

As for the Welsh, after their initial false step at Twickenham the season had been rewarding and their second place in the final table was an honourable one, to finish breathing down English necks with six points. Their gesture in the direction of fresh blood, which had seemed in earnest after their Cardiff defeat, had proved very short-lived; but perhaps selectorial minds were already focussed ahead – at the scheduled arrival of the 1953 All Blacks. Every ounce of experience, cunning and know-how would be needed to give New Zealand a warm welcome.

John Gwilliam must certainly have relished the prospect of a final tilt against a top southern hemisphere nation. Having missed the 1950 Lions tour there would be a chance, perhaps, in the coming season to mix it with a Kiwi pack; such an opportunity would certainly be his last for he had privately decided to retire from the game upon passing thirty years of age. That had happened in February 1953, and would rule him out of the 1955 Lions tour to South Africa (even had he been deemed young and brisk enough to engage with the 'Boks a second time).

For much of his Rugby career, moreover, Gwilliam had been powerfully influenced by *The Complete Rugby Footballer,* the book written jointly in 1906 by the 1905 All Black captain in Britain, Dave Gallaher, and his vice captain J.W. Stead. From this pair the Fourth All Blacks would be in direct line of descent.

THIRTEEN

In the seasons following the Lions' departure from her shores in 1950 New Zealand had time to draw breath and assess her place in world Rugby's pecking order. After the shattering whitewash by South Africa in 1949 the All Blacks had defeated the British Isles 3-0, with one Test drawn, and played five Tests against Australia of which they had won four. Not a bad come-back, you might think.

Yet, with the challenge of a 1953 expedition to Europe looming, New Zealand were enduring agonies of self-disbelief with much of the introspection centred on their erstwhile full back Bob Scott. He had been an outstanding member of the Kiwis in Britain during 1945-46 when he was a heavy scorer with the boot and created many tries for team-mates with surges into the three quarter line. This had been followed up with forty points in the four Tests of 1947 against Australia, while through the 1949 series in South Africa Scott salved some pride for his country with place kicking that kept margins of defeat to a minimum.

Despite all this, plus an appetite for counter-attack which pointed forward to Villepreux, JPR and Irvine, he never scored a Test try for the All Blacks. His goal points contributed to the defeat of the Lions, but after their departure – by now a balding veteran with a wife and kids to support – he announced his retirement from the game to concentrate on his painting and decorating business. Maybe a critical Press hastened his decision; the *Wellington Evening Post* wrote of the series:

> Scott was a disappointment. His repeated failure to find the line worked his forwards overtime... his action in at least one instance was almost inexcusable in an international full back of his experience... he strained for distance, failed, and had his hard-working pack covering ground uselessly.

At first his countrymen did not worry over his departure. But then, as their visit to Europe drew near, it was realised that the All Blacks had failed to identify and groom a successor. At the end of the 1952 domestic season two senior members of the NZRU called on him to say that it was his duty to come out of retirement and offer himself for selection to tour Britain and France. Having pondered their summons for some weeks, in 1953 at the age of thirty-two Scott declared his availability. When the news reached Wales there was general pleasure that a foe whose quality had been recognised in 1945 had endured to fight another day. At St Helens, Rodney Parade, Stradey and the Arms Park Bob Scott was remembered not for missing touch but for his style and genius.

Thorough as always, New Zealand staged a Trials week at Wellington in early October. Although the Dominion had been combed for hidden talent from the start of 1953 the first fixture in Britain, against Southern Counties at Hove, would not take place until 31 October (the last in Paris on 27 February 1954). But once the selectors had seen the action they quickly named a thirty-strong party to be captained by the Canterbury-bred Bob Stuart. This back row forward was in the veteran category and would celebrate his thirty third birthday as the tour opened. Sceptics were quick to emphasise that his only experience of Test Rugby had been in the two 1949 defeats the All Blacks suffered at Australian hands. However, Stuart was a strong character, warm-hearted, who played well-enough in the Trials to secure the plum job.

In days before modern wide-bodied aircraft could whisk touring sides across the globe in hours rather than days or weeks the prospect of this major southern hemisphere nation touring the UK stirred the Rugby community's blood like little else could. Though Kiwis and Services XVs had reminded fans in the Home Country of the Dominion's calibre, a full national squad had not been seen in Europe since 1935. Hence there was huge interest in the personnel who made up these Fourth All Blacks. Scott was a familiar figure; one or two like scrum half Vince Bevan and the brilliant wing Ron Jarden were players who had helped to put down the Lions; but the rest were mystery men. As the wires delivered names and pen portraits to Europe's media, dedicated Rugby journalists like J.B.G. Thomas filled endless column inches with personal details and statistics to whet enthusiasts' appetites.

So readers got to know about 'Tiny' White, later to be hailed as the best lock forward to visit the UK since before the War. Kevin Skinner was coming: an immensely powerful prop whose ears were a reminder that he had been a champion heavyweight boxer. Bill McCaw's speed around the pitch and deadly tackling had led New Zealanders to rate him the best back row forward in the country, a man who also pushed his weight at scrums. The desire to watch New Zealand's new stars in action was intense.

But while the Home Countries waited with bated breath there was plenty to capture people's interest in the autumn of what had been a Coronation year. Another New Zealander had preceded the Rugby players to Wales – Sir Ed Hillary, knighted for the conquest of Everest by himself and Sherpa Tensing a day or two before the young Queen was crowned. It may well have been Sir John Hunt, who led the expedition to the Himalayas and lived on the Welsh border, who persuaded Hillary to come to the land where his personnel had trained for the great challenge. The Kiwi got a big welcome in Cardiff before leaving for the north and Snowdonia to take a look at some peaks that were pimples compared to a 29,000-foot giant but still gave climbers a run for their money.

Another link forged in 1953 between 'Home' and New Zealand involved a long-distance air-race between London Airport and Auckland. Ten aircraft took part, all obliged to halt several times for re-fuelling on the 12,000-mile journey in days before long-haul capability. The winner was a Flight Lt Burton whose wife, the *Western Mail* was pleased to report, was a native of Newquay.

Beyond the UK many of the problems that continue to beset the world in 2002 were already flourishing or germinating. In the Middle East Israeli attacks on Arab villages within Jordanian territory caused loss of life. Relations with Russia are nowadays cordial, but in those days the revolutionary pressures and intrigue that Moscow managed to exert within newly-independent countries like Guiana were making the Foreign Office twitchy. The onset of tensions that would result in the disastrous Suez expedition were becoming apparent.

In Wales there were internal concerns and problems, which by today have largely been solved or gone away. The business community in South Wales was appalled when German coal was first imported into the United Kingdom, while at the same time their own coalfield was slowly but certainly contracting. The infant National Health Service was admitting that there was a 'grave need' for extra hospital beds. Local authorities wanted to meet and debate the question of a capital city for Wales, a move that brought success with Cardiff's eventual promotion; but a proposal approved by the City Council in 1953 to use a major bequest in the will of Lord Pontypridd to create a National Art Gallery within the Castle grounds has failed, at the time of writing, ever to be followed up. Cardiff is fond of calling itself 'Europe's youngest capital city'; it must also be the only one that does not have a centre dedicated to displaying the output of the nation's artists.

The sporting scene in Wales contained numerous distractions and aperitifs in advance of the All Blacks' arrival. A welcome score-line in October read 'Wales 1, South Africa, 0' – but these Springboks were South Africa's amateur soccer players. At Ninian Park England were visitors, who overwhelmed their hosts (from whose team crack centre forward Trevor Ford had been forced to withdraw with a foot injury) to the tune of 4-1, with Nat Lofthouse leading the visiting forwards brilliantly and scoring twice. In fairness to Wales, however, their accomplished full back Alf Sherwood spent some forty minutes off the field each side of half time with concussion. The visiting forwards ruthlessly exploited the amount of undefended space in the Welsh half.

The Rugby scene was mixed. Three Welsh clubs were down to meet New Zealand before the 19 December Test at Cardiff. Of them Swansea had made a wretched start to the season, losing in September at home and away to Newport (who were due to play the tourists in the New Year). Llanelli had struggled somewhat and the town was in mourning at the untimely death of its legendary 'master tactician' of the twenties, Albert Jenkins, aged just 58. For their part Cardiff had experienced set-backs, and many observers genuinely felt that their pack was too light to match New Zealand's. However, Bleddyn Williams was their captain: he turned out to be an inspirational one, telling his pack that if they could secure two-fifths of available possession then he and the glittering back line would reward their forwards with the victory.

Despite misgivings the age-old hunt for tickets to see the 19 December Test had got under way in early October once it was known that the little slivers of paste-boards had been printed. But, for fans who failed in their bid to buy one, there was now the consolation of television. Though Wales had yet to welcome the erection of the Wenvoe transmitter a BBC outside broadcast unit would ensure that match coverage could reach the rapidly accumulating audience, with pictures sent to London and bounced back via the Mendips mast then shared with the West Country. Television 'occasions' like the Coronation and big sports events prompted owners of TV sets to invite their deprived neighbours in to call around and sit before the screen in a viewers' party.

The Fourth All Blacks set an example for all major tour parties in the future by travelling to the UK by air. Their *Constellation*, which had been delayed by engine trouble at Basra and Beirut, was twenty four hours late landing at the up-to-the-minute but far from complete Heathrow Airport. A sizeable Press posse was allowed onto the runway to photograph and interview the visitors as they carefully negotiated the steps between the fuselage and the ground. Then they obligingly lined up on the tarmac and gave a vigorous version of the Haka war dance. The cameras clicked, and the 1953 All Blacks had won over their first fans.

Next day there was a reception for the tourists at a Mayfair hotel in London after which it was down to Eastbourne for the start of serious training. A priority was the welding of styles and approaches of players from twelve different provinces and styles into a team whose personnel could be interchangeable. This was rated even more important by the tour management than fitness, levels of which were high after the recent end of New Zealand's season. It is very easy to over-estimate the benefit of home advantage to teams who took on visitors in the old days of extended tours. The day-in, day-out bonding and hard physical activity of a tour party in between matches were influential factors in balancing the odds.

The tourists started as expected, brushing aside Southern Counties, Cambridge University, London Counties (no repeat of the famous victory over South Africa for them) and Oxford University fairly comfortably. On 14 November, with South Wales almost in sight across the Severn Estuary, they beat Western Counties at Bristol. Analysts noted, however, that the winning margins were less than emphatic. At the end of their tour, after thirty games, these All Blacks went above twenty points only seven times. Nevertheless, the Welsh recognised that five wins from five was evidence of great efficiency if not flair.

Now J.B.G. Thomas's reportage of their progress changed its tone. In the early weeks the *Western Mail* correspondent had been jocular, pulling New Zealanders' legs at the retention of the 'fractions' way of naming field positions – that is, five eighths – which he suggested might put youngsters who hated mathematics off the game. He had also expressed amusement at manager Millard's comment during the Heathrow Press conference that he didn't approve of the term 'number eight' for the third row forward. Unfair: most people would agree that 'eighthman', a Springbok invention, is cultural minimalism.

Stoking up fearfulness as few other journalists could, J.B.G.'s approach changed. Having watched two of the tourists' fixtures and wearing his heart (or ostrich feathers) on his sleeve, J.B.G wrote, "I do not think that Welshmen can match the fanaticism of All Black forwards in pursuit of loose possession". He doubted whether the Cardiff pack could hold them. As sports editor he published R.T. Gabe's warning: "Woe betide any Welsh back fumbling the ball with the tourists marauders ready to pounce. And, once they get their hands on it, New Zealanders don't die with the ball."

The tourists moved into Wales on 15 November, to be given a generous civic reception by Cardiff's Council and taking lunch at the Park Hotel as guests of Cardiff Rotary Club. Then came a swift transfer to the seaside town of Porthcawl, centrally positioned between the far east and the far west of Wales' Rugby zone. Some midnight oil was burned as manager, captain and senior players thought about taking on the sternest opposition of the tour so far. The Scarlets. Llanelli.

At that time Wales led New Zealand 2-1 in Tests played. It is amazing to recall that, by the end of their 1935 tour, of the 87 games played by the All Blacks had played in Europe, only four had been lost. Two of those had been at the hands of Wales, while Swansea had beaten Jack Manchester's side in 1935 as had England at Twickenham. The prospect of New Zealand taking the field at Stradey Park thrilled the westerners who dreamed of standing shoulder to shoulder with Swansea as only the second club side to defeat New Zealand.

Alas for their ambitions, which would have to wait until 1973 for fulfilment. The New Zealanders, who admitted afterwards that the game had been played at a pace not hitherto experienced by them in Britain, were moved and perhaps put off their game by the pre-match singing of twenty thousand fans crammed on the old popular banks of Stradey Park. After a rattling start by their hosts the tourists' superior weight began to tell and Llanelli found their defence fully stretched by half backs who were enjoying twenty-two carat possession. At seven minutes their over-eager flankers went round a scrum prematurely, and Jarden goaled the resultant penalty.

Nonetheless, six minutes later New Zealand conceded the third try of the tour after what their writers describe as the best move encountered so far. The correspondent of the New Zealand *Freelance*, John Hayhurst, wrote:

The Llanelli centre Denzil Thomas broke from behind a
loose scrum near the half way line and left the New Zealand
defence standing by a clever turn-in at the right moment. In
the Welsh manner of play Ron Thomas, left wing, and
Tucker, stand off half, were both backing up well. Thomas is
one of the few players able to say that he has beaten Bob
Scott; he drew him well and then gave on to Tucker coming
up on the outside who was over, too wide out for the goal-
kick to succeed.

The half-time score was thus 3-3. Shortly after the break,
however, as the All Blacks raised their game Llanelli's resistance
started to crumble under the sheer weight and power of the
opposing pack. 'Tiny' White was the first to benefit from this,
being sent in by Bill Clark. Then, as the Scarlets' forwards tired
and ceased covering the wide open spaces, the visitors' backs
abandoned all restraint and ran the ball incessantly. The result
was a hat-trick for Alan Elsom to lift New Zealand's winning
margin to fourteen in a 17-3 victory.

It is interesting to illustrate the touring side's fitness and
stamina by showing how they pressed home advantages in the
second half of many games. Fifteen times out of thirty matches
on tour New Zealand's lead at half time was three points or less.
In the second halves they were – mainly – able to run, pass and
penetrate to their hearts' content and in thirteen games they
finished with fifteen points or more.

The Fourth All Blacks had enjoyed their first outing in Wales,
finding the Rugby atmosphere bracing and robust. They liked
the Stradey Park experience, recognising the thirst for success
that the tumult on the terraces and vibrant singing represented.
Just one cloud had crept above the horizon: Bob Stuart had
suffered a cut on his knee which had turned septic and would
doom the skipper to a spectating role until the game against
Wales. He would miss seven matches, unable to regain full fitness
before the Test. The New Zealand writers with the tour testified
that Stuart had swiftly become a captain regarded with respect
and affection by his troops. His injury was really bad news.

The All Blacks gave Haig the captaincy and Skinner the pack

leadership for the Cardiff fixture. Stuart had been looking to play at 'number eight' (or whatever term the management preferred for the back row position). The gap was filled by McCaw, whose tactical role was to move out to support midfield attacks and – more importantly – get amongst the very clever Cardiff three quarters in defence. Both of the Welsh side's half backs (Morgan and Willis) were capped players as were three of the back line (Griffiths, Alun Thomas and Bleddyn Williams). The fourth was a budding doctor, a place-kicking wing called Gwyn Rowlands. His mother had had to restrain her son from accepting the offer of an England Trial (which was partly her fault since the baby had been born in Berkhamsted). However he fell into line, and New Zealand Rugby has cause to remember him as an opponent who did their cause some damage.

The Cardiff club had met New Zealand sides three times in the twentieth century. In 1905 a mind-boggling mistake by the brilliant Percy Bush threw the result away. His inexplicable failure to make a loose ball dead over the Cardiff goal-line led to a follow-up try by the Aucklander George Nicolson and an 8-10 defeat by the First All Blacks. Not unexpected reverses in 1924 and 1935 were by 8-16 and 5-20, but there was still chagrin in the air over the 0-3 defeat by the 1945 Kiwis. These were statistics which helped to motivate the home XV, while its skipper and senior player Bleddyn Williams would have been more focussed than most: by now he had been facing New Zealand Test sides for almost a decade without enjoying a single success.

For all that, there was guarded optimism in South East Wales as match day approached. The late Eamonn Andrews has recalled how he visited the Cardiff club a few days before broadcasting reports on the game, to be shown a blank space on a committee room wall. "That," said his guide, "is where we are going to hang our photograph of the 1953 Cardiff team that beat the All Blacks."

The morning of the game dawned dull but dry, meaning that the Cardiff backs would not be slithering around on a mudpatch and trying to handle a ball like a bar of soap. Beginning at

12.30pm the fifty thousand spectators queued and squeezed their way into the famous ground, which was now beginning to look dated. The bomb damage to the North Stand was repaired; but the South Stand was no more than a long shed. The east terrace was uncovered (and, incidentally, when dismantled for replacement in the 70s was discovered to be dangerously unstable). The 'River End' (in days when the stadium and its pitch lay at right angles to the Taff) comprised a sizeable terrace shaped like an exaggerated 'D'. Though high, it was a long way from the dead-ball line and hence not a great vantage point for spectating.

Spectators who arrived a few minutes late would have missed all the significant action. After Scott missed with an ambitious penalty attempt at two minutes, Cliff Morgan set in motion the move which effectively won the game. His chip ahead after breaking from a scrum bobbed back up into his hands, enabling him to send possession to Alun Thomas and Gwyn Rowlands. The last-named managed to cross-kick to a point near the posts on which Cardiff's main man-power was now converging. A retreating All Black eight had no chance of halting their furious drive, which swept pack leader Sid Judd over the line for a fine try converted by Rowlands.

The rest of the points all came in the next twenty minutes. First Ron Jarden kicked an astonishing penalty goal from fully fifty yards; but this was merely a blip in Cardiff's very positive opening offensive. Soon Morgan was at work again, drawing the New Zealand defence before putting Bleddyn Williams into space. Alun Thomas was the next handler, before his long pass sent Gwyn Rowlands streaking to the flag – for a score that was just too far out to be converted by him.

There were still three quarters of the game to go, during which New Zealand tested the Cardiff defence with a medley of every tactical ploy known to the game. The partisan crowd, becoming gradually more noisy and confident as the afternoon wore on, held its breath as the New Zealand forwards rolled like armoured cars into the Cardiff 25; as Haig's drop at goal missed by two yards; and as Cardiff dealt efficiently with an enormous up-and-under by Scott. But there remained five minutes of sheer torture as the All Blacks put in their final bid for victory with three scrummages almost beneath the Cardiff posts. At the final one hooker Geoff Beckingham ensured that history was made by striking successfully against the head.

"The last three minutes were the longest in my life," admitted Bleddyn Williams in *Rugger My Life*:

> Was there anyone in the great crowd who honestly believed we could hold out the torrential flood of the All Blacks' desperate offensive? Pinned with our backs to the wall and with the vibrating roar, anxious and encouraging, deafening our ears I have never experienced a more nerve-wracking situation.

He also recalls witnessing an All Black's tantrum which showed how much they hated defeat. As the final whistle went Bob Scott knelt down and smashed his fists repeatedly into the turf, shunning all Cardiff offers of a hand-shake. Williams subsequently commented that it showed how bitterly New Zealanders take defeat: "But years later we met in South Africa, where he apologised to me for his unseemly reaction to the result."

Neutral critics looked back on the result from different viewpoints. The general reaction was jubilation because Cardiff were underdogs and not expected to win. Some onlookers called the Welsh side lucky, since the opposition's midfield backs "lacked the nose for an opening". This highlighted a dilemma which existed inside the Kiwis' camp concerning the type of Rugby it would pay them to play, and which J.B.G. Thomas had outlined for the benefit of his readers. What did 'pay' mean? Well, er: if possible please the crowd with style, but most definitely win.

At the heart of the debate were the two first five-eighths, or stand-off halves, in the party. There was the veteran Laurie Haig who, as vice captain, needed to be selected against Cardiff in the absence of Stuart. But New Zealand also had Guy Bowers on board, just twenty years of age when the tourists left Auckland. It began to be perceived that when Bowers played the tourists ran up big scores, 28 for example against North of Scotland and 40 versus Combined Services at Twickenham. The latter stood for youth and adventure, Haig for experience and safety first. It appears that the two-way pull affected selection and tactics throughout the tour. In Wales, it might be observed, we recognise and understand the conflict.

The All Blacks travelled north for three fixtures against Scottish opposition, leaving the Welsh to ponder the happenings of a sensational week. A Trial was due in a few days' time, and the usual 'Red' and 'White' XVs were named. Erstwhile captain John Gwilliam was named in the Reds' second row, but surprisingly in the light of the way he had led Cardiff, Bleddyn Williams was not immediately given the captaincy, which went instead to Rees Stephens, picked to play at number eight. By the time the International XV to meet New Zealand was announced Stephens had been put back into the second row, the captaincy had been taken from him and given to Bleddyn Williams, and John Gwilliam was again a foot-soldier, albeit in his favourite position at number eight.

The weeks went by slowly, with the prospect of New Zealand's challenge dominating the Christmas season and getting closer. The tourists had spent their time defeating three Scottish regional combinations before returning towards the south west, beating Midland Counties and then South Western Counties on the way. They re-entered Wales on 11 December, holing up as usual at Porthcawl, there to begin an exacting fitness schedule ahead of the tour's first Test. But before they took on the Welsh XV there was the little matter of seeing off Swansea at St Helens on 12 December.

The conquerors of Jack Manchester's 1935 All Blacks were not in earth-shattering form just now. Their autumn 1953 record as the latest tourists arrived back in Wales included seven wins and eight defeats from seventeen games, also featuring two draws. Hence pre-match chatter was not about how Swansea would win, but how they could keep New Zealand at a decent distance from their line; and the apprehension felt

locally manifested itself in poor singing on the sidelines before
the kick-off. Interestingly, the club had targeted Haig and his
second five eighth Fitzpatrick for special treatment aimed at
neutralising New Zealand's attacks behind the scrum. His crash-
tackling was one reason for the inclusion of the fifteen-stone,
nineteen year old national serviceman, John Faull at centre.

Swansea won the toss and took the Mumbles end, consigning
New Zealand to a first half spent struggling to advance and
constantly turning to deal with astute tactical kicks placed down-
wind by Jackie Marker and Goronwy Morgan. This breeze was
also ready-made for the burly John Faull, the second reason for
whose inclusion was a capacity to kick goals from long range. It
soon assisted him to strike an early penalty for the Whites from
fifty-five yards out. The same wind was frustrating Scott and
Jarden who were missing with place kicks at goal.

Some ten minutes later a furious combined thrust by the All
Blacks' pack cleared Swansea defenders ruthlessly out of the way
and allowed Elsom to cross almost unchallenged. Bob Scott's
conversion attempt, which could have proved the eventual
winner, was blown astray by a gust that came straight off
Swansea Bay. The same powerful zephyr soon assisted Faull to
score again with the boot from even further out – some say 55
yards – and frustrated Jarden's attempt to convert a second try
by Elsom.

Six-six was the half time situation; 6-6 it still was forty
minutes later. New Zealand cursed their inefficiency throughout
a second half when they pinned the Whites in their own territory
half for twenty non-stop minutes without being able to land a
knock-out punch. Instead Scott, taking over as place kicker from
Jarden, missed with two penalty opportunities and no fewer than
four drops at goal. Only Alan Elsom could claim to be a happy
New Zealander, with his brace of tries at St Helen's to follow
three at Stradey.

Some of the Fourth All Blacks, including their Press party,
took exception to the behaviour of the Swansea fans. "Hard
man-to-man play," wrote John Hayhurst, of the *Freelance* "had

raised the anger of a section of the crowd. There was booing of Scott when he was kicking at goal". For his part, the full back has since spoken of his disillusion with the Cardiff crowd who hooted and booed as the 1945 Kiwis left the Arms Park having defeated the home side 3-0.

Scott has never pulled punches, and his recall of contact with Welsh fans is remarkably similar to that of the 1906 Springbok Paddy Carolin which I quoted in my book *Prince Gwyn*. Carolin wrote in his tour diary:

> Everywhere we have been, every man, woman, child, dog, cat, hen and even parrot has told us to 'Look Out For Wales'... I have had enough of that and will blow the next man's brains out who says 'Look Out For Wales'.

Now the Scott version:

> Even if he hasn't the slightest hope for his team a Welshman will still insist on telling you that 'Cardiff will beat you', or Newport or Swansea or whatever the next opponents might be... I can tell you, it gets very wearing to be told over and over again that your next opponents are going to beat you.

There must be some truth in a perception shared by men from such far-apart continents in the southern hemisphere. I would only add, "Very well, you two. But the people we are trying to convince are ourselves".

Although the Welsh players interviewed in the week-long build-up to the Test expected a very hard, even game (and were right) popular opinion favoured a home win with 2-1 or 5-4 on Wales. Such odds may have been rashly attributable to tradition or sentiment, but there was also a case history to justify them, based on the tourists' failure so far to beat club and regional sides convincingly. The Cardiff game had highlighted an inability on behalf of Stuart's men to go up a gear when the occasion warranted it.

This was a dimension that the management, therefore, tried

to nail and introduce during work-outs for the Test in which skipper Stuart was now well enough recovered to play. Unusually, the party had a free week before their second visit to Cardiff Arms Park which was used for what senior All Blacks declared as the hardest match preparation they had ever experienced. For this was the game that New Zealand wanted above all to win. The defeat by Wales of the 1905 All Blacks at Cardiff, the only one in thirty five fixtures, was the match they had been groomed to avenge – at this same venue. That would be achieved during the remainder of the twentieth century so often as to become commonplace. But – not just yet.

The home team chosen for 19 December 1953 was one of the most mature and self-possessed that had represented Wales. It contained much of the bone, muscle and brain-power that had nearly undone South Africa two seasons before and, crucially, Cliff Morgan was no longer the tyro that he had been then. Gareth Griffiths and Gwyn Rowlands, the only new cap, were in the back division for Alun Thomas and Lewis Jones; Hayward, Blyth and Forward had made way for Meredith, Judd (imported at the eleventh hour when Glyn Davies cried off) and Clem Thomas. These were no chickens; and they had the support of a 56,000-strong army spread around the sidelines.

Matches might have become all-ticket affairs; but all-ticket on a terrace did not guarantee a great view of the action and spectators started to enter the stadium as the gates opened soon after midday to obtain a good position. Often in those days, opponents sitting huddled in their changing room beneath a re-echoing North Stand may have thought that the singing before kick-off of great Welsh paeans was an advance appeal to some heavenly Caesar for a thumb-up. Not true; singing just whiled away the time. If it had a tactical impact as well – good, useful bonus.

Referee Dr Peter Cooper blew for the game to start and New Zealand moved straight to top gear attacking the River End. The visiting forwards picked up the momentum of their week-long training sessions and trapped the Welsh in their 25 for all of fifteen minutes. Then, a break-out brought Wales deep into All Black territory where the first score of the game went their way. Set-piece ball was delivered awkwardly to Scott who, under pressure from Rex Willis and Ken Jones, had no time to recover and find touch. He therefore attempted to reach Jarden who was well enough positioned on the goal line to have put in a clearance. The pass, however, was a hurried one and ill-directed – and who should be alive to the opportunity thus presented but Sid Judd, whose try was a replica of the one he had scored for Cardiff in November. Newcomer Gwyn Rowlands kicked the goal; and the match was on fire.

Although the Welsh XV was, as we have noted, among the most experienced ever to have represented its country, some wondered whether the down-side of this would be elderly muscles and sinews which would be unable to hold New Zealand's rampant pack. On the contrary, however, the best the visiting forwards could throw at their opposite numbers in the opening period was coolly absorbed. No-one can exactly remember who was pack leader on the day, but there is no doubt that John Gwilliam was using all his experience and weight to blunt the All Black thrusts.

The Welsh try had been against the run of play, and soon Jarden cut the deficit with a penalty goal well struck from an awkward angle. New Zealand edged her way into the lead when Scott, keen to atone for his earlier clumsiness, raced up the North Stand touchline, reached the 25 and put up a classic cross-kick towards the Welsh posts which the young centre Gareth Griffiths failed to deal with. New Zealand's Bill Clark pounced on the loose ball and scored a try which Jarden converted, so that the interval arrived with the tourists leading 8-5. The home team must have been kicking itself for a momentary lapse which cost it the lead after the resolve shown early on.

In days before replacements were allowed the third quarter was a testing period for Wales, beginning with the departure from the fray of Griffiths clutching a severe dislocation of his shoulder. In the twenty minutes of the second half that he spent having attention New Zealand ought to have made the match safe. Instead, as Bleddyn Williams still says, "We won the game, but New Zealand lost it".

From the first moments of the second half neither statement looked likely to be valid. Skipper Bob Stuart was held up inches short as he lunged for the Welsh line from a line out, 'Tiny' White nearly battered his way through the Welsh pack. And then, to cover the absence of Griffiths, Clem Thomas had to be brought out of the scrum by Bleddyn Williams, Gwyn Rowlands coming into the centre.

Now the forward disciplines that Gwilliam had been preaching and demanding since 1950, especially at the line out, came into their own to even up what had become a battle between eight men and seven: All throw-ins to be short. Bind tight on the catcher. Don't flap the ball down to the scrum half. Try to replicate a set scrum, and be satisfied with a few yards' progress down the touch line rather than thinking over-ambitiously.

And if the tourists were throwing in? Though not in New Zealand Gwilliam had talked with John Robins about All Black techniques learning that, as their jump was completed, catchers turned their backs on opponents in order to mask a slipped pass to a supporting tight forward. This could be repeated, generating penetrative power that was hard to stem. Gwilliam told his men that defender should:

> ...grab one of the ball-carrier's legs around the socks and refuse to let it go. The ball is passed among the attacking forwards and in a short time the ground is littered with huge men denied the opportunity of galloping down the field in close formation. The smaller men... get up quickly and begin their own attack.

Well. Make what you like of that; but some defensive skill or tactic certainly kept the All Black pack at bay as it bore down in waves upon the Welsh line.

It was at the end of this furious passage of play that Welsh morale received two notable boosts. First the gallant fourteen rubbed their eyes in disbelief as young Gareth Griffiths reappeared on the touchline waiting for Dr Cooper to summon him back to the action. Secondly Bleddyn Williams got in two long touch-finders which took play deep into New Zealand territory for almost the first time in the second half and gave his pack an attacking platform. "I thought we would win then," he recalls, "and the All Blacks must have feared the worst".

The re-invigorated Welsh now lifted the siege. Ken Jones, who had been isolated on his wing while the infantry battled it out, suddenly scorched away into space, putting in a cross-kick onto which the prop Courtenay Meredith latched. When support players arrived and overwhelmed defenders Bill Clark rolled to the Welsh side of the resultant ruck and conceded a penalty which Rowlands kicked for 8-8. Five minutes only were left. Could either team break this deadlock?

There followed the immortal Clem Thomas cross kick which led to the winning try. The flanker had arrived on Elsom, who had made a hash of a loose ball on the left – south – touchline, just within the All Black ten-yard line. Among the nearest Welshmen as the match reached its thirty fifth minute was Bleddyn Williams. The captain, however, had torn a thigh muscle (and was destined to miss yet another Twickenham match in January) and the last thing he wanted at that moment was a pass under pressure. "So Clem was in a tizzy," recalled 'Stoker' Williams, who was also a yard or two away. "People acclaim what was said to be a great tactical kick," he grins today. "The truth is that with three bloody-great All Black forwards bearing down on him, all Clem wanted to do was to unload at all costs." The touch-judge (the late Ivor Jones) also claimed to have shouted, "Cross kick, Clem". It is doubtful whether his voice could have cut through those of the other 55,999 shrieking onlookers, but at any rate that is what Thomas did.

A black and white record of the winning try exists on 'telecine', an early way of archiving special TV footage. It shows that the kick bounced once, favouring Ken Jones on the Welsh right wing, and wrong-footing Ron Jarden, his marker (who, had he collected the ball, could have gone all the way to the Welsh line). Jones, an Olympic sprinter whom the New Zealanders had learned to respect in their country three years earlier, gathered at full speed and had only to cruise for thirty yards to score the winning try, to which Rowlands added the extra two points.

New Zealand put up some up-and-unders into the Welsh 25, but by now the men in red were in no mood to throw the game away. Indeed it seemed as if they had finished the stronger: in the dying minutes John Gwilliam was named by E.W. Swanton as leader of a "thrilling foot rush" which also involved Clem Thomas and Sid Judd and nearly presented Dai Davies with a second Welsh try. But 13-8 it finished – as of now, the last time for Wales to defeat New Zealand in a Test match.

The headline on top of Swanton's report was 'Intuitive Skill won the Day for Wales'. Or, the Cavaliers had Beaten the Roundheads.

Some less-than-generous sentiments were voiced afterwards. In *The Bob Scott Story* ghost-writer Terry McLean comments, "Dr Cooper in the last five minutes did not see at least three breaches within shooting range of the Welsh posts" (in *All Blacks in Wales* John Billot corrects him, stating that the three penalties were indeed awarded, only for the tourists to use up-and-unders hoping for a try and conversion to save the day).

Not for the first time a hostile – envious? – London Press sought to knock the Welsh. "Wales were clearly out-done in the scrums," said *The Daily Telegraph*. As Clem Thomas spent nearly twenty minutes out of the pack covering Griffiths' absence some lack of shove was not unnatural – which also deals with the *Daily Mail* remark that the Welsh pack had one of the worst beatings he could remember. These were two newspapers which had said of Wales' 1905 victory over New Zealand that "the Welsh were not as good footballers as their opponents" and also complained when Wales began introducing miners and tinplate workers into her packs as "unfair".

Although there had been a demotion which the erstwhile captain would have preferred to avoid, John Gwilliam could nevertheless claim to have been involved in making history which for nearly fifty years our teams have failed to repeat. The nearest Welshmen have come to doing that was the 1971 Lions tour when its Welsh members, including skipper John Dawes, were the world-class players of their day. But against the Welsh National XV the fact is that since 1963 the All Blacks have won fourteen games in succession, scoring 403 points and conceding just 95.

Following this 1953 defeat of New Zealand there were heard once again, as after the Cardiff reverse, the prickly reactions of men who are not used to losing, and hate it. At the official Dinner that evening Gwilliam remembers sitting next to a young New Zealand back, who went on and on and on about brilliant 'moves' that were 'called' by All Black three quarter lines. In the end, said his hearer: "I had to remind myself that I was listening to a member of the losing side!" Cliff Morgan recalls an opposing half back saying to him, "If I never play against you one more time, Morgan, that'll be too soon" – though maybe that was a heavily disguised compliment. The habitually cynical and saturnine Terry McLean managed to grind out a Monday morning guest-piece for the *Western Mail* which for once tugged a forelock: "There were passionate hymns, good humour, big excitement, and a constant stupendous roar from the sidelines. But if the All Blacks' power was superior, your team generated the fire which won the match, burning fiercely until that definitive moment when Dr Cooper blew for time."

The reader will do well to remember that as a result of this game Wales led New Zealand 3-1 in Tests played. It is, and was, heady to appreciate that the great Dominion ranked the Welsh as opponents in South Africa's class.

The All Blacks could have gone into their shells after that fateful weekend and settled for percentage Rugby. Instead there was a perceptible tossing aside of the tactical chains that had inhibited them. The first spectators to benefit from this were those who stood on the steep hillside above Abertillery, where the home side was joined with a contingent from Ebbw Vale to give the tourists their fifteenth game. The midweek fixture policy

of the day was well-meant, permitting two Valleys clubs to benefit from the one fixture, but of course the do-or-die approach
that would have characterised the performance of a single club
was missing. John Billot, who saw more Welsh Rugby than most
writers as J.B.G's first lieutenant, comments in his *All Blacks in
Wales:* "as so often happens when Welsh clubs combine, they did
not do themselves justice."

So Abertillery & Ebbw Vale went down 22-3 after which the
tourists won two games in England, were held to a draw by
Ulster, and finished their business in Ireland with wins over
Munster and in the Test. Then it was back into Wales for successes
against two more combined XVs – Pontypool & Cross Keys and
Neath-Aberavon – before meeting another major challenge on
21 January 1954 at Rodney Parade, the home of Newport and a
great Rugby fortress.

The Black and Ambers had strengthened their bid for a first
victory over New Zealand by importing a new star in Onllwyn
Brace, who had come to Uskside from Aberavon. The Gowerton
man wanted to play regularly at scrum half, a position which was
firmly held at the Talbot Athletic Ground by Cliff Ashton. Sadly,
the tactical plan based on the newcomer and the stand off half
Roy Burnett – two out-standing players was doomed to failure
by the strained Achilles tendon suffered by Burnett against
Coventry just five days earlier.

It was a gamble, and it failed. Within ten minutes, his contemporaries recall, the effects of Burnett's pain-killing injection were
wearing off and he was limping, never to pose a real threat to the
visitors' defence. Newport went down 11-6.

For John Gwilliam, too, Father Time was about to end the
game, though with some collusion from the player himself. He
had always promised himself that he would retire once he moved
into his thirties, and that would happen in January 1954. The
fulfilment of this resolve was not entirely his making, but as it
happened it suited him. So he says, anyway. That is perfectly
feasible; in these days, when professional Rugby offers a sort of
career to young men, they are enabled to keep playing well

beyond their twenties. In bygone days once a man turned thirty he was obliged to look hard at a future career and throw all his energies into it.

Exactly four weeks after defeating New Zealand Wales were due at Twickenham, where her teams had not lost to England since 1939. Both selection and preparations were hampered and complicated by injuries: firstly, Bleddyn Williams's torn muscle precluded inclusion, his position at centre being given to Glyn John from the Garw Valley who, remarkably, had 'bought' his way back into Rugby Union after turning professional for Leigh at seventeen years of age: a "misguided immature decision" said the WRU, re-instating him as an amateur.

His selection was a knee-jerk reaction, prompted by injuries to both Williams and Gareth Griffiths and he would win only one other cap for his country. Up front, Gwilliam was now directed to partner Roy John in the second row, while the captaincy was handed to Rees Stephens, moving back to number eight. In a season notable for selectorial indecision he would quickly be succeeded as captain by Rex Willis and finally Ken Jones before the Five Nations Championship was over. Phew.

After two successful trips to Twickenham, 1954 was not to bring Wales a third triumph. The RFU were stingy ahead of this first all-ticket match at HQ, and the number of Welsh supporters who were able to obtain tickets for 16 January was put at somewhere below 10,000. But lack of support was only the least of Wales' worries on the day. Gallant little Gerwyn Williams dislocated a shoulder trying but failing to stop the giant Ted Woodward scoring England's first try; he left the action at half time, re-joining it five minutes into the second half.

The Welsh created a try by Gwyn Rowlands, who also kicked a penalty, and Woodward scored again for England. But as time ebbed away, Rex Willis and Billy Williams pulled up with injuries that forced Cliff Morgan and Gwyn Rowlands into unaccustomed positional roles. So it was that Wales eventually – and understandably – cracked in the final moments of the game. That was when Chris Winn got to the left corner flag for an unconverted try, and the 9-6 win which pointed England towards their first Triple Crown since World War II.

The selectors did not take the view that this narrowest of defeats by England merited the retention of some of their old hands who had contributed to the defeat of the All Blacks. They concluded that pace was missing from the pack so that old slow-coach Gwilliam must make way for younger, speedier legs. Leighton Jenkins, Brian Sparks, Len Davies, N. Glyn Davies and C.D. (Derek) Williams were all back-row forwards tried in Wales' packs of the mid-fifties which never quite achieved dominance to equal those which played under Gwilliam. The former captain's name was missing from the next Welsh XV to be named, and never re-appeared.

For the fourth and final time in his lustrous International career he had been dropped; and as usual not a word of complaint passed his lips. He is, today, so dismissive about the behaviour of national selectors towards him that you almost believe protestations by him that it really didn't matter.

How could that be?

It needs to be remembered that during the period when he was in and out of Welsh teams there was a healthy amount of territory separating him from unsettling influences – fans who might have stoked self-pity in him and others who gloated at the un-seating of one who now made return trips to his native country by parachute and chose not to re-vitalise his Welsh roots. In his own words, "During my playing career I never possessed the kind of power-base which might have worked for me. Also, by 1954 I had learned that if a Welsh team lost our selectors wasted no time in identifying someone to blame. You expected something disagreeable to happen.

"And this, remember, was not a matter of life and death. Five years at War in the Royal Tank Corps lent you a sense of proportion."

EPILOGUE

With John Gwilliam now in retirement (and Bleddyn Williams soon following him that way) the bright aura which had surrounded Welsh Rugby during the fifties began to grow dim. The decade after his departure brought only one outright Championship title. It was England's turn to occupy the driving seat, while France's rising star meant that Wales would be denied victory in Paris from 1959 to 1971. Welsh successes tended to be secured, not by great running and handling, but through goal points supplied by men like Viv Evans and Garfield Owen. Clive Rowlands cheered the nation up in 1963 with a Triple Crown, but style went out of the window as opponents were contained rather than overwhelmed.

A couple of backs, however, made sure that Welsh Rugby's Second Golden Era manifested a radiant after-glow. As long as Cliff Morgan was on the pitch some glory trailed in his wake. Despite a short business sojourn with Bective Rangers this dynamo on legs stretched his International career to twenty-nine caps before bowing out in 1958 after Wales' defeat in Paris. Phil Bennett drew level with him, but not until the advent of Neil Jenkins was his haul overtaken by another stand off half.

Now in his seventies Morgan looks back with quiet satisfaction at the vivid-in-his-memory days of mid-century. The trip that, surely, gave him most pleasure was his visit to South Africa with the 1955 British Lions where he showed the Springboks what a Welsh half back could do when an occasion brought the best out of him. He loved to tell anyone who would listen about the stand off halves who came from his Valley, explaining how they developed their will o' the wisp capability:

> As small boys, you see, when I and the rest stepped out of our terraced houses each morning to go to school we were almost under a lorry in the road – you had to side-step out of its way. The chances were then that a car was bearing down on you – prompting a fast skip the other way. Now, if you went too far, you were almost on the railway line and a

train had you in its sights. Again, beware: another misjudg-
ment would have you in the river.

Thus the artful dodgers of the Rhondda Valley learned to live
dangerously on the field of play – and love it. In due course
Morgan used to enjoy other great escapes in the face of opponents who thought they had him cornered: "Then perhaps a
change of pace or direction would leave them grasping thin air –
yes, even my great Springbok adversary Basie Van Wyk – and the
crowds would go, 'O-o-o-oh! – how did he do that?' The sounds
from terraces and grandstands were music in the ear".

And just as European admirers had acclaimed him, and the
way he played, so the hard men of the high veldt loved watching
him. The Lions' attacking strategy centred on their first-choice
stand off half and, on firm surfaces, he took the chance to show
that 1951 was firmly in the past and at twenty-five he was not
only older but a whole lot better. The statistics of the 2-2 Test
rubber are well documented, including the great understanding
he reached on the field with England centre Jeff Butterfield and
Jeeps at scrum half. Morgan scored a dazzling try in the 23-22
result at Johannesburg, but the vital win was 9-6 at Pretoria since
it meant that the Lions could not lose the series. Billy Williams,
who led the pack, recalls that he and Cliff had gone to church the
previous Sunday – a visit that paid off.

These days Cliff Morgan prefers to reflect on the long ago
culture, as opposed to the business, that was Rugby Football in
his day: "Teams spent time with opponents in those days. After
hitting lumps out of each other on the field, making defenders
look stupid, hurting them – we always had a beer or three
together afterwards."

The friends he made in the game and after the action included
the Springboks that he had first met in South Wales. Besides Van
Wyk there were 'Chum' Ochse, Hansie Brewis (the 'brown fox'),
Stephen Fry from Natal, and the great Hennie Muller: "fast,
mobile, without an ounce of fat on him – like a long, lean slice of
biltong." The Springboks' fluency in English varied according to

their background, but Morgan found it possible to have enjoyable conversations with a number of them. Among the Lions, his compatriot R.H. Williams (lock) was always eloquent on the subject of teaching, while of the other nationalities, he best remembers Dickie Jeeps (scrum half) on fruit farming, Tug Wilson (flanker) on police work and Tony O'Reilly (record try-scoring, nineteen-year-old wing) on great Irish legal cases. The last-named was to become a life-long friend: "Though only just out of his teens he always seemed twenty years more mature than the rest of us. That must have been because he was well brought up and educated."

Speculates Cliff, a trifle sadly: "These days young tourists seem to play cards endlessly. My Lions – we talked." However, he spurned the chance of more chat and the renewal of other memorable friendships in New Zealand by retiring after the 1958 European season: "I had a family. They couldn't eat caps. I needed a career. The other factor was a feeling that I felt that I had just played the best Rugby of my life – again in South Africa – with the Barbarians. I thought that I would not like to play the All Blacks at a point, in 1959, when perhaps I would be over the top."

The reality is that Morgan had been identified by the infant BBC Wales as a likely first holder of the Sports Organiser post in Cardiff. Since a substantial expansion of coverage was about to take place there was a certain urgency in their approach to him, which came from the urbane Head of Programmes of the day, Hywel Davies. Clearly it suited Morgan to turn down a New Zealand trip – desperate though Australasia was to have sight of him – and remain in Cardiff. He had deserved it – and there would be other trips Down Under to look forward to in other capacities.

Curiously, or indeed perhaps not, when he went to London to further his career in 1964 Cliff Morgan was succeeded at BBC Wales by another blithe spirit of the Welsh decade, Onllwyn Brace. A couple of years younger than Morgan this product of Gowerton Grammar School was a sportsman through-and-through: a crack hurdler and no mean all-rounder at cricket, but primarily a gifted and innovative scrum half. Though they were strictly in different Rugby age-groups, John Gwilliam led the senior side at a Trial game in the early fifties when Brace was introduced to this level of Rugby in the Possibles. Afterwards the perspiring Wales skipper of the day wanted to know exactly who was the outrageous whippersnapper working the scrums for the Whites: "I couldn't get my hands on him all afternoon".

The outrageous number nine was a product of a great school which had fashioned the pre-War half backs Tanner and W.T.H. Davies and, latterly, Lewis Jones. Well taught, and motivated, by a teacher-enthusiast called Bill Bowen, Brace was soon developing original tactics for the game which were based on his own capacity to initiate smart manoeuvres but surely remain valid for all scrum halves. He believed firmly in "making his presence felt" at the earliest appropriate juncture in a match, to pose immediate threats to opposing back rows and sow doubt in their minds about where the next attack would come from. He reflects now that, if an early break by the scrum half later caused an open side flanker to check his stride momentarily, then his midfield backs were given more precious space through which to penetrate.

He is forever associated with the 1955 Varsity match, which is rated the out-standing Oxbridge afternoon of the twentieth century for its style and movement. The Dark Blues won, but Cambridge truly contributed, gaining an early lead before succumbing to Oxford's relentless fifteen-man approach. However, the foundations of this win were laid after Brace joined Newport late in 1953 and found the dazzling Roy Burnett more than ready to dance to his tune. Here, 'switch' moves were brought to perfection, with the scrum half running laterally from set pieces and feeding a stand off half running straight past wrong-footed back rows. The variant was a 'dummy switch', where the scrum half kept on running and linked instead with a centre.

The Oxford captain of 1955, one Roy Allaway, had been on the receiving end of this magic at Rodney Parade early in the year, and persuaded Brace to come up to University College that autumn to read for a post-graduate degree. The rest is history, with a vintage team containing outstanding players like Welshman Robin Davies, John Currie and Peter Robbins, both soon to be capped by England, supporting the half back duo in which the gifted M.J.K. Smith (also capped in January 1956) was Brace's partner. People called their style 'basketball in boots' – but it worked. And today, decades after his heyday, John Gwilliam pays the man from Gowerton a grand tribute, maintaining that his leadership of Oxford "had an amazing effect by bringing the Varsity match out of some torrid years, showing how this high-profile fixture could and should be played."

You might say that Onllwyn Brace fanned the embers of the Second Golden Era of Welsh Rugby, and he certainly declined to compromise style or principles after returning to Wales and its clubs. But, though he says that Cliff Morgan was sympathetic, even laudatory, about tricks up Varsity sleeves, the two men never developed into the earth-shattering partnership that the Big Five had hoped for. They played together just five times, before Lloyd Williams stepped in for an unbroken run of thirteen caps which sidelined Brace until a brief run at the outset of the sixties.

People speculated that two hyper-active men like Morgan and Brace at half-back were one too many. Equally, many think that that the selectors broke the partnership prematurely after the 1957 defeat by England at Cardiff. When dropped, the scrum half had won three games from five; and at the end of his International career had six wins from nine games. Defences feared him; when other nations spoke of imaginative, inventive Welsh Rugby they had the likes of Onllwyn Brace in mind.

Here I need to declare an interest: later in life we spent many seasons as colleagues in BBC Wales' sports department working on televised Rugby coverage. That was some years after I captained the OU Greyhounds in the annual match against the Blue (senior) team at Iffley Road, when I was another who couldn't lay a hand on D.O.B. But I have forgiven him.

This book has been about the old amateur approach to playing Rugby Union football which, by definition, meant that while large bundles of money found their way into the game its priorities had to do with 'the general good' rather than that of individuals. It was feudal, in that the primacy of the earliest competitive pace-makers – Neath, Swansea, Cardiff, Newport and Llanelli – was never threatened by revolution and indeed was hardly challenged until the last quarter of the twentieth century. Those clubs were lords of the local Rugby manors, who gave the sport continuity of aims and purposes.

It differed from the game we know at the outset of the Third Millennium in a major respect: its amateur participants knew no undercurrent of fear and apprehension which might inhibit top players and point them away from inspirational and carefree attitudes. There were no leagues, which could bring triumph and prestige but carried a concomitant threat of under-performance and relegation that coaches dreaded lest they be sacked; and no Cup competitions in which failure might result in half a squad being put on the market. Men did not fear to take risks for glory, maximising enjoyment on both sides of the touchline; and if moves went wrong there was no stigma – even amusement, that extravagant action on the field had been stopped in its tracks. One of John Gwilliam's basic maxims was that teams should find something to laugh about at least once in each half to de-fuse tensions and stress.

Matches could, of course, be dull, very dull; and the point has been made in these pages that half a century ago the Laws of the period made it easier to close a game down. But the upside of this is that great players tried even harder to outwit and unlock tight defences; and when they achieved their aim the results were hugely spectacular and spell-binding. Occasionally, the teams of the twenty-first century can play riveting Rugby – as in the league decider between Cardiff and victorious Llanelli in May 2002 and the subsequent Cup Final that also featured a Llanelli side which went down under Pontypridd's final assault. But nowadays the enjoyment and entertainment quota is regularly under delivered until a losing side abandons safety-first in a frenzied, eleventh-hour, bid for victory or the eventual winners are so far out of sight that their mood can be wholly uninhibited.

John Gwilliam knew his Rugby realities, and appreciated that defences had to be teased and stretched and turned – and battered – until their will to resist was broken. Often this might yield no more than vulnerable moments; but these were enough for his match-winners to score decisive points. For the latters' part, they were men who sought space rather than collision. The generation that, although elderly now, well remembers mid-century Rugby cannot imagine Cleaver, Bleddyn Williams, Burnett or Lewis Jones (or, later, Dawes, John and Gerald Davies) deliberately running into opponents to create rucks and mauls. This is what New Zealanders, South Africans and Englishmen do; and it seems to me regrettable that the Welsh have picked up their habits. Maybe this has to do with our coaches in recent years.

You may be thinking: defences are much more crowded in 2002 and attackers have less space in which to operate. If so, you should be aware that, under the Laws of the nineteen fifties, defences could take their stance level with the ball at scrummages and the line out. It needed golden skills to penetrate such line ups.

John Gwilliam duly completed the 1954 season with Gloucester, where he had enjoyed his time immensely, before, as he had privately promised himself, hanging up his boots. Looking back on his career from what is now a distant vantage point, he insists that to him "Rugby has always been a game to enjoy." He certainly played it hard, possessing a physique which allowed him to compete robustly. Moreover he had reached peaks of fitness which make it possible for him to state, "I never seemed to want a game to end – with just two exceptions to this: the closely-fought Twickenham matches in which my Welsh teams held on for hard-grafted victories!"

He made two final career moves, the first as a result of an outstanding performance by the same schoolboy called Dunn whom we met earlier. Inspired by him, in 1955 Bromsgrove defeated Campbell College, Belfast, then the strongest school side in Ireland, "with a display," recalls Gwilliam, "that caused the visitors' coach to call for a stiff reviving brandy." News of this fine result reached a former Headmaster of Campbell College, who was by now the Master of Dulwich College in south London. On his behalf an intermediary suggested to Gwilliam that, should he fancy a change, an application to Dulwich would be viewed favourably. It was indeed; and the Welshman joined the London school's staff in autumn 1956, appointed by his new employers as Head of Lower School.

Also, of course, he was master-in-charge of Rugby, which he comes close to describing as a doddle, since a complement of over 1,000 pupils was ample to choose from and some of them were very fast and strong. Assisting him were two gifted coaches in Alan Cooper (offered terms by Bradford Northern RL after playing on the wing for Oxford) and Alan Barter, a Cardiff High School product who won three Blues at centre for Cambridge. Under this triumvirate Dulwich College did not lose at home for four seasons, and went through a winter unbeaten before Gwilliam moved on.

Among his vivid memories of that period are the publication of his lively manual entitled *Rugby Football Tactics*, which he says he had to write in order to help pay for the London house that he and Pegi were buying. It is a thoughtful volume, in which he suggests that thirty players are four too many on a Rugby Union field, which they over-populate. He also pursues vigorously the concept of a team formation numbering seven forwards and eight backs (which he had tinkered with at Glenalmond without having the 'clout' to make it the first XVs habitual line-up) and says that this made Dulwich water-tight in defence and menacing in attack.

It was in London, too, that the Gwilliams completed their family. The arrival of Catherine at Glenalmond had been followed at Bromsgrove by those of David (1953) and Peter (1955). Philip and Rhiannon were born in London in 1959 and 1963. But now a final move would be made by their father to Birkenhead School, set in a leafy suburb of the (then) shipbuilding town across the Mersey from Liverpool.

The post was Headmaster, which carried a house to live in (a rather large, pleasant one, to judge from the pictures that hang on the Gwilliams' walls), and the School had fine traditions. The best testimony to the new man's enjoyment of his final job is that he stayed in it for a quarter of a century, from 1963 to 1988. Though by now a Rugby geriatric, qualified to wear a 'golden belt', he occasionally donned a track suit to fine-tune his school XVs when Rugby masters were absent. The boys' approval of Mr Gwilliam was whole-hearted; but that did not prevent one of the more daring members of Birkenhead School's Rugby squad uncovering a Press photograph of their Headmaster (in his pomp) being left for dead by the Irish stand off half Jackie Kyle and displaying it all too prominently for the First XV's enjoyment. No doubt it drew a bleak smile from the Head.

Eventually came retirement, the Gwilliams settling for a hill-side residence at Llanfairfechan, a pleasant village on North Wales' coastal plain between Conwy and Bangor. Immediately above it to the south rise two of Eryri's highest mountains, Foel Fras and Carnedd Llywelyn. Up their rampart-like contours winds the start of a long-distance footpath which, Pegi Gwilliam enjoys assuring visitors, terminates at the other end of Wales near her place of upbringing, Llanelli. In the direction of England, were it not for the massive Great Orme dominating the horizon, the couple could probably see as far as the Wirral and Birkenhead on a clear day.

Nowadays there is a speedy dual carriageway, the A55, connecting north west Wales with the wider world. This is important, for even at an advanced age the Gwilliams are fond of travel. They still enjoy London, where Catherine, has raised four grandchildren. Early 2002 found them in northern France at Cambrai, a battlefield where Bert Gwilliam had seen action during World War I. In early summer they called at the gracious county ground at Worcester, where their son Peter teaches history at Kings School, to take in an afternoon's Championship cricket. David, a Professor at Aberystwyth and Philip, a Manchester actuary, are each an hour's drive away, while Rhiannon, who is severely handicapped, is at Deganwy where she can benefit from her parents' care and attention.

Some years ago the couple built a house at Moelfre on Anglesey's east coast, where they go for short breaks and which they let from time to time to favoured tenants. The island's climate is agreeable and, looking south, the storm clouds gusting over Snowdonia can be seen dispersing and permitting the sun to shine as they arrive over the Menai Straits.

For the most part, it might be said, such a life-style amounts to an idyllic way of spending retirement years.

The other journey that John Gwilliam makes from time to time is southwards, often claiming his 'old International' ticket to visit the Millennium Stadium and watch Wales in action. If his era was a 'golden' one, judged by results and panache, he nevertheless does not speak unkindly of today's action: "What is sure is that many of the matches I see at the grounds or on TV are very exciting."

Yet in almost the next breath he will say that "it is difficult not to agree with Sir Tasker Watkins's reported opinion that professionalism is the worst thing that has happened to the game of Rugby Union." In a general sense, you gather that he is talking of the big money which dominates the game today at its highest levels. More than once in these pages his own measured attitude to participation in the game has been noted, which on the face of it was the opposite of 'win at all costs'. In 2002 we discussed Neil Back's calculated action in the dying moments of the Heineken Cup final, when he knocked the ball from the hand of Munster scrum half Stringer as he was about to feed a critical scrum on the Leicester line; the Tigers won the ball against the head and their clearance to touch made the match safe. Gwilliam's view of the incident was imperfect, and he declined to pass a comment on it. However, he does admit wryly that, at set scrums, front rows in his day were not above putting a hand over an opponent's eyes as the ball came in.

The other nuance which may be present in his dislike of

professionalism is the 'comfort zone' which players may enter once a regular pay-packet is guaranteed. It is expensive for clubs to end contracts with players; and once a player does a deal with a club, or a country, he can in practice decide how hard he will train and play to justify what he earns – this is a dilemma for every person in the world who obtains a job which provides money in exchange for his or her services. For professional Rugby players, going to work on a Saturday morning is the equivalent of getting out of bed on a Monday morning for most of us; and it by no means follows that the former are raring to go any more than clerks and factory workers are bursting to reach the workplace for a new, demanding week's labour. It was, undeniably, different for top amateurs under the old regime for whom Saturday's game was a wonderful opportunity to let off steam after a week at a desk or coal-face, when no player would dream of giving less than total commitment. Rugby in those days was recreation, when men's morale and appetite for life were 're-created'.

To be more specific about the modern game, John Gwilliam laments the inevitability of set-piece possession: firstly at scrums. In his time he recalls that the ball was 'frequently' taken against the head by his players, notably Maldwyn James and Dai Davies who were adept at wriggling around between their props, often quite detached from the support. Today's scrummages resemble those of the Rugby League code, allowing defences to prepare for every and any stratagem employed by the attackers; so their net result is negative.

Equally, says John Gwilliam, it is difficult for 'old timers' to come to terms with the modern line-out where he declares that, with reasonable throws from touch the ball should never be lost. He does, however, refrain from stating the obvious – that Welsh play at the line out has been unreliable during recent seasons. It touched a nadir during the Cardiff Test against Scotland in April 2002 when three successive throw-ins by Wales gifted possession to the visitors. Until the National XV unearths a thrower who can hit double-top unerringly – especially in defence within the

22 – it seems folly to aim for jumpers way out on the 15-metre line, turning line-out possession into a kind of lottery.

How, then, does a thrower-in improve his aim and accuracy? The Gwilliam way says that there is no substitute for practice, endless practice, however boring. How to practise? The skipper and line out jumper of old counsels, "Begin by trying to throw the ball over the crossbar from in front of the posts to a jumper on the other side. This will certainly enable the thrower to measure his accuracy and fine-tune it. Eventually he will probably discover that he has enough control of the ball to drop it anywhere he wishes."

Used to referees who controlled games with nothing more than a whistle and a sometimes stern demeanour, it is to be expected that Gwilliam feels that "officials tend to dominate the game nowadays". The reference is to televised coverage, in which the harangues of today's referees often drown professional commentators. Purists, and they still exist, deplore teams being commanded to "roll away!" or "let it go!" If they are breaking a Law, why not simply penalise them? Possibly one of the most superfluous routines to be witnessed in today's media game is the ref dancing a jig close to a loose scrummage, flapping his hands wildly, and bellowing "Play on! Play on!" Why would any right-minded team not do so? By the way, if referees insist on shouting "Play on!" why don't they also shout "Stop!" when they note an infringement?

John Gwilliam, however, resists the temptation to wade into Third Millennium Rugby. Like any self-respecting Welsh supporter he must grieve at the Welsh game's decline. Yet I think he takes comfort in the golden legacy that he and his contemporaries laid down for successor generations. His teams approached each game, perhaps, obeying a tactical imperative laid down by the skipper which decreed that opponents had, first and foremost, to be subdued. Only then could they be knocked down or knocked out, delivering a dazzling pay-off to overjoy both the men he led and the onlooking nation.

After many exchanges by post and long, absorbing conversations with Gwilliam, there are still aspects of him which defy analysis. If you ask him why he never came back into Wales to teach, his reply is that none of the schools here held out a particularly attractive prospect to him and his wife Pegi. Dig a little deeper and you obtain the admission, "In my thirties I applied for three headships in Wales, two at independent schools and one at a famous state school – without success. The fact is that the two independent schools appointed men who were academically better than I was; while the state school was probably worried that I had never bothered to take a teaching diploma."

Sadly for the Welsh game, however, remaining in Scotland and England, where his abilities were clearly appreciated, has meant that Gwilliam has been unable to influence its development. That is regrettable if only because he might have communicated his own vision to those who serve it today at 'shop window' level, and perhaps uplifted the ambitions of those who carry its good name, at both representative and club level. Then again, perhaps he never wanted to. Corinthians, in a sporting context, are athletes whose commitment to their sport is total and absolute. The description suits Gwilliam very well. But such people often lack the will, the patience and the good temper to sit on committees and ruling bodies.

Therefore the legacy of the Second Golden Era of Welsh Rugby is, I suggest, not just about studying winning methods and tactics, but primarily the pulsating inspiration that it offers from half a century ago. This suggests that though the Welsh may be physically too slight to box toe-to-toe with the behemoths of world Rugby Football, we yet possess a special craft and cunning that can win games at the highest level by playing in our native style. What is that? It means the forging of packs which can offer something near parity of possession to gifted, decision-taking backs with uniquely magical footwork. For consider: in what other part of the world, has any player in Rugby's history been able to create space by side-stepping like Bleddyn Williams? – or indeed, later on, Phil Bennett and Gerald Davies? It would appear to be a skill that is, somehow, innate in a small number of special Welshmen and it can bewilder defenders. However, those who possess it have to be identified and nurtured, before, in due course, they can become the high-risk selections of daring coaches.

Until lately the role of coaches in the modern professional age was not remote from that of the highly-successful Carwyn James three decades ago. They prepared teams with vision and attention to detail before sending them out to do battle under a carefully-chosen captain. The latter was under orders to bring the best out of his men. Our own coaches accepted that fifteen Welsh International players down on the pitch would – should – read a game well enough to counter any developing threat from opponents and to be able to exploit the smallest chinks in their defence.

Now the command post is far behind the conflict. Am I alone in seeing the modern coach, with his headphones and lip-microphones, as rather a risible figure? What is he telling his messenger boys who rush up and down the touchline gesturing and offering water-bottles to the players? How about, "Don't do as I do. Do as I say." And if he orders, "Send on number 21, bring off number 4," what sort of consternation, puzzlement and demoralisation may he be causing down on the pitch? That is when players look up at the grandstand, point at their chests, raise their eyebrows, frown, shake their heads – and finally trot sheepishly into the tunnel. What damage is done to team spirit and fervour (and a player who has given his all) by the sending-on of yet another replacement? – who, in the remaining three minutes must instantly reach sixty mph and remember all the moves (no doubt a cap is some consolation plus the enhanced fee he can charge for representing his country).

What was golden about the Second Golden Era (and the Nicholls years and, later, the seventies) was that the man in charge was at the heart of the action – panting and perspiring, experiencing in turn delight and dismay, able to groan with the troops if a try was conceded and shout with joy like the rest of his pack when the backs turned on their clever tricks. I suspect that such a figure can get more out of fifteen players than any would-be talisman seated in the twentieth row of the grandstand.

It is certain that, in situations where 'putting the body on the line' is necessary, players will respond better to the exhortations of someone in the same plight than to dictats from afar. Urgent encouragement from a captain at his elbow is surely better for a man having a poor game than abrupt demotion to the sidelines.

Those who witnessed and applauded the outstanding achievements by Welsh sides of half a century ago took pleasure and deep satisfaction from the way their national representatives played the handling game, responding positively to the leadership of John Gwilliam. The feel-good factor uplifted his players, and the nation.

It seems to follow that, for the eighty minutes of a big game, it is the captain's role which should be paramount. The coach is the civil servant, who knows the laws outlines the feasibilities, and contributes to pre-match morale. The captain is the deciding influence – who may suggest to his scrum half, "Under move number 34 you are supposed to send the ball to the open side. I can see acres of space on the touchline side. Try that way!" A top flight scrum will quite possibly have noted the possibility already, but the extra word from the skipper is what persuades him to have a go.

And his side scores.

That is captaincy: it's about lighting fuses and cooling fevered brows. More than half a century later, a man like Lewis Jones still remembers how as an anxious, if precocious, teenager about to make his International debut in front of 72,000 spectators at Twickenham he was called to the half way line by his captain, given the bright new match ball and told, "Lewis: you're the man to kick off today."

Captaincy's also about encouraging men's chests to swell.

Index